EXTREME
METAL II

EXTREME
METAL II

JOEL MCIVER

OMNIBUS PRESS

Exclusive Distributors
Music Sales Limited, 8/9 Frith Street, London W1D 3JB, UK.

Music Sales Corporation,
257 Park Avenue South, New York, NY 10010, USA.

Macmillan Distribution Services,
53 Park West Drive, Derrimut, Vic 3030, Australia.

To the Music Trade only:
Music Sales Limited, 8/9 Frith Street, London W1D 3JB, UK.

Photocredits:
Steve Eichner/PhotoWeb/WireImage, Rolf Klatt/WireImage,
LFI, Rex Features, Hans Arne Vedlog/Rex Features.

All Photos used by kind permission.

Every effort has been made to trace the copyright holders of the
photographs in this book but one or two were unreachable.
We would be grateful if the photographers concerned would contact us.

Printed and bound in Spain by Bookprint, S.L., Barcelona

A catalogue record for this book is available from the British Library.

Visit Omnibus Press on the web at
www.omnibuspress.com

Acknowledgements

The following loinclothed warriors of metal made the compiling
of this book possible, nay enjoyable:

PR lovies and record company staff: Karl Demata at Eleven PR, Jaap Wagemaker
at Nuclear Blast, Darren Edwards at Eagle, Sarah, Debra and Becky at EMI, Hammy
and Lisa at Peaceville, Andy Turner, Philipp Schulte and Donna O'Connor at Century
Media, Michelle Kerr and Alison Edwards at Roadrunner, Nik and Roland at
Work Hard, Dorothy Howe, Patrick Savelkoul at Karmageddon Media, Louise and
James at Mercury, Daryl Easlea at Universal, Carlos Anaia at Warners

Fellow writers: Alan, Tim, Jake and Jack at Record Collector, Jonathan Selzer,
Damien and Ian Glasper at Terrorizer, Jamie Hibbard and Tommy Udo at Metal
Hammer, Luke Lewis at Kerrang, Mario Mortier at Rock Tribune, Christof Leim
at Metal Hammer (Germany), Adrian Ashton at Bass Guitar, Hugo Montgomery-Swan
and Steve Harvey at Acoustic, Scott Rowley, Stephen Lawson and Henry Yates at
Total Guitar, Andy Jones at Future Music, Nev Pierce at Total Film, Patrik Wiren
at Close Up, Martin Forssman at Sweden Rock, Paul Stenning, Stephen Daultrey,
Martin Popoff, Joe Matera, Ian Fletcher, Gillian Gaar, KJ Doughton,
Chris Charlesworth and Helen Donlon at Omnibus Press

Musicians: Jeff Dunn (Venom/Mantas), Tony Dolan (Atomkraft/Venom),
Killjoy (Necrophagia), Mirai Kawashima (Sigh), Katon W DePena (Hirax), Dennis Pepa
(Death Angel), Dan Lorenzo (Hades), Mille Petrozza (Kreator) for the foreword and
the many fine musicians who agreed to be interviewed for this book

Headbangers: Dan Balaam, Frank Livadaros, Elton Wheeler, Quinn Harrington,
Dora the Winter Sprite, Bruce Zombie

Normal people: The Parr, Houston-Miller, Everitt-Bossmann and Tominey dynasties,
Vinay, Dave and Dawn, Woody and Glynis, Helen and Tony, Simone, the Corky Nips

The NCT crew: The Barnes, Ellis, Johnston, Legerton and Maynard families:
give 'em five years and they'll all be listening to thrash metal

Always and forever: Emma, Alice, Robin, Dad, John and Jen

**Extreme Metal II is dedicated to all the metal fans who have contacted
me since Extreme Metal was published in 2000.**

You Rule!

FOREWORD

Foreword by Mille Petrozza of Kreator

Welcome to Extreme Metal II.

It must have been around 1982. I was a metal kid hanging out in a local club, where they had a Monday night three-hour metal special from 7–10pm. Back then, the New Wave Of British Heavy Metal was the most exciting thing, until one night the DJ played a song that sounded unlike anything I've heard to this day. To me it felt like a mix between metal and hardcore punk, with a dark and evil touch. I found out later that the band I was listening to was Venom. I was infected and bought all their albums and singles. Soon other great acts like Bathory, Metallica and Slayer appeared – the rest is history.

Today in 2005 extreme metal is stronger then ever! Looking back over the 20-year transition, the genre has experienced a variety of different developments from black, thrash, grindcore and death metal to metalcore. Even a controversial mainstream phenomenon like nu-metal is partly rooted in extreme metal. A worldwide legion of fans, bands, magazines, fanzines, independent radio stations and webzines present an alternative to mainstream, corporate brainwashed music, played by puppets of the music industry, that are trying to shove the newest hype down the throats of those who don't know (or don't want to know) any better. Bands that commit their sound to the more intense side of metal will always be more exciting then your average 3.30 rockin' radio tune!

Mille Petrozza

INDRODUCTION

Hello again, five years on from *Extreme Metal*, this volume's predecessor, which appeared in early 2000. In the introduction to that volume I stated, only half seriously, that the metal scene was developing so quickly that in five years' time I'd need to revise the book completely. As it turns out, a complete reformat hasn't been necessary – a simple A–Z of bands was what the readers wanted, judging by your feedback and, of course, the book's sales figures – but a comprehensive reshuffle of the actual bands included has been essential, thanks to various developments in the ever-shifting environment of extreme music.

First off, there are more bands on the scene than ever before. The first years of the new century have seen an entirely unexpected rise to prominence of mainstream metal bands such as Slipknot and Nightwish, both of which have sold vast numbers of records, scored high chart placings in many countries and attracted the attention of millions of previously non-metal-aware music fans. Although neither band is particularly extreme (although the former just about qualify for inclusion in this book thanks to the death metal element in their sound), the knock-on effect of their success on the metal scene in general has meant that there is more room for metal, from the big sellers to the underground.

This means that although nu-metal has come and gone, power metal flourishes and gothic rock dominates, the darker, scarier extreme metal scene has gone from strength to strength. Truly extreme acts – which for me, are confined to today's death metal, black metal and grindcore bands, plus the small-but-stubborn thrash metal scene – are proliferating. To reflect this I've expanded the original list of 260 bands to almost 400, and included many new interviews.

This time around, I've also been a bit tougher on the definition of what is truly extreme and what is not. *Extreme Metal* had an intentionally broad remit, taking in not just death, black, grind and thrash metal groups but also a few doom metal acts such as Black Sabbath, Candlemass and Anathema – all great bands, but in 2005's extreme stakes, not appropriate for inclusion. Slipknot can stay in, as can Soulfly and Fear Factory, two bands who came dangerously close to nu-metal territory but have veered back towards a more extreme approach of late. The odd power metal and stoner-rock act which I included in *Extreme Metal* out of stubbornness (my book, my rules!) such as Stratovarius and Queens Of The Stone Age are also out.

In the last volume I included a fair bit of discographical information, which I've omitted this time. In the interests of space (and because the internet now contains discographies for practically every band ever formed), I've focused on one single recommended album per act. There's also a web address, official or otherwise, where possible.

All this makes *Extreme Metal II* the best single-volume guide to the scene currently available. Hundreds of readers have let me know where I got it right (or wrong!) with the first volume: keep your comments coming, and who knows – perhaps I'll be writing another introduction in 2010.

Joel McIver
Spring 2005
www.joelmciver.co.uk
Email: joel@joelmciver.co.uk

Extreme metal is, by definition, music which is faster, harsher, heavier or more aggressive than the mainstream heavy metal performed by classic bands such as **Iron Maiden** (right)**, Judas Priest** and **Motörhead** or new bands such as **Korn, Deftones, Limp Bizkit, Staind** and **Linkin Park**. Historically, extreme metal tends not to receive much airplay or achieve high chart positions because most people find it thematically intimidating or sonically abrasive. They're right, too. That's what makes it so entertaining. However, 'metal-friendly' countries such as Sweden have begun to regard extreme metal as worthy of Grammys and other industry awards: times are changing.

In this book we're concentrating solely on four genres: thrash metal, black metal, death metal and grindcore. **Thrash metal** is a faster, heavier, more precise take on traditional heavy metal and began life with

HISTORY

Venom's debut album, *Welcome To Hell*, released in January 1981. By the following year thrash had spread to the US, and specifically to San Francisco's Bay Area, where **Metallica** (left) became the first band to receive global acclaim in the field. The movement spread rapidly and by 1986, the peak year of thrash, pundits were referring to The Big Four Of Thrash Metal: Metallica plus **Anthrax, Megadeth** and **Slayer**. All four received major exposure throughout the Eighties, but by the mid-Nineties Metallica had become an MTV-friendly stadium-rock band, Anthrax and Megadeth had taken up a less prominent, less aggressive position and only Slayer were still flying the flag for thrash. Today they remain the scene leaders, with a few new acts such as **The Haunted** and **Carnal Forge** emulating the classic style: however, a full-scale 'return of thrash' is always being predicted, and one day it might actually happen. In the meantime, an American mini-movement of thrash-influenced bands

such as **Shadows Fall** (above), **Chimaira** and **God Forbid** is gaining exposure.

Death metal took a while to come to prominence, with **Possessed** and **Death** on their feet by the mid-to-late Eighties, but when it finally took off at the turn of the decade, it did so with a vengeance. Typified by guttural, often indecipherable vocals, a deeper, more bass-heavy production than the thrash bands and the use of blastbeats (a super-fast drumming style borrowed from **grindcore**, a parallel movement spawned from the punk scene), bands such as **Morbid Angel, Deicide, Obituary, Entombed** and **Cannibal Corpse** were attracting huge crowds by the early Nineties. These days death metal has split into 'melodic' and 'brutal' strands, with the former emerging from the Swedish city of Gothenburg in the early to mid-Nineties and currently led by **In Flames**. The harsher edge of death metal is upheld by **Insision, Vader** and **Decapitated** from Europe as well as the American **Nile**. Grindcore, meanwhile, was initially the province of **Napalm Death** and **Carcass** but lives on in the music of super-heavy bands such as **Lock-Up** and **Pig Destroyer**.

But it's **black metal** that pulls the biggest crowds nowadays. The scene's first incarnation centred on three early-Eighties bands, **Venom, Bathory** and **Mercyful Fate,** and was basically primitive thrash metal with satanic lyrics (the 'black' element). As thrash and death metal took off, black metal foundered and by the end of the Eighties had vanished underground. However, it reappeared with fearsome rapidity and charisma in the early Nineties, when a group of Scandinavian acts including **Mayhem, Darkthrone, Burzum, Immortal, Enslaved** and **Unleashed** grew tired of death metal and took the old black metal template for their own. Hitting on a blend of speedy riffs, screamed or growled vocals and massive doses of Satanism, the bands formed a scene and fuelled the movement with controversy (including church-burnings, graveyard desecrations and homicides). By the mid to late Nineties the genre had become sophisticated, with the classical dexterity of the now-defunct **Emperor** and the layered keyboards of **Dimmu Borgir** bringing in huge sales figures. The most successful extreme metal band of all (if you discount the partly death metal, partly mainstream rock band **Slipknot**) is currently the British black metal act **Cradle Of Filth** (below), a sex-and-vampires-focused quintet who startled everyone in 2002 by signing to Sony, the first major label to sign an extreme metal band.

The result in 2005 is a multilayered, thriving scene made up of thousands of bands. Extreme metal's time is now.

Abbatoir

A competent Eighties thrash act, Abbatoir (initially vocalist Steve Gaines and later Mike Towers, plus guitarists Danny Oliverio and Mark Caro, bassist Mel Sanchez and drummer Danny Anaya) debuted – like many others before them – on a *Metal Massacre* compilation. The band are primarily known for harbouring John Cyriis and Juan Garcia, who would later go on to join Agent Steel. Abbatoir also recorded an interesting version of Motörhead's 'Ace Of Spades'. Sanchez would also later form Evildead with Garcia.

RECOMMENDED ALBUM:
Vicious Attack (Combat, 1985)

Abhorer

A now-defunct Singaporean black metal band, Abhorer consisted of Crucifer (vocals), Exorcist (guitar), Imprecator (bass) and Dagoth (drums) and were formed in 1988. A laughably-titled demo, *Rumpus Of The Undead*, saw them attract local attention and a split 7" with Necrophile. However, progress was slow and tortuous, with a highlight the release of a single, 'Upheaval Of Blasphemy', by the Shivadarshana label. By 1998 the band had split.

RECOMMENDED ALBUM:
Zygotical Sabbatory (Anabapt, 1996)

Abhorrence

Formed in 1997 and comprising Rangel Arroyo (guitar/vocals), Kleber Varnier (bass, later replaced by Marcello Marzari) and Fernando Arroyo (drums), Abhorrence are a Brazilian death metal band whose music bore the hallmarks of the South American extreme metal scene – intense riffing and minimal production values. Like many of their countrymen, they gained exposure through the Relapse label's *Brazilian Assault* compilation of 2000, although two demos (*Ascension*, 1997, and *Triumph In Blasphemy*, 1999) had gained them a local following. A break came in 2000 from the American 'extreme war metal' label Evil Vengeance, run by Angel Corpse's Gene Palubicki,

which released the *Evoking The Abomination* album (licensed to Listenable Records in Europe), mastered by then-Morbid Angel guitarist Erik Rutan.

RECOMMENDED ALBUM:
Evoking The Abomination
(Evil Vengeance, 2000)

Abhorrent

Founded in 1988, Abhorrent are a thrash/death metal act from Brazil and, like Abhorrence, benefited from their inclusion on an early compilation, *Brazil Alternativo 6*. The early line-up split after the recording of the *Horrible Slaughter* (is there any other kind?) demo, but re-formed with Robson Aldeoli (vocals), Fabrício Moraes (guitar), Leandro Soares (bass), and Gabriel Teykal (drums). An album, *Rage*, was issued in 1994 and was followed by a UK tour, bizarrely commencing in the small town of Rugely in Staffordshire. Another demo, *Live In Rage*, was recorded amid line-up shuffles and contained a cover of Slayer's 'Raining Blood'. A serious road accident didn't deter the band from contributing covers of Sepultura's 'Clenched Fist' and Megadeth's 'She-Wolf' to Dwell Records' tribute album series and another album, *Blasting*, was scheduled to appear on the Zenor label at the time of writing.

RECOMMENDED ALBUM:
Rage (1994)
www.abhorrent.com.br

Abhoth

The Swedish death metal outfit Abhoth (named after a supernatural HP Lovecraft creation) formed in 1989, when they were also known as Morbid Salvation Army. Singer Jorgen Broms left to join Afflicted in 1990, while guitarist Jorgen Kristensen and drummer Mats Blyckert have also worked with Suffer. Abhoth only stayed together long enough to record one 1993 single, the vaguely doom-laden 'The Tide', for the Corpsegrinder label.

Abigor

After a series of successful demo recordings – *Ash Nazgh*, *Lux Devicta Est*, *II/94*, *Moonrise* and *In Hate & Sin* – the black metal band Abigor signed to Austria's prolific Napalm label. Dumping their original vocalist Tharen (known as Rune at the time) for his lack of dedication, the band entered the studio with new frontman Silenius and the album *Verwuestung/Invoke The Dark Age* was recorded in June 1994. Gaining recognition for their atmospheric, proficient songs, Abigor swiftly issued a follow-up, the concept album *Orkblut – The Retaliation*. Although the narrative was a little naive (a warrior remembers his pagan origins and his life is traced until his eventual death) it was a lyrical and musical step forward and the band became one of Napalm's most popular acts. Silenius was replaced by Thurisaz in 1999 and the band recorded a version of Slayer's 'Crionics' the same year. The latest in a string of well-received albums is *Satanized (A Journey Through Cosmic Infinity)*, released in 2001.

RECOMMENDED ALBUM:
Orkblut – The Retaliation (Napalm, 1994)
www.infernalhorde.com/abigor

Aborym

Currently one of the leading lights of the electronic/black metal crossover micro-scene, Italy's Aborym were formed in 1991 by vocalist/bassist Malfeitor Fabban and guitarist Mental Siege. Honing their act by performing covers of tracks by bands such as Celtic Frost, Mayhem and Darkthrone, the duo recorded the *Worshipping Damned Souls* demo in 1993 and then fell silent for four years. When the band reconvened with the *Antichristian Nuclear Sabbath* demo in 1998 it was an entirely different beast: Siege was gone, replaced by ex-Satanik Terrorists/Alien Vampires axeman Nysrok, plus a temporary singer, Yorga. However, for Aborym's debut album *Kali Yuga Bizarre*

(Scarlet Records, 1999), the band took the step of recruiting black metal vocalist extraordinaire Attila Csihar (see Mayhem entry) and Yorga departed.

A second album, 2001's remarkable *Fire Walk With Us*, amply demonstrated the unique, somewhat futuristic vision of the band, but Aborym truly arrived on the international scene with the *With No Human Intervention* album two years later, which featured the talents of guest lyricist Bärd 'Faust' Eithun (ex-Thorns, ex-Emperor, later briefly drummer in Dissection). Eithun, serving a jail sentence at the time for a murder he committed in 1992 (see Emperor entry), recorded some spoken-word vocals by phone. Carpathian Forest frontman Nattefrost also contributed lyrics and vocals to the song 'The Alienation Of A Blackened Heart'.

RECOMMENDED ALBUM:
With No Human Intervention
(Code666, 2003)
www.aborym.org

A cheery message from Nysrok
❝We are the Chernobyl generation. Our musical breed is just at the beginning, but we won't get fucked as other bands have done in the past. We'll destroy this fucking dump you call Earth.❞

Abramelin

Australian death metal and grindcore is a well-developed scene and one of its more interesting bands (along with The Berzerker and Blood Duster) is Abramelin, formed in 1988 under the name Acheron. However, the band has not achieved much live exposure due to constant personnel shifts. Founder member and singer Simon Dower, accompanied at first by the initial line-up of Jason Black (guitar), David Abbott (guitar), Derek (bass) and Michael Colton (drums), recorded a series of demos, 7" singles and EPs, including *Eternal Suffering* (1989), *Deprived Of Afterlife* (1991) and *Transgression From Acheron* (1993), on a variety of European and local labels. A name-change came after a request from the US black metal act Acheron and Dower selected the name Abramelin after a medieval wizard.

A self-titled debut album appeared in 1995 but was banned in Western Australia due to the state authorities' objection to its

Abramelin – Aussie grind specialists

supposedly offensive lyrics: it was reissued (without lyrics) shortly afterwards. A second album, *Deadspeak*, came out on the Shock label in 2000. Abramelin have toured with international acts such as Cradle Of Filth, Carcass, Morbid Angel, Cathedral, Paradise Lost, Napalm Death, Deicide and Cannibal Corpse.

RECOMMENDED ALBUM:
Deadspeak (Shock, 2000)
www.abramelin.live.com.au

Simon Dower on metal overload

"For several years I listened to death metal exclusively, only straying on rare occasions to delve into other genres of music. Unfortunately this saturation of extreme metal always left me wanting more (heavier, faster and more brutal) until I got to a point where I think I'd pretty much heard it all and there wasn't much new stuff coming out that really impressed me. I've heard the heaviest, the fastest, the most brutal, the most hideous gore-ridden lyrics, and I'm not sure where else the music can go apart from just re-hashing itself. But there will always be a solid fanbase of people who want to seek out the buzz that extreme metal delivers."

Abruptum

Black metal to the limit, Abruptum is the work of two bandmembers – Evil, who claims to be responsible for "guitars, sounds, piano and darkness", and It, who provides "cries, screams, violin, drums and torture". The band first made an impression with their demos *Abruptum* and *The Satanist Tunes* (both 1990), while a further recording, 'Orchestra Of Dark' (1991) led to a deal with Mayhem guitarist Euronymous' Deathlike Silence Productions. Their debut LP, *Obscuritatem Advoco Amplectere Me*, was released in 1993. A snappily-titled follow-up, *In Umbra Malitae Ambulabo, In Aeternum In Triumpho Tenebrarum*, was released the following year, but with Euronymous' untimely death (see Burzum and Mayhem entries), Deathlike Silence folded and Abruptum signed to Head Not Found. Their next album, *Vi Sonas Veris Nigrae Malitiaes* (1997) continued with the previous ultra-evil themes.

RECOMMENDED ALBUM:
Obscuritatem Advoco Amplectere Me
(Deathlike Silence, 1993)

Abscess

Deliberately raw death metal played as the logical extension of the classic gore band Autopsy, Abscess was formed in 1994 in California and released two tapes, *Demo #1* and *Raw Sick & Brutal Noise*, the same year. Two more demos, *Crawled Up From The Sewer* and *Filthy Fucking Freaks*, appeared the following year. Some of this material was later remastered and reissued in the form of the *Urine Junkies* album by Relapse. A series of albums has been released since then, all of which mark the pedigree of the musicians (ex-Death drummer and Autopsy frontman Chris Reifert and guitarists/bassist Danny Coralles and Clint Bower). Reifert, a scene figure since its earliest days, also contributes to The Ravenous (see separate entry plus Necrophagia and Nuclear Assault) and produced the second album by Swedish Autopsy tribute band Murder Squad.

RECOMMENDED ALBUM:
Through The Cracks Of Death
(Peaceville, 2002)

Absu

Dallas, Texas black metal act Absu (named after a netherworld ocean and/or deity) were formed in 1989 under the name Dolmen by Equitant Ifernain (guitar, bass) and Shaftiel (guitar, bass, mouth harp, vocals). A demo, *Return Of The Ancients*, led the Gothic label to release a 1992 EP, *The Temples Of Offal*. A deal was signed with Osmose and three albums followed through the Nineties. Tours with labelmates Impaled Nazarene and Sadistik Exekution led to the growth of a live reputation, but the high point of Absu's career is, if we're honest, a 2002 audition by drummer Proscriptor McGovern for Slayer.

RECOMMENDED ALBUM:
Barathrum: Visita Interiora Terra
Rectificando Invenies Occultum Lapidem
(Osmose, 1993)
www.absu.ws

Abysmal

Abysmal were a Norwegian black metal band who released the promising *Pillorian Age* album in 1994. Frontman Endre Begby later moved to the Viking outfit Carpathian Full Moon, but further personnel problems proved to be too much for the band to continue.

RECOMMENDED ALBUM:
Pillorian Age (Avantgarde, 1994)

The Abyss

A side project of Hypocrisy (see separate entry) frontman and producer extraordinaire Peter Tägtgren, The Abyss features that band's musicians on different instruments (Tägtgren on drums and drummer Lars Szöke and bassist Mikael Hedlund playing guitars). An outlet for the trio's love of fast black metal, the band is an unremarkable if competent adjunct to the much more engaging Hypocrisy.

RECOMMENDED ALBUM:
The Other Side (Nuclear Blast, 1994)

Abyssic Hate

A side project by Shane Rout, drummer with the Australian band Blood Duster: Rout used the project as a vehicle for his fondness for very raw, primitive black metal. The genocide of the human race is one of the themes and the music itself is deliberately very hard going. Abyssic Hate's three demos have gained popularity in Germany, while the band have gone on to release a series of EPs. The first, a split with Det Hedenske Folk, featured Blood Duster's guitarist Brad Johnston and was a reworking of the material of one of the demo tapes, although 'remaster' is probably a misnomer given its minimal production values.

RECOMMENDED ALBUM:
Eternal Damnation
(EP, Darker Than Black, 1998)

Accuser

Accuser were one of many German technical thrash bands of the Eighties, inspired by the success of their countrymen Kreator and Sodom, but lacking the individuality to achieve similar heights. The tidal wave of grunge that weeded out all but the strongest thrash outfits was too powerful for them and their earliest work remains their best.

RECOMMENDED ALBUM:
Experimental Errors (Atom, 1988)

Acheron

An American act led by singer/bassist Reverend Vincent Crowley, Acheron play keyboards-laden black metal. Their first demo, *Messe Noir*, was released as a 666-copy limited run by Reaper Records in Belgium before the band signed to the US Turbo label in 1991. A debut album, *Rites Of The Black Mass*, did what it said on the sleeve, combining traditional Black Mass texts with orchestral sounds, and caused some controversy when Crowley was interviewed on a NBC talk show, *Cristina*. More albums followed and Crowley was invited to join the Church Of Satan by its founder, Anton Szandor Lavey. Eventually the Christian radio presenter and evangelist Bob Larson challenged Acheron to a couple of broadcast debates: both sides did well out of the predictable media coverage. The band continues to issue records on the Moribund label.

RECOMMENDED ALBUM:
Compendium Diablerie: The Demo Days (Moribund, 2001)

Acid Bath

A US death metal band, Acid Bath only released two albums before splitting to form other projects. The split also largely came about due to the early death of bassist Audie Pitre, who together with singer Dax Riggs, guitarists Sammy Duet and Mike Sanchez and drummer Jimmy Kyle had combined hints of hardcore and doom to create a hybrid sound. The first album, *When The Kite String Pops*, was released in 1994 and along with its many-faceted sound, was also notable for its artwork, a series of paintings by the serial killer John Wayne Gacy.

Its successor, *Paegan Terrorism Tactics*, continued the multi-style theme, with its acoustic touches and moments of vocal clarity a sharp contrast to Riggs' death metal roar. 'Old Skin' in particular boasted psychedelic hints, a possible indication that had the band remained together, an interesting, innovative direction might have emerged. After the split Duet founded a black metal outfit, Goatwhore, and also became a member of Crowbar. In the meantime, Riggs and Sanchez formed Agents Of Oblivion.

RECOMMENDED ALBUM:
When The Kite String Pops (Rotten, 1994)

Acid Reign

Although they were a competent enough thrash metal band, Harrogate's Acid Reign demonstrated only too clearly why Eighties thrash metal belonged to the Americans.

H (vocals), Kev (guitar), Gaz Jennings (guitar), Ian Gangwer (bass) and Ramsey (drums) attempted to ape the twisted humour of Anthrax et al without much success. After their split in 1990, some of the members went on to form the much more credible doom metal band Cathedral, alongside ex-members of Napalm Death. Acid Reign are really only memorable for their bizarre cover of Blondie's 'Hangin' On The Telephone'. The high point of their career was undoubtedly a support slot with Flotsam And Jetsam at the London Astoria.

RECOMMENDED ALBUM:
The Fear (Under One Flag, 1989)

Acrophet

A speed metal band from Brookfield, a suburb of Milwaukee, USA, Acrophet – originally known as Stalker – were formed when the members were only 16. Nonetheless, they immediately recorded an album, *Corrupt Minds*, for Roadrunner, who had signed them after hearing their technically nimble-fingered demo of 1986, *The Answer Within*. The album was briefly noted for the speed and technical prowess of Acrophet's drummer, Jason Mooney, who even came close to filling Dave Lombardo's role in Slayer when he left the band in 1996. A North American tour followed in 1989 with another local band, Realm, and a buzz started to build around Acrophet; however, after the disappointing follow-up, 1990's appropriately-titled *Faded Glory*, the band split, with two members going on to medical school in Des Moines, Iowa. Both albums were produced by Eric "Griffy" Greif, who had previously managed Death before making his living as a producer.

RECOMMENDED ALBUM:
Corrupt Minds (Roadrunner, 1988)

Aeternus

Norwegian black metallers Aeternus (not to be confused with the American Christian metal band of the same name) were formed in 1993 in Bergen. Vocalist Ares has sessioned for Immortal and Gorgoroth, while the latter group have also utilised the talents of drummer Vrolok. Their first release was the *Dark Sorcery* EP for the Czech label View Beyond, and a debut album followed on Hammerheart entitled *Beyond The Wandering Moon*. Support slots with Emperor, Cannibal

Corpse and others bolstered their progress and they remain near the vanguard of Norway's considerable BM scene.

RECOMMENDED ALBUM:
Shadows Of Old (Hammerheart, 1999)

Afflicted

The Swedish band Afflicted (initially Afflicted Convulsion), consisting of Jesper Thorsson (guitar), Michael van de Graff (vocals), Yasin Hillborg (drums) and Christian Canalez (bass), released two classic black metal albums in the early- to mid-Nineties, but felt (rightly) that newer styles had taken over the extreme scene. They split in late 1995 after the lukewarm reception of their second album and devoted their attentions to a new outfit, Molosser.

RECOMMENDED ALBUM:
Prodigal Sun (Nuclear Blast, 1992)

Agathodaimon

Founded in 1995 and consisting of Vlad (vocals and keyboards), Sathonys (guitars), Marko (bass) and Matthias (drums), Agathodaimon are a melodic black metal band whose early demos impressed the major European labels Nuclear Blast and Century Media enough to spark a minor bidding war. After the latter secured the band's signatures, sessions for a demo album, *Blacken The Angel*, were scheduled: however, Vlad (Rumanian by birth) was detained during a visit to his home country, accused of breaking emigration laws by leaving the country under the reign of Ceaucescu. Singer Akaias of Asaru deputised in Vlad's absence and the album was recorded. Tours with major acts followed and on Vlad's eventual return, more albums were recorded. In recent months the line-up has changed but the band continues to reap rewards for its inventive take on the black metal idiom.

RECOMMENDED ALBUM:
Higher Art Of Rebellion
(Century Media, 1999)
www.agathodaimon.de

Sathonys on the wheel of fashion
"Everything goes in circles. One moment a certain style is out, the next year it might be in again. Black and death metal are two styles which can be described as the most extreme, and both will continue to develop – but I think the most important experiments have been made, apart for some freaky mixtures of different styles. So I doubt this decade will see as many new interesting, extreme bands as the last one had to offer."

Agathodaimon – melodic black metallers

Agent Steel

An American power/speed metal band, Agent Steel revolved around singer/guitarist John Cyriis (real name John Camps), a graduate of that quintessential school of Eighties hair-metal, the California Guitar Institute of Technology. Although other musicians remained in the band for extended periods of time – notably guitarist Juan Garcia and drummer Chuch Profus – Agent Steel housed many different players, among them the itinerant six-stringer James Murphy.

Cyriis met Garcia in the short-lived Abbatoir before leaving to form Agent Steel (originally known as Sanctuary) with Profus. Recruiting Mark Marshall and Sill Simmons (guitarists) and bassist George Robb, the demo *144,000 Gone* was recorded in 1984. Garcia and Kurt Colfelt replaced the two guitar players and the debut album, *Skeptics Apocalypse*, was recorded for Combat in 1985. The personnel merry-go-round continued and Colfelt was replaced by the teenage Bernie Versailles, who helped to record the *Mad Locust Rising* EP, released in 1986. George Robb was then exchanged for Michael Zaputil and Agent Steel began recording another album, *Unstoppable Force*, at the legendary Morrisound Studios in Tampa.

At this point major label interest was awoken and Capitol – who had recently signed the rapidly-rising Megadeth – briefly flirted with the idea of a deal. For technical reasons and a lack of communication between the band and their management, the offer fell through, causing friction between band members and contributing to Agent Steel's eventual split. Yet more personnel changes ensued – including the recruitment of Murphy – but despite the success of *Unstoppable Force*, the band parted ways in 1988. A bizarre postscript to the first instalment of the Agent Steel story was that Profus and Cyriis, on their way back to California after a visit to Florida, were arrested in a Phoenix hotel, supposedly because they were performing Satanic rituals. Charges were dropped, however. 1999 brought an Agent Steel reformation and the release of a new album, *The Omega Conspiracy*, which was hailed as a return to form.

RECOMMENDED ALBUM:
Unstoppable Force (Combat, 1987)
www.agentsteelonline.com

Aggressor

Founded in the French-speaking Antibes, this death metal band (singer/guitarist Alex Colin-Tocquaine, guitarist Manu Ragot, bass player Joel Guigou and drummer Steiphan Gwegwam) debuted with a split EP with Loudblast. The band then signed to Black Mark and four albums ensued, but none rose above the mediocre and the band parted ways in 1995.

RECOMMENDED ALBUM:
Satan's Sodomy (Black Mark, 1987)

Agoraphobic Nosebleed

An enormously heavy grindcore act from Massachusetts, Agoraphobic Nosebleed is centred on sometime Anal Cunt guitarist Scott Hull. Formed in 1994, Hull and a series of musicians from bands such as Ulcer, Thug and Suppression released a sequence of split releases with various bands but didn't debut a solo record until 1998, when Relapse released their Honkey Reduction album. Like fellow extremists Mortician, Hull and vocalist Jay Randall used a drum program for high-speed percussion. After a second album, PCP Torpedo, AN recorded split releases with Converge and Benümb. Enemy Soil's Richard Johnson and Prosthetic Cunt's CA Schultz were recruited for 2002's *Frozen Corpse Stuffed With Dope*, which received a degree of media coverage that elevated the band to a new, internationally popular level. The tempo of some songs exceeded the 2000bpm mark at points, but perhaps the ultimate statement of extremity came in 2003 with the *Altered States Of America* 3" CD, which contained over 100 songs.

RECOMMENDED ALBUM:
Frozen Corpse Stuffed With Dope
(Relapse, 2002)
www.agoraphobicnosebleed.com

Richard Johnson on grindcore
"I'm a huge fan of grindcore when it's done properly. Sometimes you need a kick in the pants and Napalm Death is one to give it to you. Discordance Axis is another one. Their music is like listening to razor blades having a fight. But there's structure there at the same time, and progression. The death metal scene crossed with grindcore a great deal. Now all those bands have blasts in them. Maybe we need another band like Carcass to come along and shake things up a bit."

Akercocke

Certainly the most credible band that the British black metal scene has to offer alongside Cradle Of Filth, the appeal of the London-based Akercocke comes from the power and intricacy of their music, their studied, besuited image and the evident sincerity of their satanic beliefs. These combine to provide a charisma that the metal press has been soaking up since the band's debut release in 1999, *Rape Of The Bastard Nazarene*, on their own Goat Of Mendes label. Consisting of vocalist/guitarist Jason Mendonca, guitarist Paul Scanlan, bassist Peter Theobald and drummer David Gray, the band then released *The Goat Of Mendes* through Peaceville in 2001 and *Choronzon* on Earache two years later. Probably the black metal band most likely to achieve international recognition in the near future, Akercocke have supported established heavyweights such as Deicide with an insouciance that seems sure to serve them well.

RECOMMENDED ALBUM:
Choronzon (Earache, 2003)
www.akercocke.com

Akercocke (above) – black metal's new hope

Alastis (below) – Gothic black metal

Alastis

Switzerland's Alastis were founded in the late Eighties with War D on guitar, Zumof on vocals, Acronoise on drums and his brother Masmiseim on bass. Recording two strong, innovative demos in 1989 and 1990, the band signed to the Norwegian label

Head Not Found, and an album, *The Just Law*, was issued. Various personnel changes hindered the progress of the band, with War D taking on vocal duties when necessary, but Alastis still found time to develop their sound, moving from primitive black metal to more melodic, Gothic territory.

Moving to the French label Adipocere, a follow-up *...And Death Smiled*, was released in 1995, showcasing a more intricate, technical direction. A further label-change followed, this time a step up to Century Media, for whom Alastis recorded 1997's *The Other Side*. A successful tour with Anathema came the following year and the band accepted an invitation to play on the Twilight Of The Gods tour with Theatre Of Tragedy and Saviour Machine. In 1998 Alastis issued the *Revenge* album, which has garnered much praise from both doom and black metal fans, and 2000's *Unity* saw them continue to cover metal and gothic-rock territories with a certain panache.

RECOMMENDED ALBUM:
The Other Side (Century Media, 1997)
www.alastis.ch

Algaion

A Swedish black metal band at a time when that country's extreme metal scene is focused sharply on the death metal movement, Algaion were formed in 1993 by Mathias Kamijo and Mårten Björkman, formerly of the band Abernal. A two-track demo with the songs 'On The Reach Of Zaphonia' and '...And With Darkness I Pierce Him' led to a deal with the legendary Florida label Fullmoon. The *Oimai Algeiou* album was released in 1995, having been recorded with Peter Tägtgren at the newly-opened Abyss studio. After Björkman had spent some time in prison for arson and was paroled, the Italian labels Avantgarde and Wounded Love co-released a new mini-CD, *Vox Clamentis*. Touring followed, with Tägtgren guesting, and after a couple of years of silence the *General Enmity* album appeared in 1997, with some mainstream heavy metal and doom touches added to the early black metal template.

RECOMMENDED ALBUM:
Vox Clamentis
(Avantgarde/Wounded Love, 1995)

Allegiance

The Swedish Viking/black metal band Allegiance was formed in 1989 by Marduk collaborators Roger 'Bogge' Svensson and Fredrik 'Froding' Andersson and spent the ensuing six years recording a number of demos, including *Sick World*, *Odin Åge Er Alle* and *Höfdingadrapa*. These received a positive response among Swedish underground fans and ultimately led to a deal with No Fashion Records in 1995. The debut album *Hymn Till Hangagud* was released in 1996, followed swiftly by *Blodörnsoffer*. Peter Tägtgren was the producer. After a third long-player, *Vrede,* the band called it a day.

RECOMMENDED ALBUM:
Blodörnsoffer (No Fashion, 1997)

Altar

A Dutch death metal band formed in 1992, Altar first gained exposure through their *And God Created Satan To Blame For His Mistakes* demo and a debut album, *Youth Against Christ*, two years later. Local controversy due to the satanic nature of Altar's music provided more publicity and 1996's Ego Art led to major festival appearances. Although subsequent albums were increasingly polished, with a melodic death metal approach, the band have never really broken through internationally and are currently in stasis after a brief split in 2001.

RECOMMENDED ALBUM:
Red Harvest (Spitzenburg, 2001)
www.altar.nu

Amestigon

Austria's Amestigon were formed by the ex-Abigor singer Rune, also known as Tharen. They produce black metal with melodic and folk elements, successfully creating the required atmosphere with keyboards. Their music bears a resemblance to the Viking metal of Enslaved and the bands also share lyrical themes; one of Amestigon's best-known songs is 'Samhain', about the idealised pagan/Norse society so popular among a certain strand of the black metal audience.

RECOMMMENDED RELEASE:
EP (split with Angizia, Napalm Records, 1998)

Amnesia

Like Acid Reign, Barnsley's Amnesia played a lame Dixon of Dock Green to the Dirty Harry of Slayer and Anthrax, producing melodic thrash resembling (but inferior to) Megadeth. At the forefront of the Brit-thrash genre in the Eighties, they toured with other UK acts such as Toranaga, Xentrix and Slammer. Their sole album showed off the meaty riffing of Simon Fairhurst and Clive Heely, but the band were ultimately destined to be consigned to the C-league of UK extreme metal.

RECOMMENDED ALBUM:
Unknown Entity (independent, 1991)

Amon Amarth

From Tumba, a southern suburb of Stockholm, Amon Amarth (vocalist Johan Hegg, guitarists Olli Mikkonen and Johan Söderberg, bassist Ted Lundström and drummer Fredrik Andersson) formed in 1992. Two demos, *Thor Arise* and *The Arrival Of The Fimbul Winter*, led to a one-off deal with Pulverised Records, a label based in Singapore. *Sorrow Throughout The Nine Worlds* was released in April 1996 and sold in sufficient quantities to attract the attention of Metal Blade, to whom the band signed later that year.

Recorded with Peter Tägtgren, Amon Amarth's next LP, *Once Sent From The Golden Hall*, was followed by a major tour with heavyweight deathsters Deicide in June 1998. For the third album, *The Avenger*, recorded in 1999, the band decided to produce themselves: the result was a combination of death and black metal and retained the Viking themes. Subsequent albums *The Crusher* (2000), *Versus The World* (2003) and *Fate Of Norns* (2004) have kept Amon Amarth's profile extremely high.

RECOMMENDED ALBUM:
Once Sent From The Golden Hall
(Metal Blade, 1997)
www.amonamarth.com

Amorphis

Singer and guitarist Tomi Koivusaari, guitarist Esa Holopainen, bassist Olli-Pekka Laine and drummer Jan Rechberger form Amorphis, one of Finland's best-known extreme metal bands. Their first album, *The Karelian Isthmus*, was released in 1992 and contained competently-played death metal. However, over their next three recordings the band refined their sound to a much more progressive hybrid of doom, death and even rock influences.

An additional singer, Pasi Koskinen, now provides clear, melodic vocals in place of Koivusaari's death metal grunts as the band move away from their traditional death roots, and the band have introduced acoustic guitars into their songwriting.

However, Amorphis still pack a punch and recently reduced the amount of keyboards in their sound to allow the guitars to come through more brightly. The *Tuonela* album of 1999 was a much tougher beast and reassured those who had begun to doubt the band's status in extreme metal, as did the *Far From The Sun* album of 2003, released by major label Virgin.

RECOMMENDED ALBUM:
Tuonela (Relapse, 1999)
www.amorphis.net

Amorphis – prog-death metal?

Amsvartner

Amsvartner were formed in 1994 by the then-12-year-old Johansson twins Alfred (drums) and Albin (guitar/bass). Initially known as Awakening, the line-up eventually stabilised with another brother, Marcus, on vocals, and the 16-year-old guitarists Jonathan Holmgren and Daniel Nygaard. An EP containing fairly competent death/black metal was released to moderate praise, but it wasn't until 1999's impressively-performed album *Dreams* that the band started to be taken seriously. However, since 2000 band activity has been minimal.

RECOMMENDED ALBUM:
Dreams (Blackend, 1999)

Anaal Nathrakh

A much-praised British black metal band, Anaal Nathrakh recorded two demos in 1999 which were reissued as an album, *Total Fucking Necro*, by the Leviaphonic label. A barrage of brutal black metal, the old-school album title and feel led to credits from Norwegian pioneers Mayhem and the UK underground label Mordgrimm signed AN up for a debut album. *The Codex Necro* caused waves on the British scene and the band's reputation was bolstered by the appearance of Seth and Attila from Aborym on the follow-up, a mini album entitled *When Fire Rains Down From The Sky, Mankind Will Reap As It Has Sown*. The late Radio 1 DJ John Peel asked Anaal Nathrakh to do a session for him in December 2003, and a new deal with the Season Of Mist label points to a future in the black metal mainstream.

RECOMMENDED ALBUM:
The Codex Necro (Mordgrimm, 2002)
www.anaal-nathrakh.tk

Anacrusis

Formed in 1987 by guitarist Kevin Heidbreder and bassist John Emery, St. Louis' Anacrusis grew from a talented thrash outfit to one of the most highly respected progressive metal bands in the United States. Signed to Axis Records after winning a demo competition in *Metal Forces* magazine, the band recorded and mixed their debut *Suffering Hour* in one week for $1,000. Although technically competent, it was more or less a traditional thrash metal album and the 1990 follow-up, *Reason*, represented a step forward in musical terms - the songs were more innovative and experimental and showcased singer Kenn Nardi's surprising vocal range.

After a tour and a move to Metal Blade, Anacrusis' founder, drummer Mike Owen, left the band and joined the US navy. Chad Smith, who had played drums for Nardi's high school band Heaven's Flame, stepped in to perform on *Manic Impressions*, the next album, which would be hailed as a progressive thrash masterpiece. *Screams And Whispers* saw another change in the drum seat, with Paul Miles providing a solid, technical base to the increasingly complex song structures. Their most mature album, *Screams* also proved to be the band's swansong, the group parting ways in 1994.

Strokes singer Julian Casablancas namechecked the band at a 2002 gig, telling the audience that Anacrusis "will change your life".

RECOMMENDED ALBUM:
Manic Impressions (Metal Blade, 1991)

Anal Cunt

Formed in March 1988 by guitarist Seth Putnam, Anal Cunt (who had to be referred to by industry personnel as 'AC' for many years for obvious reasons) had a long, chequered and always deliberately offensive career until their split in the late Nineties for more serious projects. Targeting women, homosexuals and all ethnic and religious minorities in their songs with a moronic, schoolboy-level humour, it was hard to know if AC really intended their violent, misanthropic lyrics to be taken seriously, but many observers did and the band was never destined for major success. Perhaps the most memorable thing about them was their song titles, some of which were idiotically amusing whether you objected to their content or not: 'I Snuck A Retard Into A Sperm Bank', 'I Just Saw The Gayest Guy On Earth', 'Being A Cobbler Is Dumb', 'I Intentionally Ran Over Your Dog' and so on.

Seth Putnam on *Extreme Metal II*
❝Thanks for putting us in the book. It's so great. It's such an important book, you're so important too. It's such an honour. Are we in the first book? I hope not. Writers are a bunch of parasites who are usually failed musicians. I hope whoever reads this didn't have to buy this gay book.❞

Anata

A Swedish death metal act fomed in Varberg in 1993 by Fredrik Schälin (lead guitar, vocals), Mattias Svensson (guitar), Robert Petersson (drums), and Martin Sjöstrand (bass), Anata produce dense death metal with thrash and doom influences. Early tours with Dissection, Lake Of Tears and Beseech honed the band's live act and a demo appeared in 1995 entitled *Bury Forever The Garden Of Lie*. Svensson and Sjöstrand left the band in 1996 and were replaced by new bassist Henrik Drake and Andreas Allenmark as second guitarist.

A second demo, *Vast Lands Of My Infernal Dominion* (1997), led to a deal with the French label Season Of Mist and a debut album, *The Infernal Depths of Hatred*, appeared the following year. Tours followed before a follow-up, *Dreams Of Death And Dismay* (2001), which included more progressive elements than its predecessor. Drummer Petersson was replaced by Conny Pettersson, a member of the Anata side-project Rot Inject, in time for the recording of the band's most recent album, *Under A Stone With No Inscription*, released after a switch to the Earache label.

RECOMMENDED ALBUM:
Under A Stone With No Inscription (2002)
www.anata.se

Anatomy

Australian band Anatomy, made up of Marty (vocals), Hippy Slayer (guitar, keyboards), JA (bass), Chris Masochist (guitar) and the memorably-named Marcus Hellcunt (drums), perform mega-aggressive black metal. They were formed in Melbourne in the mid-Nineties and supported Impaled Nazarene in various states of Australia but, as they have been through various line-up changes, output has remained minimal.

RECOMMENDED ALBUM:
The Witches Of Dathomir (Bleed, 1999)

Ancient

Ancient's line-up revolves around primary composer Aphazel (vocals, guitar, bass, keyboards) although other members have come and gone. Notable among them was Lord Kiaphas, a singer previously known as Lord Vlad Luciferion, who had handled grunt/scream duties in Thokk as well as Grand Belial's Key.

After the first demo, 1992's *Eerily Howling Winds*, sold in droves, Aphazel and original vocalist Grimm signed to the French label Listenable and the *Svartalvheim* album was recorded. In 1995 the band went on to produce an EP, *Trolltaar*, but Grimm had had enough of black metal and left the band. Aphazel took his project to the US, signed to Metal Blade and recruited Kiaphas, a Norwegian drummer, Kjetil, and a female vocalist, Kimberly Goss. The new line-up then recorded their most well-known album, *The Cainian Chronicle*, a concept album based on the story of Cain and Abel. The record was followed by a 1997 tour through Europe.

Erichte then replaced Kimberly Goss, and a guitarist, Jesus Christ (yes, really), also joined the band. 1997's *Mad Grandiose Bloodfiends* was a record admired for its expansion into newer musical territories. During the subsequent tour Aphazel met the singer Deadly Kristin in Italy, relocated to Europe and took over the vocals, with Kristin as the new female vocalist. The latest recruit, Krigse (drums) completed the 1999 line-up and *The Halls of Eternity*, an aggressive, unrelenting return to the old-style Ancient, garnered critical praise. The latest album, *Night Visit*, sees the band's position at the forefront of the black metal B-league remain strong.

RECOMMENDED ALBUM:
The Cainian Chronicle (Metal Blade, 1996)
www.ancientband.com

Ancient Rites

Founded in 1988, although some of the members had been together since 1981, the Belgian black metal band Ancient Rites consist of Gunther Theys (vocals, bass) Bart Vandereycken (guitar) and Walter van Cortenberg (drums). The success of a 1990 demo, *Dark Ritual*, prompted the trio to set up the Fallen Angel label and self-release an EP, *Evil Prevails*. Touring followed and as the black metal scene flourished, the band's reputation spread. Despite personnel problems, two albums were recorded: *The Diabolic Serenades* was another self-release, while *Blasfemia Eternal* was a Mascot Records issue.

1998's *Fatherland* was a musical change in direction and received much critical praise, leading to festival appearances despite the perception by some that AR's lyrical themes were politically sensitive. A move to the Hammerheart label was followed by a new album in 2001, *Dim Carcosa*, which contained medieval themes. A live CD and DVD, *...And The Hordes Stood As One*, was released in 2003.

RECOMMENDED ALBUM:
Blasfemia Eternal (independent, 1999)
www.ancientrites.be

Ancient Wisdom

The Swedish side project of Bewitched frontman Marcus Norman, Ancient Wisdom was formed (initially as Ancient) in 1992 and recorded two early demos, *In The Eye Of The Serpent* and *Through Rivers Of The Eternal Blackness*. These led to a deal with Avantgarde and a debut album, *For Snow Covered The Northland*, was recorded in 1994. Technical problems forced a two-year delay. Norman, accompanied by guitarist Andreas Nilsson, bassist Fredrik Jacobssen and keyboard player Jens Ryden, continued with *The Calling* (1997), *And The Physical Shape Of Light Bled* (2000) and *Cometh Doom, Cometh Death* (2004).

RECOMMENDED ALBUM:
For The Snow Covered The Northland
(Avantgarde, 1996)
http://ancient-wisdom.cjb.net

Angel Corpse

A technical death metal band, the American act Angel Corpse were formed in 1995 by Gene Palubicki and Pete Helmkamp. The *Goats To Azazael* demo was recorded with drummer John Longstreth and led to a deal with Osmose. The album *Hammer Of Gods* was duly recorded and second guitarist Bill Taylor was recruited to add a fuller texture to the sound.

The band toured extensively to promote the album, notably in support of Impaled Nazarene, and in 1997 two EPs were recorded. Word spread and the band played several major shows, including the Milwaukee Metalfest, before entering Morrisound Studios to record *Exterminate*. A furiously aggressive album, it led to almost universal praise among fans of the death genre. Longstreth was replaced by Tony Laureano and the band continued to record and play, notably on an eleven-date European tour featuring an ultra-heavyweight bill including Immortal, Cannibal Corpse, Obituary, Marduk and God Dethroned.

1999 saw Angel Corpse move to Tampa for the recording and release of their third album, *The Inexorable*, and embark on

Angel Dust – (overleaf) extreme metal veterans

another gruelling tour of Europe and the US. However, an unexpected split came after a 2000 tour with Krisiun and Satyricon: Helmkamp's wife was injured in a confrontation at a gig and he was temporarily replaced by Krisiun frontman Alex Camargo. Osmose issued *Iron, Blood And Blasphemy* the following year, a collection of early demos; Helmkamp returned with a T-shirt company, Vomit Productions, and membership of first Terror Organ and Revenge; and Laureano took a step up to international level by joining Nile.

RECOMMENDED ALBUM:
Exterminate (Osmose, 1997)
http://come.to/angelcorpse

Angel Dust

Veterans of the German extreme scene, Angel Dust (currently Dirk Thurisch on vocals, Steven Banx on keyboards and Dirk Assmuth on drums) took almost a decade off from the metal arena but reappeared to the delight of many fans of Eighties Euro-thrash. Active initially from 1984 to 1989, Angel Dust split after the poor reception of their second album, *To Dust You Will Decay*. The first AD long-player, *Into The Dark Past*, became one of their most popular metal releases, but progress was hampered by disagreement between the band members and a split became inevitable.

Moving from thrash to more contemporary melodic power metal, the band delivered 1998's *Border Of Reality* and the band immediately embarked on tour supporting the US thrashers Overkill and Jag Panzer. Their appearance at the 1998 Wacken festival also earned them a few fans and their recent albums *Bleed, Enlighten The Darkness* and *Of Human Bondage* have been warmly received, even if the extremity that pervaded their earlier work has now been replaced by a mellower, less aggressive approach.

RECOMMENDED ALBUM:
Into The Dark Past (independent, 1984)
www.angel-dust.de

Annihilator

Seasoned US thrash metallers Annihilator are essentially the multi-instrumentalist Jeff Waters, with various other musicians involved on an ad hoc basis. Guitarists have included Neil Goldberg, Dave Scott Davis and Anthony Greenham, while Wayne

Darley played bass on the first three Annihilator albums, and several drummers have also trained under Waters. Randy Rampage contributed vocals to the band's seminal first album, *Alice In Hell*, and a later outing, *Criteria For A Black Widow*.

Waters claimed in a late-Eighties interview that one of his talents lay in writing commercial mainstream metal, but that his character was too rebellious to handle such conformity and thus that extreme metal was his ideal milieu. Pretentious as this may sound, it's a fact that his band have achieved a certain popularity through their crisply-produced, almost catchy melodies. Waters prefers to stick to what he does best, which is to say crunchy, toe-tapping speed metal with power metal elements. The Eighties live on...

RECOMMENDED ALBUM:
Never, Neverland (Roadrunner, 1990)
www.annihilatormetal.com

Jeff Waters on the birth of extreme metal
❝Energy. Aggression. Fast guitar playing. When I was younger, I always thought that there would be room for a band with those heavy aggressive speeds and riffs and attitude but with more technical and tighter guitar playing: Annihilator was born of fire!❞

Antaeus

French black metal act Antaeus operate a revolving line-up centred on frontman MKM and are almost as old-school in their approach as better-known genre bands such as Darkthrone. A debut album, the resolutely dark *Cut Your Flesh And Worship*

Satan, plus support slots with Impaled Nazarene and Thus Defiled and a track on a split EP entitled *SPK Kommando: We Hope You Die*, kept the band's profile high in 2000. A collaboration with Necrophagia was released by that band's frontman, Killjoy, on his Red Stream label later that year and was titled *Reverse Voices Of The Dead*. The band remains at the obscure, cult end of the BM genre, with MKM's habit of on-stage self-mutilation lending them a certain grisly credibility.

MKM on the frontline of extreme metal

❝Black metal bands like Funeral Mist, Katharsis, Malign, Watain and Deathspell Omega combine great musical work with strong ideology and are definitely among the most devoted individuals within the scene. Death metal-wise, we all keep on listening to demo bands from the early Nineties like Traumatic, Goreaphobia, Corpus Rottus, Immolation. I'm not too keen on newer death acts, apart from Verminous, Kaamos, Repugnant and Funebrarum from the USA.❞

Anthrax

One of the most influential of the Eighties thrash bands, Anthrax first took shape in 1981, founded by guitarist Scott Ian (nicknamed Scott "Not" Ian by fellow high school pupils) while he was still a teenager: the band's name occurred to Ian during a biology course. Recruiting the prodigiously talented Charlie Benante on drums, bassist Dan Lilker, lead guitarist Greg Walls and Neil Turbin on vocals, the debut album *Fistful Of Metal* was recorded in 1983. A primitive attempt at technical thrash, it's really only worth buying for its shrill cover of Alice Cooper's 'I'm Eighteen'.

After *Fistful Of Metal* Turbin, Walls, and Lilker departed (Lilker to Nuclear Assault, and later Brutal Truth and The Ravenous) and were replaced by singer Joey Belladonna, the band's bass roadie Frank Bello and the diminutive Dan Spitz on lead guitar. This became their most successful line-up to date, largely due to the operatic range of Belladonna, whose grasp of the high notes placed him miles apart from the then-untrained hoarseness of his main vocal competitors at the time, Metallica's James Hetfield and Slayer's Tom Araya.

Anthrax – still caught in a mosh after 20 years

Releasing the *Armed And Dangerous* EP in 1984 and *Spreading The Disease* the following year, Anthrax's popularity grew hugely. By this time they had developed a highly original and much-copied 'squeaky-clean' guitar sound – on 'Gung-Ho', an amusing sideways look at macho soldiering, complete with martial effects, the machine-gun-like velocity of Ian's rhythm guitar and Benante's kick drums has to be heard to be believed. By today's standards the band's overall sound may appear a little anodyne, but the song remains an object lesson in precision.

1987's *Among The Living* propelled Anthrax into the international limelight. The band had adopted a kind of hyperactive clown image, gurning into the camera, dressing in skatewear and generally presenting a much more relaxed, humorous image than the other three members of the so-called Big Four of Thrash – Slayer, Metallica, and Dave Mustaine's po-faced Megadeth. They built up a reputation for their crowd-pleasing shows – Ian would shave "Not" into his chest-hair while Belladonna, a natural showman, would offer up a hilarious vocal solo after the other band members had performed theirs. To this day, seasoned metallers grow misty-eyed at the memory of Anthrax's tour in support of the rapidly-rising Metallica in 1987, one of the most entertaining live bills ever – and, some say, one in which Anthrax would often unseat the headliners.

Among The Living was an instant hit worldwide, thanks largely to the catchy, witty songwriting. 'I Am The Law', a paean to the underground comic hero Judge Dredd, even charted in the UK despite the lack of radio airplay – the line "I am the law/ You won't fuck around no more" was too much for British programmers. The title track, a stamping, threatening display of power, the hugely entertaining 'Caught In A Mosh', and 'NFL (Efilnikufesin)' ensured that rock clubs everywhere caught the Anthrax virus, and for a time it seemed certain that the band would continue to dominate the metal scene.

However, Anthrax's fanbase began to decrease after the follow-up, 1988's *State Of Euphoria*, despite the fact that it was an innovative, challenging album exploring slower, more sophisticated avenues; the fans clearly preferred the wacky thrash of yore. *Persistence Of Time* (1990), was better, containing a remarkable cover of Joe

Jackson's 'Got The Time'.

At about this time the band began to experiment with rap and hip-hop. They had been impressed by Run DMC's collaboration with Aerosmith on 1987's 'Walk This Way' and approached Public Enemy's Chuck D. After some initial reluctance, D agreed to work with Anthrax: the result was the blinding 'Bring The Noise', a potent blend of Anthrax's gut-churning riffs and Chuck's powerful rap vocal, which Ian had described as "as heavy as Slayer". Awareness of the band remained high and a sense of being given a second chance was perceptible. *Attack Of The Killer B's* (1991) was an interesting stopgap for the fans, containing B-sides and remixes, and kept fans happy while Anthrax participated in the Clash Of The Titans tour with Megadeth and Slayer (they were replaced by Testament on the UK leg of the tour).

However, Belladonna had had enough and decided to leave the band. It's never been made clear exactly why he left, although rumours have persisted that the rest of the band found him lazy. The usual "musical differences" were quoted as the reason for his departure, and ex-Armored Saint singer John Bush was recruited as the new singer in time for the band's move to new label Elektra. Although Bush was, and remains, a talented, versatile singer, many fans felt that Belladonna's high-pitched wails represented Anthrax's 'true' sound and sales of the next album, *The Sound Of White Noise* (1993) were less than astounding.

Dan Spitz was the next to leave, and the image of a 'new' Anthrax was compounded. Spitz had often been quoted in interviews with guitarists' magazines as saying that he loved to mix outlandish scales, and it's a fact that his wild, unpredictable soloing was a defining feature of the band. Paul Cook took his place for 1995's *Stomp 442* and the band continued to make a respectable living, issuing *Volume 8: The Threat Is Real* in 1998. Benante also took over guitar duties, subsequently becoming the author of many of the band's most-applauded riffs.

The year 2000 saw the release of *Attack Of The Killer A's*, a compilation of many of the band's best songs, chosen by fans via the Anthrax website. Many of the tunes come from the 'classic' *Among The Living* line-up, evincing the fact that those were the days for many followers. However, Anthrax's versatility was obviously still a strong point. The Ian/Benante side project SOD (see separate entry) also produced a second album, more than a decade after their debut, while other news included the planning and then cancelling of a proposed tour with both Bush and a returned Joey Belladonna on vocals.

In 2001 the threat of anthrax being used on the American public after the 9/11 attacks led the band to jokingly consider a change of name. Ian told the press that he would be taking an anthrax immunisation, stating: "I refuse to die an ironic death".

After a move to the German label Nuclear Blast, Anthrax released *We've Come For You All* in 2004, a well-received album that indicated how much energy the band retained after two decades in the business. New guitarist and respected producer Rob Caggiano added some much-needed drive to the band and their future remains bright.

RECOMMENDED ALBUM:
Among The Living (Island, 1987)
www.anthrax.com

John Bush on the death of British metal
❝I'll always feel a kinship with UFO, Journey, Zeppelin of course, Purple and then Maiden. The Scorpions, too, Ted Nugent, too, but it was mostly British stuff. In fact I rib a lot of British people about it, I say come on, where are all the great bands nowadays? I love Radiohead and Coldplay, and even Robbie Williams, but where's the metal bands? There's Cradle Of Filth, and there's Lostprophets, but they're emulating the American bands, whereas back then we were all copying the Brits!❞

Apollyon

The Danish black metal band Apollyon was formed in 1992. The line-up has been fluid; initial personnel consisted solely of Archdemon Diabolos and Lord Worros. The *Creators Of Evil Thoughts* demo and an unnamed promo were recorded the following year, showcasing a dark, melancholic style, a precursor of the ubiquitous doom of today.

Worros was replaced by Sorgh in 1994, and a bass player, Korihor, was added. Another demo, entitled *Troldeskovens Aander*, was produced, and Korihor was swiftly replaced by ex-Denial Of God bassist Azter, although he himself only lasted two concerts. The vocalist Vrykolatios then

joined Apollyon and the song 'Omnia In Majorem Diaboli Gloriam' was recorded for the *A Tribute To Hell* compilation CD. At this point the band secured a deal with Fullmoon, and the *Diaboli Gratio* album was recorded in 1998.

RECOMMENDED ALBUM:
Diaboli Gratio (Full Moon, 1998)

Apollyon Sun

Guitarist and singer Thomas Gabriel Fischer, the frontman of avant-garde metal outfit Celtic Frost, returned to the scene in 1998 with Apollyon Sun, together with Erol Unala (guitar), Dany Zingg (bass), Roger Muller (keyboards) and Marky Edelmann (ex-Coroner, drums). Great things are expected of the Swiss outfit, which was founded in 1994, but which has spent almost five years perfecting a full-length recording, *Sub*.

As one might expect from a musician who thought nothing of incorporating opera singers and drum machines into his early work – which included metal covers of Roxy Music and Dean Martin – AS utilise a blend of influences, including industrial rock and electronic samples. Their music has been labelled 'metal for the 21st century', although whether this is merely hyperbole or the edge of a promising new direction for extreme music is as yet unknown. Rumours of a Celtic Frost reunion have also been constant.
www.apollyonsun.com

Arch Enemy

A Swedish death metal project of great popularity centring on the guitar-wielding Amott brothers Michael and Chris, along with Angela Gossow (vocals), Sharlee DiAngelo (bass) and Daniel Erlandsson (drums), Arch Enemy started out as an extreme metal supergroup. Michael Amott, once of Carcass, plays in three bands simultaneously – he's also a member of doom super-metallers Candlemass and the Kyuss-like Spiritual Beggars – while bassist DiAngelo has an impressive CV, having played with Mercyful Fate as well as Witchery and Dismember.

Arch Enemy began life with vocalist Johan Liiva and made some acclaimed albums with him. 1996's *Black Earth* album was a combination of melodic thrash and progressive influences; fans loved the

Arch Enemy – the death metal band du jour

classic-style duelling guitars and Liiva's meaty vocals, a recipe repeated on *Stigmata* in 1998. However, it was only with the recruitment of the formidable Gossow, who has become an iconic example for women in extreme metal, that the band really took off. They remain at the forefront of European death metal.

RECOMMENDED ALBUM:
Wages Of Sin (Century Media, 2001)
www.archenemy.net

Arckanum

Arckanum's music is – according to the band – "primitive, raw, medieval, grieved and trollish". This last adjective may be a little startling for some, but the image ties in perfectly with the band's vision, a view not unlike that of Burzum, whose ideal of a pagan-values lifestyle bears comparison. The band consists of only one member, Shamaatae, whose day job is as the singer of the black metal band Sorhin.

Shamaatae originally started the band in 1992 with Loke Svarteld on guitar and Sataros on vocals, recording a demo in 1993 containing six tracks of 'Old Black Metal'. Dumping the other musicians, Shamaatae ventured alone into billy-goat-gruff territory, producing the 15-song *Trulen* demo which led to a 1995 deal with Necropolis. Entering the Abyss Studio

(previously home to fellow Swedes Dark Funeral and the super-evil Abruptum) Arckanum's debut album *Fran Marder* (*From The Forest*) was recorded. The lyrics were, helpfully, written in Ancient Swedish, and the music is raw, atmospheric black metal.

RECOMMENDED ALBUM:
Fran Marder (Necropolis, 1996)
www.arckanum.se

Arcturus

An intriguing symphonic black metal project formed by various members of the current Norwegian A-league, Arcturus were founded in the early Nineties by Garm (vocals), a member of Ulver and Borknagar, Mayhem's Hellhammer (drums) and Sverd (initially guitar, later keyboards). Their first recording, the *My Angel* EP, was a dark work focusing less on traditional black metal fury than on the ambient bombastics of the synths. The band then concentrated on other work for two years, but Arcturus was rejuvenated when the guitarist Samoth of Emperor – in whose band both Sverd and Hellhammer were playing – joined temporarily. Ulver's bass player Skoll also helped out and Samoth released *Arcturus' Constellation* demo on his Nocturnal Art label in 1994.

Imprisoned for church-burning, Samoth played no part in the band for some time, but as Hellhammer and Sverd both left Emperor at around the same time, Arcturus took precedence once again and the Tritonius guitarist August was drafted in to replace Samoth. The *Aspera Hiems Symfonia* album was issued by Ancient Lore Creations, part of the UK's Misanthropy label, and was licensed to the metal major Music For Nations. Another guitarist, Knut, was recruited and the fourth (and at this point, last) album was recorded: *La Masquerade Infernale*. The album hints at classical influences but remains a gloomy, introspective work. The band acknowledge the influence of composers such as Kurt Weill and Tricky, which may go some way to explaining the lo-fi nature of the music.

RECOMMENDED ALBUM:
Aspera Hiems Symfonia
(Ancient Lore/Misanthropy, 1996)
www.arcturus.tk

Arkhon Infaustus

A deeply satanic metal band from France, who straddle the line between death and black metal with aplomb, Arkhon Infaustus were formed in 1997 by guitarist/vocalist D Deviant and bassist 666 Torturer. Committed to their beliefs, the band put together a powerfully grim set of songs and recorded a demo, *In Sperma Infernum*, which was released by the Mordgrimm label. A 2000 EP, tastefully called *Dead Cunt Maniac*, appeared on Spikekult and a full-length debut album, *Hell Injection*, followed shortly afterwards.

A tour with Mortician and signing to Osmose preceded a new album, *Filth Catalyst*, which garnered much praise. The current line-up is completed by drummer AZK6 and second guitarist Toxik H.

RECOMMENDED ALBUM:
Filth Catalyst (Osmose, 2003)
www.evilness.com/arkhon666

Artillery

Artillery are a thrash metal band from Denmark, who in the early to mid-Eighties often appeared to be about to ascend to the heights achieved by their German contemporaries Sodom and Kreator. Formed in 1982, the band signed to Neat and released the impressive *Fear Of Tomorrow* album in 1985. Due to budgetary problems, however, the 1987 follow-up, *Terror Squad*, failed to receive the promotion it deserved and the band shifted to Roadrunner, for whom a further album was released. However, Artillery never achieved the attention they deserved and split in 1991 after internal disputes.

In late 1999, the band reformed with Flemming Ronsdorf, Michael Stytzer, Morten Stytzer and Per M. Jensen and released *B.A.C.K.*, produced by Andy Sneap, which was hailed immediately as a return to form. Since then, however, activities have been minimal.

RECOMMENDED ALBUM:
Fear Of Tomorrow (Neat, 1985)

Asgaroth – a rare Spanish metal act

Asgaroth

Spanish black metal bands are few and far between, but Asgaroth do the job with commendable malevolence. Initially the solo project of Daniel Rubi Piero (stage name Lord Lupus), who recorded a demo in 1995 entitled *Songs Of War*, the band soon assembled a line-up (currently Piero plus Christopher Baque-Wildman, Oscar David Raventos and Oison Martinez). An EP, *The Quest For Eldenhor*, appeared in 1996, with another two years later entitled *Absence Spells Beyond*, which contained a cover of King Crimson's 'Epitaph'. In between they recorded an album, *Trapped In The Depths Of Eve*. Touring with Alastis

was followed by a signing to Peaceville and a 2002 album, *Red Shift*.
RECOMMENDED ALBUM:
Trapped In The Depths Of Eve
(New Gotia, 1998)
www.asgaroth.com

Assuck

A grindcore act from Florida, the oddly-named Assuck were formed in 1992 by singer Steve Heritage alongside Pete Jay (bass) and Rob Proctor (drums) and released two albums. The first, *Anti Capital* (1993), made little impact, but protracted touring in Europe raised the band's profile and 1996's *Misery Index* did better. However, personnel problems plagued the band and they split soon after, with a late-entry drummer, Daryl Kahan, going on to join Abazagorath.
RECOMMENDED ALBUM:
Misery Index (Sound Pollution, 1996)

At The Gates

The legendary Swedish death metal band At The Gates, made up of Tomas Lindberg (vocals), Anders Björler (guitar), Alf Svensson (guitar), Jonas Björler (bass) and Adrian Erlandsson (drums), were among the first to combine melody and brutality to found the 'Gothenburg sound' and were at the forefront of the New Swedish Wave Of Death Metal (NSWODM) until they disbanded in 1999.

Shortly after their formation in 1990, the band recorded the *Gardens Of Grief* EP for the Dolores label and embarked on a prolonged Swedish tour accompanied by such accomplished acts as Dismember, Bolt Thrower, Massacre and Immolation. ATG built up a reputation for their charismatic live presence and a deal with the UK's Peaceville Records led to 1991's *The Red In The Sky Is Ours* album. Two years of intense touring followed and a successor, *With Fear I Kiss The Burning Darkness*, followed in 1993. Svensson was replaced by Martin Larsson and the band started to become more well-known internationally, with their first UK show – at Nottingham's Rock City venue – filmed for an MTV Headbangers Special.

1994's *Terminal Spirit Disease* was hailed as their best work yet, bearing similarities both to their countrymen Entombed and a more refined Carcass. The band moved to

Earache in the following year and the more melodic *Slaughter Of The Soul* was produced, which included keyboards for the first time. The album gained a nomination in the Best Hard Rock category at the Swedish Grammy Awards for the 'Blinded By Fear' single, which was also nominated at the 1996 *Kerrang!* awards for Headbanger's Ball Best Video.

At The Gates then toured the US, more than holding their own despite the accompaniment of Morbid Angel and Napalm Death. However, as the band were at their commercial and musical peak, they decided to split, the pressure of the incessant touring culminating in the decision of the principal ATG singwriters, the Björler twins, to form another band, The Haunted (see separate entry), which has achieved enormous recognition for spearheading a microcosmic return of thrash metal. Lindberg has since gone on to provide vocals for The Great Deceiver and Lock-Up (see entries) among other bands.
RECOMMENDED ALBUM:
The Red In The Sky Is Ours
(Peaceville, 1991)

Atheist

Initially a late-Eighties Florida thrash metal band, Atheist evolved into a death metal outfit with heavy jazz and progressive influences. They managed to record three successful albums but never recovered from the death of bassist Roger Patterson, the founder member and linchpin of the band. The other personnel, Kelly Shaefer (vocals), Rand Burkey (guitar), Frank Emmi (guitar) and Marcel Dissantos (drums), leaned on the talents of the session bass player Tony Choy on their last two albums, but the core was gone and the band split in 1993.
RECOMMENDED ALBUM:
Piece Of Time (Active, 1989)

Atrocity

A German band who progressed from a death metal stance on their earlier work to a less popular electronic/sampling style, Atrocity were founded in 1985 and after four years of gigs and demos, signed to Nuclear Blast. The primitive *Blue Blood* EP (1989) was less developed than the Scott Burns-produced *Hallucinations* LP of 1990, one of whose high points was its cover artwork, a painting by the Swiss artist H.R.

Giger of *Alien* fame. Atrocity went on to support Carcass in 1990, Sodom in 1991, Deicide in 1992 and Obituary in 1994, but despite their live successes, the move towards electronic music which they displayed on their later albums deprived them of a fanbase and the band called it a day in 1996.

RECOMMENDED ALBUM:
Todessehnsucht (Roadrunner, 1992)

Atrophy

The Arizona band Atrophy, consisting of Brian Zimmerman (vocals), Chris Lykins (guitar), Rick Skowron (guitar), James Gulotta (bass) and Tim Kelly (drums), played thrash metal along the lines of the established San Francisco Bay Area bands Exodus, Forbidden or the early Metallica. Their first album, *Socialized Hate*, displayed a technically competent feel, but the follow-up, *Violent By Nature*, proved that whatever finesse Atrophy possessed would not be enough to lift them above the crowd of Hetfield wannabes.

RECOMMENDED ALBUM:
Socialized Hate (Roadrunner, 1988)

Aura Noir

A Norwegian black/thrash metal band, Aura Noir was founded by Aggressor (a member of the avantgarde BM band Ved Buens Ende) and Apollyon, who recorded the *Two Voices, One King* demo. Signing to Dimmu Borgir singer Shagrath's Hot label, they released *Dreams Like Deserts* in 1995, a record labelled 'retro-thrash' by some critics. Live dates and a debut album, *Black Thrash Attack*, featured the talents of Mayhem guitarist Blasphemer. Moving slightly away from the Eighties thrash template, 1998's *Deep Tracts Of Hell* (released after a label switch from Malicious to Hammerheart) sounded more like a black metal record and was supported by tours with Dødheimsgard; the band also formed a new act, Cadaver Inc. A rarities collection, *Increased Damnation*, appeared in 2000, and as Cadaver Inc. has taken off, so Aura Noir has been put on hold. However, Blasphemer has rejoined for more sessions and the band is still in existence.

RECOMMENDED ALBUM:
Dreams Like Deserts (Malicious, 1995)
www.on.to/internet-damnation

Autopsy

Although Slayer and Death had used slasher themes in early songs, Autopsy are recognised as the inventors of gore metal. The line-up of Chris Reifert (ex-Death), Danny Coralles, Eric Cutler and later Steve DiGiorgio emerged from the metal scene of San Francisco with their own brand of music, signing to Peaceville after a series of innovative demos. Controversy came quickly after Australian customs officials seized import copies of an album, *Acts Of The Unspeakable*, and impounded it due to its cartoon-horror artwork. The band released a series of albums before splitting in the mid-Nineties and reforming as Abscess. Their legacy is such that a tribute band, made up of musicians from Dismember and other death metal bands, occasionally tours Sweden under the name Murder Squad.

RECOMMENDED ALBUM:
Severed Survival (Peaceville, 1989)

Autumn Leaves

Not to be confused with the German pop-folk outfit of the same name, the Danish Autumn Leaves were formed in 1992, initially calling themselves Decrial, and recorded the *Desires Unfold* demo. The tape attracted attention nationwide and after the name-change in 1994, some personnel changes and another successful demo, 1995's *Hope Springs Eternal*, a deal was signed with Serious Entertainment.

The debut Autumn Leaves LP, *Embraced By The Absolute*, was recorded in 1996 at Borsing Studios, where acts such as Illdisposed, Invocator and Infernal Torment had worked. The album was released in 1997 and critics labelled it a strong debut, combining aggression with atmosphere. Two years of touring followed before another album, *As Night Conquers Day*, was produced; once again it was welcomed by metal fans in Denmark and abroad. Since then, however, the band have fallen silent.

RECOMMENDED ALBUM:
Embraced By The Absolute
(Serious Entertainment, 1997)

Avulsed

A Spanish death metal outfit, Avulsed is composed of Dave Rotten (vocals), Cabra (guitar), Juancar (guitar), Furni (drums) and

Tana (bass). The band's career kicked off with the Carnivoracity EP in 1994, followed swiftly by a split LP with the Greek band Acid Death. They played their first gig as support to the UK death act Cancer and a reputation as a powerful live act began to develop. Rotten subsequently founded the Repulse label and issued the *Eminence In Putrescence* album two years later, a rapid success in death metal circles.

However, Avulsed then made the notoriously risky move of recording an electronic remix album of some of their old tunes; the result was 1998's *Cybergore* CD. Attempts to achieve a crossover between the worlds of extreme metal and techno have rarely been successful (see Atrocity; Celtic Frost; possibly Fear Factory) but the band survived the negative response of their fans, largely by virtue of the fact that they are signed to an independent, self-owned label.

The same year saw the Colombian label Quirofano release a collection of Avulsed demos and old recordings, *Seven Years Of Decay* – a welcome return to form for many fans. The tapes were mastered by James Murphy in California, ensuring a meaty, layered sound. In November 1999 the band played their biggest show to date in front of 5,000 people on the second Barbarian Rock Festival. The bill also featured Manowar, Cradle Of Filth, Napalm Death and Hammerfall. A series of albums has followed and the most recent recording, *Gorespattered Suicide*, was hailed as their best yet in 2004.

RECOMMENDED ALBUM:
Stabwound Orgasm (Repulse, 1999)
www.avulsed.com

Axis Of Advance

A Canadian 'militant war metal' band fusing the black and death genres to innovative effect, Axis Of Advance were formed when the band Sacramentary Abolishment split in 1998. Two of the members, Wör and Vermin, continued with the new band and recruited J Read as a session drummer. 1999 saw the release of the *Landline* EP through the Catharsis label. Axis Of Advance remained more or less an underground act until 2004, when the superb *Obey* album – a brutally extreme record based on genocidal themes – appeared on Osmose.

RECOMMENDED ALBUM:
Obey (Osmose, 2004)
http://aoa.ark11.net

Bal-Sagoth - British war metal

B

Bal-Sagoth *(Left)*

Currently Byron Roberts (vocals) plus Chris Maudling (guitar), Jason Porter (bass) and Johnny Maudling (drums and keyboards), UK metallers Bal-Sagoth first came together in 1993. Roberts' idea was to assemble a symphonic metal band which would concentrate on his preferred themes – the darker forms of fantasy and science fiction, laced heavily with doses of cod-mythicism. Bal-Sagoth duly signed to Cacophonous and recorded the *A Black Moon Broods Over Lemuria* album, a competent attempt at epic grandeur. It was not until 1996's *Starfire Burning Upon The Ice-Veiled Throne Of Ultima Thule* that fans began to accumulate, and after the next album, *Battle Magic*, on which Byron began to experiment more with themes of warfare, Bal-Sagoth embarked on European tours with the black metallers Dark Funeral and Emperor.

A move to Germany's Nuclear Blast label followed and *The Power Cosmic* was released in 1999. The band have labelled themselves 'True Britannic War Metal' (the Manowar parallels are obvious) and the Bal-Sagoth war fetish reached its logical conclusion when a sponsorship deal was reached with the Sussex-based replica arms and armour manufacturers Battle Orders Ltd. *Atlantis Ascendant* was released in 2001 and the BS saga continues.

RECOMMENDED ALBUM:
Battle Magic (Cacophonous, 1997)
www.bal-sagoth.freeserve.co.uk

Byron Roberts on growing up with metal
❝My first experience of heavy metal was when my brother and sister used to steal my Lite Brite to make the Kiss logo when I was a kid. I also remember the old Kiss action figures and comic books, even though I never listened to their music. Years later, my first experience of metal proper was probably Iron Maiden's *Number Of The Beast* album.

My favourites were Bathory, Hellhammer, Celtic Frost, Kreator and Slayer. The dynamic power, speed, anger and aggression of these bands, as well as their apparently sinister nature and often occult imagery, immediately appealed to me. It was so much more exciting than standard turgid heavy metal and the dark aspect was more enticing than a lot of the more 'street level' thrash bands.**❞**

Baphomet

German thrash metal band Baphomet was founded in 1986 with Thomas Hertler (vocals), Gernot Kerrer (guitar), Hansi Bieber (bass) and Manuel Reichart (drums). The peak of their career was undoubtedly a support slot with the Jim Carrey-endorsed gore-merchants Cannibal Corpse on their tour of Germany in 1992. Their second album, *Latest Jesus* (1992), was an attack on the superficiality of the consumer society and received positive reviews, but Hertler left the band to pursue other interests and the band split shortly afterwards, later becoming Banished.

RECOMMENDED ALBUM:
No Answers (Massacre, 1991)

Barathrum

Finnish black metallers Barathrum, originally called Darkfeast, formed in 1990 and consisting of Demonos Sova (vocals and bass), Aki (guitar) and Ilu (drums). After a self-titled demo and the temporary replacement of Aki by Jetblack Roima in 1991, the name-change to Barathrum came. Members came and went before the recording of a second demo, *Witchmaster*, produced by Beherit's Holocausto, which sold 600 copies. The band then split up after internal dissension and Demonos continued with new members, the even more metallically-nicknamed Bloodbeast (guitar) and Necronom Dethstrike (drums); the band's musical approach became more experimental, utilising a second bass player and playing a so-called 'witchdrum' with human bones for a more morbid effect. A deal was struck with the Finnish label Spinefarm and a series of albums, culminating on 2002's *Venomous*, has brought Barathrum a respectable degree of attention.

RECOMMENDED ALBUM:
Okkult (2000)
http://barathrum.poro-tuotanto.org

Bathory

The Swedish one-man black metal project Bathory was far more in its fans' eyes than just a band, due to the cult of personality that enveloped it over years of secrecy. The band first attracted attention after contributing two songs, 'Sacrifice' and 'The Return Of Darkness And Evil', to an obscure but acclaimed compilation called *Scandinavian Metal Attack*, released by Tyfon Records in 1983. After the release of *Bathory* (1984), the band started to attract a cult following: it soon became apparent that the music was more or less the work of one individual, the multi-instrumentalist Thomas Forsberg (commonly known by his stage name, Quorthon), about whom personal information was for a long while thin on the ground. Although he did acknowledge the sporadic contributions of two other musicians, Kothaar (bass) and Vvornth (drums), Quorthon later revealed that more than one musician used these *noms de guerre* and that he himself was normally responsible for all guitar, bass, drums, keyboard and production duties.

Quorthon sang of hell, damnation and other demonic subjects in a choked, hacking style which might sound rather outmoded today but which helped to establish the entire Scandinavian black metal scene. Along with Venom and Mercyful Fate, Bathory were hailed as the inventors of the new black metal style, with their profile helped along by the grim, murky production of their music. Quorthon revealed in later interviews that the conditions in which Bathory's successors, *The Return* and *Under The Sign Of The Black Mark* (both 1985) were recorded were inconvenient, to say the least. Heavenshore Studios, where these early albums were recorded, functioned as a garage and general store room, and he often recorded his vocals surrounded by boxes of washing powder and used car parts, wondering if the noise of nearby traffic and dripping water would filter through to the tapes. The recording technology itself was primitive and there was very little light to work by.

Looking to the Nordic legends of Odin and Valhalla for inspiration, as well as the music of Wagner and Beethoven, Quorthon shifted the thematic emphasis of his music from a satanic to a Wotanist standpoint, releasing *Blood Fire Death* (1989), *Hammerheart* (1990) and *Twilight Of The Gods* (1991) in quick succession. Predictably, many fans resented this change of direction, but others were attracted to this newer approach and appreciated the intelligent, non-misanthropic themes. However, the death metal generation passed Bathory by in the Nineties and he remained at cult level, releasing three best-ofs under the title *Jubilaeum* and winding up the decade with a two-album concept, *Nordland*. Sadly, Bathory's career was cut permanently short when Forsberg died of a sudden heart attack in 2004 at only 39 years old. His legacy lives on.

RECOMMENDED ALBUM:
Under The Sign Of The Black Mark
(Black Mark, 1987)
www.bathory.se

Quorthon on the birth of a genre
"Everything that didn't sound like the NWOBHM in those days was called black metal. In fact, by 1984 when people were asking us how long we'd been into black metal, we were embarrassed because we thought they were referring to the Venom album of the same name. I used to say that we were into death metal, just for fun, and I challenge anyone to show proof that anyone else came up with that subcategory before September 1984."

Beheaded

Beheaded's line-up of Marcel Scalpello (vocals), David Bugeja and Tyson Fenech (guitars), David Cachia (bass) and Chris Brincat (drums) first formed in 1991 and became what probably remains the only Maltese death metal band to make much impact away from the island.

The *Souldead* demo was recorded in March 1995 and was favourably reviewed by several underground publications, who praised its technical, aggressive combination of death metal and atmospheric keyboard passages. Omar Grech replaced Tyson Fenech and the band signed with the Swedish label X-Treme Records. The *Perpetual Mockery* album was released in 1998 and Beheaded played a series of shows in mainland Europe, playing alongside Vader and Deranged. On their return, Marcel Scalpello left the band and was replaced by Lawrence Joyce. The latest album, *Recounts Of Disembodiment*, continues along standard death metal lines.

Perpetual Mockery (X-Treme, 1988)

Beherit

This Finnish black metal quartet's debut album, *The Oath Of Black Blood* (1992) was reminiscent of early Bathory, both in content and in its hamfisted production values, but it sold respectably and a certain cult following has developed around the band. Formed in 1989, Beherit recorded a number of demos which later formed the basis of the *Oath...* album. The *Demonancy* demo in particular contained powerful, evocative songs and is now much sought-after. The Beherit live show is said to be one of the band's strong points, in which blood-drinking and other "very metal" activities take centre stage.

The Oath Of Black Blood (independent, 1992)

Benediction

One of the better UK death metal bands along with Desecration, Birmingham band Benediction (Dave Ingram (vocals), Darren Brookes (guitar), Peter Rew (guitar), Frank Healy (bass) and Neil Hutton (drums) released their first album, *Subconscious Terror*, in 1989 with soon-to-be-Napalm Death vocalist Barney Greenaway. Touring consistently led to a reputation for a powerful live show, in particular successful appearances with Bolt Thrower, Paradise Lost and Autopsy. At one point Benediction took over the headline spot from Bolt Thrower, due to administrative problems: Ingram joined Bolt Thrower full-time in 1999. The band have also played with Slayer and Biohazard, covering one of the latter's tunes for a 2000 compilation. The recent *Grind Bastard* and *Organised Chaos* albums offer a glimpse of the better end of the UK death scene.

Grind Bastard (Nuclear Blast, 1998)
www.benediction.tk

Benümb

San Francisco Bay Area hardcore/thrash band Benümb were formed in 1994, releasing a split 7" with Short Hate Temper a year later and more releases on the same format over the next three years. 1998 saw the release of *Soul Of The Martyr*, with some songs clocking in at mere seconds in length in the best grindcore tradition. *Withering Strands Of Hope* was even heavier and led to a split release with Pig Destroyer. The most recent record, *By Means Of Upheaval*, saw the Benümb recipe refined still further.

By Means Of Upheaval (Relapse, 2003)
www.benumb.net

The Berzerker

Initially a hardcore techno/gabba DJ act, Australian band The Berzerker upped the stakes to an intense death metal approach on two internationally-released records to date, both from the Earache label. Based on the studio work of frontman Luke Kenny, the songs are anchored by an insanely fast blastbeat played on live drums and consisting of triggered, distorted kick drums and snare which make the guitar riffs almost irrelevant. Kenny was quoted recently as saying that his music is designed "to take the diseased shell of the mundane human rituals and habits that exist on this planet and destroy them to reveal a being with a greater purity than man", which explains the intensely misanthropic song-titles and lyrics. The second album, *Dissimulate* (2002) contains grim, spoken-word samples from pathology films and contained drumming of such enormous speeds (1148bpm at points) that at one point the *Guinness Book Of Records* was called in to investigate. The grisly masks

which the band wear on stage add to their intimidating image.

RECOMMENDED ALBUM:
Dissimulate (Earache, 2002)
www.theberzerker.com

Luke Kenny on the bigger picture
❝I would like to hope that some of the songwriting skills come back and that death metal and grindcore are not two separate styles of music. Although after the glory years – from the late Eighties to about 1993 – death metal started to die out, for sure as it stands today in 2005, extreme metal is here to stay.❞

Bestial Mockery

Formed in 1995 by Master Motorsåg, Warslaughter, Jocke Christcrusher and Micke Doomanfanger, Swedish black metallers Bestial Mockery recorded the *Battle* promo in 1996 and, after the inevitable line-up shuffles, the first demo, *Christcrushing Hammerchainsaw*, came out in 1997. Another recording called *Chainsaw Demons Return* was recorded one year later. Various demos and split releases led to a compilation of material entitled, yes, *Chainsaw Execution* by the German Sombre label in 2001.

Tours with Maniac Butcher and Driller Killer followed and then the first full-length album, also entitled *Christcrushing Hammerchainsaw*, was released by Metal Blood Music in 2002. More European dates followed before Bestial Mockery signed to Osmose, who in 2003 released their second album, *Evoke The Desecrator*. Recently the band played the Fucked Up In Finland tour; their next move is a split LP with Unholy Massacre and a new demo called *Sepulchral Wrath*.

RECOMMENDED ALBUM:
Chainsaw Execution (Sombre, 2001)
www.geocities.com/bestialattack

Bestial Warlust

Classic Australian black metal performed by Chris Corpsemolester (guitar), Phil Venom (bass), Marcus Hellcunt (drums), Chris Masochist (guitar) and Damon Bloodstorm (vocals), Bestial Warlust emerged from an earlier death metal band called Corpse Molestation and released *Vengeance War 'Til Death*. However, the band only remained together for one more record,

Blood And Valour, before splitting: the members went on to join Destroyer 666, Anatomy and Abominator.

RECOMMENDED ALBUM:
Vengeance War 'Til Death
(Modern Invasion, 1995)

Bethzaida

Norwegian black metal band Bethzaida (named after the supposed birthplace of Satan) were formed in 1993 by guitar player André Svee, drummer Terje Kråbøl, bass player Olav Malmin and vocalist/flute player Lars Ruben Hirsch. A 1994 demo, *Dawn*, was a combination of doom and Eighties death metal. A second demo, *Nine Worlds*, appeared in '95 and led to a deal with Season Of Mist. A debut album, also titled *Nine Worlds*, showcased Bethzaida's unusual death-metal-plus-flute approach and was the first in a sequence of albums, the most recent of which, *War Volume 2*, appeared in 2000.

RECOMMENDED ALBUM:
Nine Worlds (Season Of Mist, 1996)

Bewitched

Sweden's Bewitched, based on guitarist and main songwriter Anders Nystrom (aka Blackheim), also includes Vargher (vocals), Wrathyr (bass) and Reaper (drums) and follow the Eighties black/thrash code to the letter, as a side project for the musicians, whose main bands are Ancient Wisdom and Katatonia. Their debut album, *Diabolical Desecration*, was released by Osmose in 1995 and was the first in a line of albums which pay tribute to the thrash legends of 20 years ago. There's also a Chilean black metal band called Bewitched.

RECOMMENDED ALBUM:
At The Gates Of Hell (Osmose, 1999)

Blazemth

One of the very few Spanish extreme metal bands to rise to international attention, Blazemth rose from the Barcelona band Undivine, which released a single in the early Nineties through the tiny Drowned label. After Undivine split, three of the members went on to form Blazemth, recruiting a bass player from Beheaded Lamb.

An album, *For Centuries Left Behind*, was released in 1995, revealing the band's early preoccupation with classic black metal as well as doom and Gothic rock. Lyrically, *For Centuries…* dealt with medieval fantasy (a kind of Iberian equivalent of the Nordic themes of Ulver and Burzum) and was well-received despite the lack of a widespread extreme scene in Spain. Gigs were played with fellow countrymen Avulsed in support, and the band have remained occasionally active ever since.

RECOMMENDED ALBUM:
For Centuries Left Behind
(Abstract Emotions, 1995)

Blood Duster

Australian death metal band Blood Duster – Tony Forde (vocals), Jason PC (bass), Finn Alman (guitar) and either Shane Rout or Euan Heriot (drums) – mix grindcore and high-velocity thrash on their SOD-length tunes, although their later work has seen them slow down. Blood Duster's debut album, the charming *Fisting The Dead*, first drew attention to the band in 1994 and was followed by an Aussie tour with Brutal Truth. Personnel changes ensued, notably including the departure of Rout, who went on to form the almost unlistenable Abyssic Hate. The *Yeest* mini-CD followed, but it was only after the release of *Str8outtanorthcote* that the band rose to a semblance of international prominence. Euan Heriot left the band in 1999 and Rout briefly re-joined, leaving the future of Abyssic Hate uncertain. A certain propensity towards AC-style comedy-metal has emerged of late, with the *Cunt* album (2000) and a 2004 self-titled release on Season Of Mist boasting titles such as *Let's Fuck, I Love It When Joe Pesci Swears,* and so on.

RECOMMENDED ALBUM:
Str8outtanorthcote (Dr Jims, 1997)
www.bloodduster.com

Blood Red Throne

The new project of sometime Emperor bassist Tchort, Blood Red Throne was formed in 1998 and includes guitarist Død, singer Mr. Hustler, drummer Espen 'Beist' Antonsen and bassist Erlend Caspersen. Honing an act by rehearsing Deicide, Death and Obituary songs and recording the *Deathmix* demo, BRT scored a deal with Hammerheart and a debut album, *Monument Of Death,* was recorded. A limited

edition 'Suicide Kit' version of the CD was accompanied by a razorblade and a poster, as well as being hand-numbered in the band's own blood. A cover of a Massacre song was recorded for the *A Taste For Blood* EP in 2002 and a second album, *Affiliated With The Suffering*, was released in 2002. A new deal with Earache followed a year later.

RECOMMENDED ALBUM:
Affiliated With The Suffering
(Hammerheart, 2002)
www.bloodredthrone.tk

Bloodbath – death metal supergroup

Bloodbath

A Swedish supergroup comprising Opeth frontman Mikael Akerfeldt, Hypocrisy's Peter Tägtgren, all-round composer Dan Swanö and others, Bloodbath released an excellent, brutal death metal album, *Resurrection Through Carnage*, in 2002 as a more aggressive outlet from their more melodic day-job bands. It's not known if the band has a long-term future but it is to be hoped that a new album will appear at some point, as the initial effort was promising.

RECOMMENDED ALBUM:
Resurrection Through Carnage
(Century Media, 2002)

Body Count

Body Count's line-up consists of the rapper Ice-T (vocals), Ernie C (guitar), D-Roe (guitar), Mooseman (bass) and Beatmaster V (drums). The band members met as teenagers at Crenshaw High School in the black ghetto of South Central in Los Angeles, and remained friends while Ice-T's profile as a rapper, TV personality and political commentator went stratospheric in the early Nineties.

Ice-T had employed Ernie C as occasional guitarist on his hip-hop albums, which often sampled or otherwise included some fairly heavy riffs. He extended the metal idiom on his 1991 breakthrough album *OG: Original Gangster* by including a complete song, 'Body Count'. The band embarked on the 1991 Lollapalooza tour and received an ecstatic response. Ice-T clearly relished his role as heavy metal frontman (he told the press "I'm living out all my teenage fantasies") and would stand, poker-faced and muscles clenched, staring down the crowd while his band churned out the riffs. One or two songs reached thrash velocity, but the majority of Body Count's music was standard trad-metal fare, if perhaps a little dirtier than the norm; what made it so entertaining, however, was Ice's obvious commitment to the use of Body Count as a vehicle for his quasi-anarchist message.

1992 saw the release of a self-titled album, and the lead single, 'There Goes The Neighborhood', set out the Body Count stall succinctly with lines like "Here come those fuckin' niggers/With their fancy cars", while the album also contained the song 'KKK Bitch'. The band toured widely with B-league thrash and hardcore outfits such as Exodus, DRI and ProPain, while the heavyweight Metallica and Guns N' Roses also invited BC to support.

At this point it seemed that Body Count would never receive much publicity, as a mere side project for Ice-T, but later in the year a global furore erupted over the content of one of the band's more graphic songs, 'Cop Killer', which detailed the execution and justification thereof of a member of the police department. Body Count's record label Warner Brothers got into a pious froth about the song's putative influence on America's impressionable youth, while Warners' shareholders (including, bizarrely, Charlton Heston) made public statements condemning the song. After some months of tabloid fever the song was replaced by a spoken-word invective by Jello Biafra entitled 'Freedom Of Speech'. In due course band and label parted company.

After the media frenzy died down,

Body Count's career appeared to be in the ascendant, but the following album, 1994's *Born Dead*, failed to make much of an impression; the metal-buying public had perhaps tired of Ice-T's rather monotonous message and moved on.

Although Ice-T recorded a track, 'Disorder', with Slayer for the *Judgement Night* soundtrack in 1995 and appeared with Motörhead's Lemmy and Ugly Kid Joe's Whitfield Crane on the 1996 collaboration, *Born To Raise Hell*, it was clear that Body Count would return to side-project status. Ice-T's hip-hop, acting and book-writing careers were all in relatively healthy shape, and perhaps his heavy metal urges had almost been satisfied. A third album, *Violent Demise: The Last Days*, was issued, but vanished without trace; at the time of writing, Body Count is in hibernation and the 'Cop Killer' controversy is fast becoming a distant memory. Ice-T himself provided a typically pithy epitaph to his beloved metal project: "They did everything they could to take us out, but like any good monster, that just made us stronger."

RECOMMENDED ALBUM:
Body Count (Warners, 1992)
www.bodycount.com

Bolt Thrower

UK death metal act Bolt Thrower's line-up is Karl Willets (vocals), Barry Thompson (guitar), Gavin Ward (guitar) Jo Bench (bass) and Andrew Whale (drums), although several line-up changes have occurred. The band was formed in 1986 by Ward and Whale, taking its name from a role-playing game, Warhammer Fantasy Battle (a bolt thrower is a weapon resembling a crossbow that launches arrows). The band recorded two demos in 1987, *In Battle There Is No Law* and *Concession Of Pain*, which led to a deal with Vinyl Solution. The former was released to underground acclaim, and Bolt Thrower were snapped up by Earache, with whom the 1989 EPs *Realm Of Chaos* and *Cenotaph* were recorded. The following year saw the release of *Warmaster* and the band came to the attention of the late Radio 1 DJ John Peel, who recorded a Peel Sessions album with them and issued it on Strange Fruit in 1991.

The warlike themes continued with 1992's *The IVth Crusade* and 1994's *For Victory* before Bolt Thrower moved to

Metal Blade, touring incessantly and requiring some years to write a new album. The result was 1998's *Mercenary*, after which Karl was briefly replaced by Benediction's Dave Ingram. Festival appearances and more recordings for Metal Blade have kept the band's progress steady.

RECOMMENDED ALBUM:
The Peel Sessions 1988-1990
(Strange Fruit, 1991)

Borknagar

A black metal supergroup, Borknagar first formed in 1995 and consisted of ex-Molested guitarist Øystein Garnes Brun, vocalist Garm of Ulver and Arcturus, guitarist Ivar Bjornson of Enslaved, drummer Grim of Immortal and Gorgoroth, and Gorgoroth bassist Infernus, who was, however, rapidly replaced by a musician named Kai.

A self-titled debut album was recorded for the Norwegian Malicious label, receiving some underground recognition. Its production was slightly murky, however, and the band decided to give their music a higher budget for the second long-player, 1996's *The Olden Domain*. The album contained acoustic guitar, piano and choir, and fully deserved the label of epic metal which Øystein assigned to it. Borknagar then toured Europe with In Flames and Night In Gales, while a Borknagar song appeared on a *Darkness We Feel* compilation, included as a bonus disc with Rotting Christ's 'A Dead Poem'.

The last Borknagar album was 1998's *The Archaic Course*, employing the vocal talents of Simen Hestnæs in place of Garm and a new guitarist, Jens Ryland. The band then completed a successful tour with Cradle Of Filth and Napalm Death throughout Europe. More line-up changes have occurred but the band remains active.

RECOMMENDED ALBUM:
The Olden Domain (Malicious, 1996)
www.borknagar.com

Broken Hope

Death metal band Broken Hope – Jeremy Wagner (guitar), Joe Ptacek (vocals), Brian Griffin (guitar), Shaun Glass (bass) and Ryan Stanek (drums) – were founded in the late Eighties, recording two demos which led to a deal with Grind Core and their primitive-sounding debut, *Swamped In Gore*. The band signed up with Metal Blade and a slightly more sophisticated follow-up was recorded, 1993's *The Bowels of Repugnance*. A national tour supporting Unleashed followed and Broken Hope found themselves popular for their combination of harmonic riffs with touches of doom, which counterbalanced the raw grind of their more brutal songs. Broken Hope also contributed a version of Twisted Sister's 'Captain Howdy' on their next album, *Repulsive*, inviting the itinerant guitarist James Murphy in to play a solo.

RECOMMENDED ALBUM:
The Bowels Of Repugnance
(Metal Blade, 1993)

Borknagar – progressive black metal from – yes! – Norway

Brujeria

Grindcore band Brujeria is a group of Americans and Brits posing as Mexican bandits. Their stage names are Juan Brujo (vocals), Asesino (guitars), Guero Sin Fe (bass), Fantasma (bass), Grenudo (drums) and the mysterious Jr. Hozicon (diabolic director). A press kit was released at the time of the first Brujeria album, *Brujeria*, which was issued by Roadrunner in 1997, claiming that DEA agents are searching for the bandmembers of Brujeria, that they have become the most wanted criminals in the US, and even that 50% of the drugs smuggled into North America are the responsibility of Brujeria and their organisation. The ultimate in Bond-like subterfuge, however, was the claim that the band were using submarines to bring drugs into the US, although whether anyone actually believed them is unknown.

The line-up actually revolves around ex-Fear Factory guitarist Dino Cazares, Billy Gould of Faith No More and Shane Embury of Napalm Death, along with a succession of vocalists, guitarists and drummers. The high point of their career was undoubtedly the song 'Razo Odiero', a tirade against right-wing California politician Peter 'Pito' Wilson. Gould left in 2003 when it became apparent that the band was going to be a successful act, rather than the amusing side-project it was at its inception.

RECOMMENDED ALBUM:
Brujerizmo (Roadrunner, 2000)

Brutal Truth

After the demise of the Eighties thrash outfit Nuclear Assault and the apparently-permanent descent into hibernation of SOD, the bassist Danny Lilker (also ex-Anthrax) assembled Kevin Sharp (vocals), Brent McCarthy (guitars) and Scott Lewis (drums) to perform the rawest grindcore possible, combining this with a range of disparate influences to create a kind of industrial/techno/noise metal hybrid. The Brutal Truth debut album, *Extreme Conditions Demand Extreme Responses*, was released in 1992 by Earache, after which the band embarked on the US Campaign For Musical Destruction Tour, also featuring the talents of Napalm Death, Carcass and Cathedral. The following year saw the band tour Europe on a 30-date co-headlining

jaunt with Fear Factory. The subsequent Perpetual Conversion single, recorded with the UK techno band Larcency, was a grindcore remix which included a cover of Black Sabbath's Lord Of This World.

The following year saw the band tour with Pungent Stench and Macabre as a buildup to the release of *Need To Control*, another versatile album. The band had included two more covers, 'Dethroned Emperor' by Celtic Frost, and perhaps less predictably, a stab at Pink Floyd's 'Wish You Were Here'. A new drummer, Rich Hoak, replaced Lewis, and a fourth record was rapidly assembled, the Tarzan-themed *The Sounds Of The Animal Kingdom*, graced with sleeve art depicting a kind of grindcore *Lord Of The Apes*. The band split in 2000 with the *For Drug Crazed Grindfreaks* EP.

RECOMMENDED ALBUM:
Sounds Of The Animal Kingdom
(Relapse, 1997)
www.brutaltruth.com

Burzum

Rarely has the politics of a band so dominated its output. Like Bathory (with whom Burzum share certain thematic and musical similarities), the band is more or less the work of one man, the Norwegian Varg Vikernes, also known by his stage name of Count Grishnackh. Both this name and that of the band come from J.R.R. Tolkien's *Lord Of The Rings*, Grishnackh being a particularly repulsive Orc and Burzum ("darkness" in Orcish) their hell-like home. Ironically, Vikernes' name was originally Kristian; he later changed it legally to Varg.

Having played in the Eighties death metal bands Satanel and Old Funeral, Vikernes' career in black metal began when he gravitated towards the centre of the Inner Circle, a group of Satanists devoted, they announced, to making Norway resemble hell. In practice this meant the vandalism and arson of churches and the desecration of graveyards. The leader of the Circle was Euronymous (real name Øystein Aarseth), the owner of a record label, Deathlike Silence, an Oslo record shop named Helvete (Hell) and the guitarist of the black metal band Mayhem (see separate entry).

Euronymous was impressed by the young Vikernes' talents and invited him to play bass on the Mayhem album

Burzum – permanently on hold?

De Mysteriis Dom Sathanas. A spate of church burnings led to Vikernes' arrest, but he was subsequently released after evidence was found to be inconclusive. Enjoying the attention this brought him, both from the other members of the Inner Circle and the Norwegian press, Vikernes started to play a more prominent role in the Circle's activities. As Burzum began to gain recognition, Euronymous grew increasingly disillusioned with his young protegé and a rivalry developed between the two musicians. Although it's likely to be apocryphal, it's rumoured that Euronymous visited a medium and was warned that his death was imminent.

In August 1993, Vikernes and the Thorns and ex-Mayhem musician, Blackthorn, paid a late-evening visit to Euronymous, who answered the door in his underwear. An argument began and as Euronymous turned to walk away, Vikernes attacked him with a knife. Euronymous was stabbed repeatedly in the back and neck and ran screaming out of his flat, where Vikernes stabbed him to death.

Unfortunately for the killer, several pieces of evidence pointed to him, including his bloodstained record contract — which he had forgotten to take out of Euronymous' flat — as well as sets of fingerprints. He was soon arrested and charged with murder, and is now serving 21 years in prison, the maximum penalty a Norwegian court can award. This sequence of events has made Vikernes a notorious public figure. The Norwegian press made the most of the story, of course, and the issue of Satanism in the metal scene remains topical. However, it is his political stance which makes Burzum such a controversial project.

Growing up in Bergen, Norway, and spending a year as a child in Iraq, Grishnackh became obsessed firstly with fantasy fiction such as the Tolkien works before graduating to more serious, weighty sources such as Norse legends and folk myths, which appealed to him as he began to question the society in which he lived. In one interview he said, "If you like forests and wilderness, you would love Bergen. We have a lot of Urwälder (ancient forests), wild animals, grim mountains and wilderness. Some places the forest is so dense you have to crawl to get anywhere. Some places the best – if not only – way to move around is to find a brook, and move along its course, jumping from rock to rock," and claimed that those wanting to understand his political and spiritual ideology should "take a walk in the middle of a winter night in a forest all alone... it actually speaks."

In essence, Vikernes believes that Judeo-Christian beliefs are a plague on Norway and the Scandinavian/Germanic peoples, and that a return to the religious system and social structure of ancient times would benefit those countries spiritually and sociologically. Many fans find Burzum attractive - the idea of a pagan, balanced society might seem a delicious fantasy to some. However, it's also a racist stance. Certain aspects of the Burzum vision resemble those of Nazism - the concept of a master race, the purge of undesirable elements, the forbidding of art and technological progress, and so on – which has rightly led to more or less universal condemnation.

Musically, Burzum was until Vikernes' imprisonment the blackest of black metal (long, gut-wrenching screams and hyper-fast riffs), although the production quality of Burzum's six albums progressed from a primitive murk to the latest in digital clarity. The last two were issued from prison, where he was not permitted to use guitars, and are therefore primarily ambient, keyboard-based music. Thematically, Burzum moved away from Satanism and towards a pagan/Wotanist standpoint. A look at the various Burzum album covers should be enough to let you know what Vikernes was thinking of – he often used artwork by the artist Theodor Kittelsen, who is well-known for his idealistic paintings of a supposedly untamed 'pagan' Norway.

It appears that 1999's *Hlidskalf* will be the final Burzum release for the foreseeable future. Whether Vikernes will emerge from prison after the projected 21 years (or longer: he bungled a prison escape attempt in 2003) and resume his position as the simultaneously most revered and despised figure in black metal is unknown. What is certain is that a precedent has been set, and that the politics of extreme metal have been thrown sharply into focus. Black metal can no longer be dismissed as just a game for teenagers.

RECOMMENDED ALBUM:
Det Som Engang Var (Misanthropy, 1994)

Cadaver/Cadaver Inc.

Formed in 1989, Cadaver's line-up of Ole Bjerkebakke (vocals/drums), Anders Odden (guitar), Espen Sollum (guitar) and Rene Jansen (bass) knocked out a technically competent death-brew but never quite managed to ascend the heights of popularity enjoyed by their black metal countrymen. Still, their first album, a 1990 split release with Carnage entitled *Hallucinating Anxiety*, was hailed as Norway's first death metal album, something of a an

honour. However, that country's rapidly-rising black metal scene caused Cadaver to take an extended break in 1993.

Six years later, Anders Odden recuited drummer Czral, bassist LJ Balvaz and frontman Apollyon (also of Aura Noir) and reformed the band with a slight name-change. Cadaver Inc. re-signed with Earache and toured with Morbid Angel and Extreme Noise Terror. An album in 2001, *Discipline*, caused some controversy when the band launched it with a fake (but serious-looking) 'campaign' selling alibis for murder. Returning to their death metal roots with a move to the Candlelight label and the *Necrosis* album in 2004, Cadaver Inc. seem ready to consolidate their position.

RECOMMENDED ALBUM:
Discipline (Earache, 2001)
www.cadaverinc.com

Anders Odden on classic extreme metal
❝My favourite bands had their heyday in the Eighties. It's not my job to search the underground for the next big thing, as I already regard thrash/death metal as a classic genre that has settled like rock and heavy metal has. I hope that the kids find more extreme stuff on the far side of the scene and that someone is creating music out of pure evil with no thoughts of the music business bullshit involved.❞

Cadaverous Condition

This Austrian doom/death outfit consists of Wolfgang Weiss (vocals), Rene Kramer (guitar), Peter Droneberger (bass) and Paul Droneberger (drums). Along with many mid-Nineties German and Austrian bands, Cadaverous Condition have covered a song from the so-called Neue Deutsche Welle (New German Wave) of the Eighties – in their case the very New Romantic 'Eisbaer'. Recent albums have included Weiss' guttural vocals and death-like riffs over a drum machine program to interesting effect.

RECOMMENDED ALBUM:
The Lesser Travelled Seas
(Perverted Taste, 2001)
www.cadaverouscondition.com

Callenish Circle

Holland's Callenish Circle were founded in 1992 under their former name Genocide by vocalist Patrick Savelkoul. Recruiting a steady line-up, Savelkoul changed the band name and in 1995, the band recorded a demo entitled *Lovelorn*. It went on to become Demo Of The Month in the Dutch magazine *Aardschok*, and CC signed to the Dutch label Hammerheart for one record.

The debut album, *Drift Of Empathy*, followed; it was snapped up immediately by fans of melodic death metal, a fairly uncommon genre in the Netherlands at the time. The *Escape* mini-album was subsequently released by Polar Bear Records, all of which led to a more permanent deal with DSFA, for whom a third melodious, death/doom record was recorded, *Graceful… Yet Forbidding*. Savelkoul, who works at the Karmageddon Media label, continues to divide his time between band and label.

RECOMMENDED ALBUM:
Drift Of Empathy (Hammerheart, 1996)
www.callenish-circle.com

Cancer

This death metal act – John Walker (vocals, guitar), Ian Buchanan (bass) and Carl Stokes (drums) – from Telford, UK showed signs of Florida-style death influences on their first album, 1990's *To The Gory End* (which took a mere four days to record) before recruiting guitarist James Murphy, fresh from the excesses of Obituary. The second album, *Death Shall Rise*, showed signs of the nimble-fingered Murphy touch, introducing the melodic elements from which his later bands Disincarnate and Testament have since benefited. Leaving the smaller Vinyl Solution label for Flametrader, *The Sins Of Mankind* proved to be the high point of Cancer's career, hailed by fans from far and wide as a leap forward in the genre. The next Cancer album, *Black Faith*, was a far more commercial proposition, reflected in its unlikely release by the major EastWest label. Its cover art was slightly unnerving, however, and the popularity of the band plateaued.

RECOMMENDED ALBUM:
The Sins Of Mankind (Flametrader, 1993)

Cannibal Corpse

Buffalo band Cannibal Corpse are perhaps the most devoted brutal death metal act in this book, rarely diverging from the path of the blastbeat and the throaty roar. Despite the pious proclamations of US Republican Bob Dole (who once identified them as a symptom of America's falling moral

standards), the line-up – George 'Corpsegrinder' Fisher (vocals), Paul Mazurkiewicz (drums), Pat O'Brien (guitar), Jack Owen (guitar) and Alex Webster (bass) – won't be going anywhere for some time.

Due to the consistently shocking nature of their album sleeves and lyrics, many of the world's larger record shops choose not to stock their records, while CC are banned entirely in Australia, New Zealand and Korea and, in an oddly specific ruling, are not allowed to perform songs from their first three albums in Germany. Publicity, positive or otherwise, has always surrounded them; surreally, gurner-extraordinaire Jim Carrey, a big fan, requested their appearance in his *Ace Ventura: Pet Detective* film. The band's American supporters are also sufficient in number to bring about another unexpected coup – in 1996 they became the first death metal band to debut on the *Billboard 200*, with their *Vile* album.

Cannibal Corpse continue to maintain a prolific work rate. Whether or not they contribute to the USA's "falling moral standards" or not is difficult to assess, but it seems that the international metal community wants them around, and what the public wants, the public gets.

RECOMMENDED ALBUM:
Tomb Of The Mutilated (Metal Blade, 1992)
www.cannibalcorpse.net

A Canorous Quintet

Swedish death metal band A Canorous Quintet (guitarists Linus Nirbrant and Leo Pignon, drummer Fredrik Andersson, bassist Jesper Löfgren and vocalist Marten Hansen) were first founded in 1991, when only four members existed; thus, the name was initially A Canorous Quartet.

The 1993 demo *The Time Of Autumn* led to live appearances with Edge of Sanity, Katatonia and Hypocrisy, while the following year saw Chaos Records sign them up on the strength of a second tape, *As Tears* (later released as an mini-CD). Further tours ensued and in 1995 the Quintet entered the famed Abyss studio to record the *Silence Of The World Beyond* album for No Fashion. Reviews were positive and in 1997 a follow-up was released, the more aggressive *The Only Pure Hate*.

RECOMMENDED ALBUM:
The Only Pure Hate (No Fashion, 1997)
http://acanorousquintet.8k.com

Carbonized

Carbonized was a moderately successful side project of some of the members of Therion – Jonas Derouche (vocals, guitar), Lars Rosenberg (bass) and Piotr Wawrzeniuk (drums) – and was founded in 1988. Despitely the aggressively death-metal name, Carbonized played experimental, psychedelic music which found favour among fans of Therion or other more unorthodox extreme metal.

After two albums of psych-death, Carbonized went the whole hog on *Screaming Machines*, a bizarre combination of influences including Sonic Youth, Pink Floyd and the tinny narcissisms of Voivod. Very few people enjoyed it, even though the record company, Foundations, had remixed it and delayed its release by three years to make it more public-friendly. After this non-event, Carbonized was put on ice and its over-experimental members returned to Therion, maintaining that the psychedelic death genre will be back when the world is ready for it.

RECOMMENDED ALBUM:
Screaming Machines (Foundations, 1996)

Carcass

Combining the speedy blastbeats of Napalm Death with lyrics taken straight from pathology manuals, Liverpool grindcore legends Carcass inspired two whole movements in metal across six albums. Carcass' line-up – guitarist Bill Steer, drummer Ken Owen and ex-Electro Hippies vocalist/bassist Jeff Walker – stabilised in 1987 when Steer left his main band, Napalm Death. 1988's debut album, *Reek Of Putrefaction*, and the following year's *Symphonies Of Sickness*, contained 'songs' consisting of practically unlistenable blasts of guitar, drums and grunts – and contained graphic lyrics that would inspire the gore metal of Cannibal Corpse and Autopsy, such as "Globular tissue decomposed, hydrogen sulphide is evolved/Reek of putrefaction secreted by necrotrophic mould", resulting in a deeply disturbing set of songs, including 'Vomited Anal Tract', 'Swarming Vulgar Mass Of Infected Virulency', 'Excoriating Abdominal Emanation' and 'Cadaveric Incubator Of Endo-Parasites'. Perhaps unsurprisingly, the members of Carcass were all vegetarians.

However, fans were surprised when the recruitment of ex-Carnage guitarist Michael Amott gave 1991's *Necroticism: Descanting The Insalubrious* album a

Carcass – grindcore pioneers

Carnal Forge – neo-thrashers extraordinaire

progressive, very melodic edge, inspiring bands at the forefront of the new Swedish death metal movement such as In Flames and Dark Tranquillity. Two more new albums and a best-of, 1996's *Wake Up And Smell The Carcass*, were released amid further line-up changes, but Steer decided to leave and Carcass folded shortly after. They leave two legacies for the world of extreme metal: time will tell if they are given the recognition they deserve.

RECOMMENDED ALBUM:
Heartwork (Earache, 1993)

Carnage

Michael Amott's Swedish death metal band – also featuring Matti Karki (vocals), David Blomkvist (guitar), Johnny Dordevic (bass) and Fred Estby (drums) were only really notable for the bands they went on to join. Dordevic became the singer of the very successful death-metallers Entombed, Amott went to Carcass (see above), while the others reformed the dormant Dismember. Formed in 1989, Carnage issued a Mexico-only EP, a split CD with the short-lived Cadaver (later Cadaver Inc.) and one full-length album, 1990's *Dark Recollections*.

RECOMMENDED ALBUM:
Dark Recollections (Necrosis, 1990)

Carnal Forge

Formed in 1997 by In Thy Dreams members Stefan Westerberg and Jari Kuusisto, Carnal Forge refined a fast, thrash metal approach with a demo, *Sweet Bride*,

which led to a brief deal with Wrong Again and later a more permanent home with Century Media. The line-up was expanded with Johan Magnusson, Dennis Vestman and Jonas Kjellgren and an album, *Who's Gonna Burn*, atttacted praise for its committed, but not merely plagiaristic, take on Eighties thrash. The next record, *Firedemon*, came out in 2000 and established a style with which the band have more or less stuck ever since – bass-light production with clean, staccato guitars and raw vocals. Vestman was replaced by Petri Kuusisto, Jari's brother, also of In Thy Dreams.

After a 17-date tour with The Haunted (who share the neo-thrash approach) and US death metal gods Nile, more line-up changes took place, but didn't hinder the recording of *Please… Die!*, which was released in 2002. A long European tour with Mortician followed, as did another album, *The More You Suffer*. The following year CF were booked, somewhat incongruously, onto the 2003 Metal Gods Tour (Halford, Testament, Primal Fear, Immortal, Amon Amarth) of the US. In 2004 a new album, *Aren't You Dead Yet?*, and a DVD, *Destroy*, were both released. Although CF are riding a wave of popularity, the fact is that their music is much the same from album to album: hopefully this won't end their career prematurely.

RECOMMENDED ALBUM:
Please… Die! (Century Media, 2001)
www.carnalforge.com

Carpathian Forest

A Norwegian black metal band, Carpathian Forest – the work of two musicians, Nattefrost and Nordavind – first emerged in 1992 with the *Bloodlust & Perversion* demo. The more pagan-themed *Journey Through The Cold Moors Of Svarttjern* tape of the following year dropped the lechery, containing more atmospheric, proficient composing, and led to a deal with Avantgarde in 1994.

The first CF album, the extremely black metal mini-album *Through Chasm, Caves And Titan Woods* was released in 1995 to great acclaim from Norwegian fans. The band then ceased activities entirely for three years, despite the popularity of *Through Chasm...*, prompting rumours of the band's demise. However, 1998 saw the band release what appeared to be a return to *Bloodlust & Perversion* form, with the full-length *Black Shining Leather*, containing a remarkable cover of The Cure's 'A Forest'. The *Strange Old Brew* and *Morbid Fascination Of Death* concept albums kept the band in the public eye and they continue along their way with the help of Tchort (Blood Red Throne) on guitar and Vrangsinn (World Destroyer) on bass. Nattefrost also performs and records in the the latter musician's band, as well as another act called Grimm.

RECOMMENDED ALBUM:
Strange Old Brew (Avantgarde, 2000)

Carpathian Full Moon

A Norwegian doom/death band featuring Henrik Pettersen (drums/vocals), Jorgen Hansen (guitar), Endre Begby (guitar), Lars Lie (bass) and Jon F. Bakker (keyboards), Carpathian Full Moon incorporated Gothic, acoustic and classical sounds on their sole album, 1994's *Serenades In Blood Minor*. The songs contained plenty of melody and the odd spoken-word and folkie pretension, although black metal touches were also to be heard. The song 'De Praestigiis Daemonum' even included a double bass, and although the net result was an album with much potential, the band failed to gain much attention and split soon after its release.

RECOMMENDED ALBUM:
Serenades In Blood Minor
(Avantgarde, 1994)

Cattle Decapitation

San Diego death metal band Cattle Decapitation has evolved from a gore metal side-project of the art-metal band The Locust to a sophisticated grind act in its own right, despite the many line-up changes that have taken place since its formation in 1996. Originally comprising David Astor (bass), Gabe Serbian (drums) and Anal Flatulence (yes) vocalist Travis Ryan, the band recorded two albums, *Human Jerky* (on the Nevada label Satan's Pimp) and *Homovore*. Adding bassist Troy Oftedal, CD recorded *To Serve Man*, released in late 2002 by Metal Blade. The members of Cattle Decapitation also perform in side projects such as DisreantiyouthhellchristbastardassmanX, 5/5/2000 and UUM.

RECOMMENDED ALBUM:
Humanure (Metal Blade, 2004)
www.cattledecapitation.com

Cemetary

Sweden's Cemetary, including Mathias Lodmalm (vocals, guitar), Anders Iwers (guitar), Tomas Josefssen (bass) and Markus Nordberg (drums) executed a complete change-around in musical style over their six-year career, starting life as a pure death metal band on 1992's *An Evil Shade Of Grey* but moving towards far more doom and even trad-metal territory on subsequent albums.

Last Confession saw the band producing Gothic doom with hardly any death references, but despite this new sound, mainman Lodmalm split the band in 1997, claiming that Cemetary had said everything they needed to say. He has since gone on to form and disband another act, Sundown, named after one of Cemetary's albums.

RECOMMENDED ALBUM:
An Evil Shade Of Grey (Black Mark, 1992)

Centinex

The Swedish death metal outfit Centinex were formed in 1990, recording a demo, *The End Of Life*, in 1991. A deal with Swedish Underground followed and 1992 saw the release of the *Subconscious Lobotomy* album, which was ultimately released in 1993 on tape only by Wild Rags Records, who also issued *Transcend The Dark Chaos* on cassette the following year.

After some confusion over labels, a compilation of promo and unreleased tracks formed 1996's *Malleus Maleficarum*, which paved the way for another deal with Die Hard, the small but influential Danish label. The next year's *Reflections* album led to yet another deal, this time with Repulse, who issued *Reborn Through Flames* in 1998. A Centinex gig was recorded on video and also released by Repulse.

1999's *Bloodhunt* mini-album was released as a six-track CD, and was also issued as a 10" picture disc by Oskorei, including a cover of a song by Death. The band have also issued a best-of album, *Subconscious Lobotomy/Malleus Maleficarum: The Early Years '92-'95* CD. The *Decadence: Prophecies Of Cosmic Chaos* album of 2004 sees them continue to make progress.

RECOMMENDED ALBUM:
Reborn Through Flames (Repulse, 1998)
www.centinex.org

Cephalic Carnage

A grindcore/death metal act from Denver, Colorado, Cephalic Carnage (initially just vocalist Lenzig and drummer Zac) recorded three demos – *Scrape My Lungs* (1994), *Fortuitous Oddity* ('96) and *Cephalic Carnage* ('97) – before signing to the Italian Headfucker label for a split release with Adnauseum and a debut album, *Conforming To Abnormality*. A drummer and guitarist were also recruited from the band Molester, plus the bassist from Origin. They also recorded a cover of Slayer's 'Jesus Saves' for a Dwell label tribute album and a split CD with Anal Blast. A tour the same year with Internal Bleeding and Deeds Of Flesh, as well as the support slot with Kreator and Destruction two years later, raised the CC profile further. A 2002 album, *Lucid Interval*, introduced elements of jazz fusion to the CC sound and they toured with Cannibal Corpse and Mastodon to promote it.

RECOMMENDED ALBUM:
Lucid Interval (Relapse, 2002)
http://cephaliccarnage.infamos.com

Lenzig on the future of extreme metal
❝I see it getting faster and more brutal like it was in the early Nineties. Some of the newer bands will rise and become the new Obituary or Morbid Angel and pull those kinds of crowds and sell the same amounts of records, and reach a new mass of children's minds to raise awareness.❞

Ceremonial Oath

The side project of Tiamat guitarist Anders Iwers, this Swedish melodic death metal outfit also consisted briefly of Oscar Dronjak (vocals), Mikael Andersson (guitar), Jesper Stromblad (bass) and Markus Nordberg (drums). The band, formed in 1990, were originally known by the very Eighties name of Desecrator. In 1993 the band issued their *The Book Of Truth* debut album through Modern Primitive, also covering 'Disposable Heroes' on the Metallica tribute album of the same year, *Metal Militia*. Dronjak and Stromblad departed to join the very successful Hammerfall and In Flames, but Iwers assembled a new line-up and recorded the album *The Carpet*, released by Black Sun in 1995 with singers Tomas Lindberg (ex-At the Gates) and Anders Friden (now also of In Flames). Since then their activities have been minimal.

RECOMMENDED ALBUM:
The Carpet (Black Sun, 1995)

Children Of Bodom

A Finnish death metal band highly acclaimed for their intricate riffing and grasp of both melodic and aggressive approaches, Children Of Bodom were named after Bodom Lake, the scene of a triple murder in 1960. Formed in 1993 in the town of Espoo by singer Alex Laiho and drummer Jaska Raatikainen, COB began life as Inearthed but change the name after a line-up shuffle and signed to the Finnish label Spinefarm. A debut album, *Something Wild*, was distributed in 1997 through Europe by Nuclear Blast, and to their surprise, a self-titled single made No. 1 on the national charts. Tours with Hypocrisy, Dismember and Night In Gales followed. A second No. 1 single, 'Downfall', came in 1999. Their next album, *Follow The Reaper*, was a similar success.

Recognising that singles success in their home country was clearly not only desirable but possible, COB released 'You're Better Off Dead' in 2002, backed with a cover of The Ramones' 'Somebody Put Something In My Drink'. The third album, *Hate Crew Deathroll*, was released by Century Media the following year in the US, where a tour alongside Dimmu Borgir and others took place. They continue to

Children Of Bodom – chart-bound death metal

achieve levels of success unprecedented outside their home country.
RECOMMENDED ALBUM:
Hate Crew Deathroll (Motor Music, 2003)
www.cobhc.com

Chimaira

At the forefront of the new wave of US metal bands who combine anthemic elements with classic thrash and death metal, Cleveland quintet Chimaira (named after a mythical creature) are a rare thing: an extreme metal act that sells well. The line-up (vocalist Mark Hunter, guitarists Matt De Vries and Rob Arnold, bassist Jim LaMarca, keyboards/programmer Chris Spicuzza and drummer Kevin Talley) first gained attention with 1999's *This Present Darkness*, released by the East Coast Empire label. A move to Roadrunner proved highly profitable for the band and tours with Slayer, Fear Factory, Machine Head and Danzig have kept them in the public eye. *Pass Out Of Existence* appeared in 2001 and dealt with Fear Factory-esque cybermetal themes – a successful gambit at the height of nu-metal – but it was 2003's *The Impossibility Of Reason* which propelled

Chimaira to the international limelight. Their future seems assured.
RECOMMENDED ALBUM:
The Impossibility Of Reason
(Roadrunner, 2001)
www.chimaira.com

Cirith Gorgor

Named after the haunted pass to the land of the dead in *The Lord Of The Rings*, black metallers Cirith Gorgor (initially Dark Sorceress) were founded by guitarists Asmoday and Astaroth Daemonum in 1993. Levithmong (drums), Mystic (bass) and Nimroth (vocals) completed the line-up, which finally bore fruit with the *Mystic Legends* demo in 1997. Osmose signed them and a debut album, *Onwards To The Spectral Defile*, appeared in 1999. Asmoday was replaced by Marchosias and tours with Behemoth, Aeternus, Asphyx and Testament followed. The 2001 album *Unveiling The Essence* was followed by gigs with Enthroned, Dead Head and Hades Almighty, and although the other founder member Astaroth also chose to depart at this point the band continued. After a move to the Ketzer label, the *Firestorm Apocalypse – Tomorrow Shall Know The Blackest Dawn* album was released.

Cirith Gorgor – possibly black metal

RECOMMENDED ALBUM:
Unveiling The Essence (Osmose, 2001)
www.cirithgorgor.tk

Mystic on black metal
"I prefer primitive black metal without keyboards, female vocals or any other useless 'progressive' or 'original' instruments that could ruin the purity and the whole cold, harsh atmosphere that black metal should have. Bands that meet these characteristics and which I therefore also prefer are, among many others, Trelldom, Darkthrone, Inquisition, Arckanum, Burzum, Gorgoroth, Graven and Tsjuder."

Comecon

Swedish band Comecon were originally known as the industrial-sounding Omnitron before becoming The Krixjhalters. No-one outside Scandinavia could pronounce this, however, and thus Comecon was born. The band were made up of Martin van Drunen (vocals), Pelle Strom (guitar), Rasmus Ekman (bass) and Andres Green (drums), although future Entombed frontman Lars Goran Petrov handled vocals on the debut album, 1991's *Megatrends In Brutality*. The record was a substandard thrash effort and after Petrov's departure, van Drunen took over. Two more albums followed but Comecon weren't getting the attention they craved and, despite the efforts of Morgoth singer Marc Grewe on 'Fable Frolic', the band folded. Their song 'Soft Creamy Lather' qualifies for Most Un-Metal Song Title Of All Time.
RECOMMENDED ALBUM:
Megatrends In Brutality
(Century Media, 1991)

Control Denied

When the late Death frontman Chuck Schuldiner decided to dissolve his band and move forward with a newer, more contemporary direction from the crunchy death metal of before, Control Denied was the result. Also featuring Tim Aymar (vocals), Shannon Hamm (guitar), Steve DiGiorgio (bass) and Richard Christy (drums), Control Denied combined Death's uncompromising power with a melodic awareness which delighted many metal critics. An album, *The Fragile Art Of Existence*, was recorded by the well-known death metal producer Jim Morris in 1999, but the cancer to which Chuck tragically succumbed two years later prevented any further activities.
RECOMMENDED ALBUM:
The Fragile Art Of Existence
(Nuclear Blast, 1999)

Convulse

A Finnish band consisting of Rami Jamsa (vocals/guitar), Toni Honkala (guitar), Juha Tetenius (bass) and Janne Miikkulainen (drums), Convulse combined death metal with rock'n'roll influences. Two albums were issued in 1992 and 1994, but their musical direction was not to the metal-buying public's taste and the band separated.
RECOMMENDED ALBUM:
Reflections (Nuclear Blast, 1994)

Coroner

Founded in 1985, Swiss band Coroner – Ron Royce (bass/vocals), Marquis Marky (drums) and Tommy T. Baron (guitar) – (actually Ron Broder, Marky Edelmann and Tommy Vetterli) turned out six albums of avant-garde thrash metal that took in death and black influences and bore certain similarities to the work of their countrymen and labelmates Celtic Frost. In fact, the band's first demo, *Death Cult*, featured Frost frontman Tom G. Warrior on guest vocals. Death Cult led to a deal with Noise, who issued 1987's *R.I.P.* A leftfield thrash album, it attracted a fanbase, perhaps helped along by Edelmann's eye for a theatrical stage-show.

The next two albums, *Punishment For Decadence* and *No More Color*, were rather more sombre. Tours with Motörhead and

Watchtower, as well as MTV appearances, broadened the band's profile. The fans also responded positively to two singles, covers of Jimi Hendrix's 'Purple Haze' and The Beatles' 'I Want You (She's So Heavy)'. The next album, the almost psychedelic *Mental Vortex*, proved that the band were becoming a force to reckon with on the European scene.

However, 1993's unusual *Grin* was a shade too laid-back for many of Coroner's fans, and it became apparent that the band were in something of a rut. An eponymous compilation album was assembled, and in 1994 the band quit while they were ahead – even before *Coroner* was released. The members had no plans to retire: Edelmann went on to join Tom G. Warrior's Apollyon Sun and Tommy Vetterli joined Kreator. A reunion seems likely at some point.

RECOMMENDED ALBUM:

Mental Vortex (Noise, 1991)

Corporation 187

Heading up the Swedish thrash metal movement alongside The Haunted and Carnal Forge, Corporation 187 began their career as a Slayer tribute act before writing original material. Unsurprisingly, the line-up – initially Pelle Severin on vocals, guitarists Magnus Pettersson and Olof Knuttsson, and drummer Robert Eng – retain something of the LA thrash gods' sound in their music, but that is, as they say, no bad thing.

A demo tape, *Promo 98* (on which Pettersson played bass), attracted the Earache imprint Wicked World and a deal was signed. Ex-Séance bassist Johan Ekström joined up in 1999 and an album, *Subliminal Fear*, was released early the following year. It was deemed a success and C187 toured with Decapitated and grindcore supergroup

Corporation 187 – thrash for the masses

Lock-Up. Singer Severin was replaced by Filip Carlsson of Satanic Slaughter, who had been Corpration 187's bass player in the Slayer tribute days, and Ekström made way for Viktor Klint. The next album, recorded in 2002 with Peter Tägtgren at the Abyss Studios, was *Perfection In Pain*, an utterly Slayer-esque title which was well-received.

RECOMMENDED ALBUM:
Perfection In Pain (Wicked World, 2002)
www.corporation187.com

Cradle Of Filth

After over a decade during which the leading lights of the black metal scene were Scandinavian (Mercyful Fate, Burzum, Mayhem, Emperor) it came as something of a surprise to find at the turn of the century that the biggest BM band in the world was from the UK. Much of their appeal lies in the Gothic good looks of their singer, Dani Davey, as well as his partiality to quotable soundbites.

Formed in 1991, Cradle Of Filth initially consisted of Dani, Paul Ryan (guitar), his brother Ben (keyboards), John Richard (bass) and Darren (drums). A demo, *Invoking The Unclean*, was recorded, and a new guitarist, Robin Graves, joined up for a second tape, *Orgiastic Pleasures*. Richard left Cradle soon after and Robin returned, taking over bass, and yet another guitarist, Paul Allender, became the latest Filth. After the *Total Fucking Darkness* demo, the band recruited the drummer Nick Barker and signed with Cacophonous. The music that the band would go on to make across all their recordings is a mixture of the usual black metal warp-speed and a pseudo-classical keyboard wash, laced with Dani's evil vocals and sound effects and strings straight from Hammer horror movies.

The first Cradle album, *The Principle Of Evil Made Flesh*, was released in 1994. Further personnel difficulties ensued and the Ryans left the band, rapidly replaced by guitarist Stuart Anstis and keyboard player Damien. 1996's mini-album, *Vempire: Dark Faerytales In Phallustein*, caused hackles among some of the more mainstream record-buying populace for its devilish porn/Christ images, as did the full-length *Dusk And Her Embrace* of the same year, released after Music For Nations signed the band.

At around this time the band's merchandising included a T-shirt with the infamous slogan 'Jesus Is A Cunt' spread across it, which led to a serious outcry and increased media coverage. A BBC *Living With The Enemy* documentary was screened in 1997, in which Dani was asked to explain the T-shirt, as well as some of his more inflammatory statements, to the mother of a devout fan.

A new keyboard player, Les Smith, replaced Damien and another album, *Cruelty And The Beast*, was released in 1998. Barker left to pursue other projects – notably with Dimmu Borgir, then Lock-Up – and his place was taken by Adrian Erlandsson of At The Gates. More personnel shuffles took place, but COF have gone on to exploit their position at the top of the black metal tree with a series of well-crafted (if broadly similar) albums and remain a unique act on the scene. The movie *Cradle Of Fear* starred Dani as 'The Man' in 2001 and was enjoyed by the more committed members of the vampire fetish movement, and a brief dalliance with Sony lent COF an air of respectability as the first extreme metal band to sign to a major label. The experiment was not a success, however – the band claimed that Sony didn't know how to handle their kind of music – and at the time of writing they are signed to Roadrunner.

RECOMMENDED ALBUM:
Cruelty And The Beast
(Music For Nations, 1998)
www.cradleoffilth.com

Paul Allender on the 'Jesus Is A Cunt' T-shirt controversy
"The number of people that got arrested for wearing that shirt was ridiculous. I find it amusing the way that people get so offended so easily. People said, oh, blasphemy! But if you want to be in a successful band, the image has to suit the music."

Crematory

A German band admired for their inventive take on Gothic metal, Felix (vocals), Lotte (guitar), Heinz (bass) and Markus (drums) first formed Crematory in 1991, producing a 1500-selling demo tape. Signing to Massacre in late 1992, their debut album, *Transmigration*, was released the following year; successful concerts in Germany followed and a keyboard player, Katrin, joined the band. The album and its successor, 1994's *Just Dreaming* – for which Heinz was replaced by new bassist Harald – established Crematory's dark, textured version of heavy metal, and tours with Tiamat and UK gloomsters My Dying Bride followed.

Just Dreaming also provided the first Crematory hit, 'Shadows Of Mine'. The videos for both this song and a second single, 'In My Hands', were played on European MTV and the band's audience grew steadily. A third album, *Illusions*, was released in 1995 and further semi-mainstream success ensued with the suitably elevated 'Tears Of Time' single, which boasted a big-budget video.

The *Crematory* album was released in May 1996 and sold well, enabling the band to headline the Out Of The Dark festival of 1996 and release a live video from the OOTD festival for the single 'Ist Es Wahr'.

They then founded their own label, CRC (Crematory's Record Company) before moving to Nuclear Blast. For the next album, *Awake*, the band recorded a cover of The Sisters Of Mercy's Eighties hit, 'Temple Of Love' – a suitably dark vehicle for the Crematory vision. 1999 was an eventful year for the band, with another single, 'Fly', and another album, *Act Seven*, both charting, as well as some line-up changes. Lotte was replaced by Matthias Hechler, and the album contained guest appearances from singers Michael Rohr of Century, Kalle Friedrich of Giants Causeway and Lisa Mosinski of Dark. The band continues to be popular despite a three-year cessation of activities: they made a comeback in 2004.

RECOMMENDED ALBUM:
Act Seven (Nuclear Blast, 1999)
www.crematory.de

Crematory – long-time Euro-metallers

Crisis

Karyn Crisis (vocals), Afzaal Nasiruddeen (guitar), Gia Chuan Wang (bass) and Jason Bittner (drums and percussion) performed complex, layered music with a variety of metal influences, and stood out thematically for their penchant for challenging lyrics that addressed personal and social issues with an unfliching zeal. The New York quartet formed in the early Nineties, issuing the *8 Convulsions* album in 1992 before signing with Metal Blade, who nurtured their experimental style through two further albums. The last, *The Hollowing*, featured guest performances from no fewer than four drummers, guitarist Norman Westberg of the Swans and the Acid Bath vocalist, Sammy Pierre. After a lull in activity, Crisis made a new album in 2004, *Like Sheep Led To Slaughter*.

RECOMMENDED ALBUM:
The Hollowing (Metal Blade, 1997)
www.karyncrisis.com

The Crown

Swedish melodic thrash band The Crown were formed as Crown Of Thorns in 1990 and recorded demos, *Forever Heaven Gone* and *Forget The Light*, three years later. A deal with Black Sun and a cover of Slayer's 'Mandatory Suicide' for the *Slaytanic Slaughter* tribute album progressed their career and a debut album, *The Burning*, received great reviews. *Eternal Death* (1996) was a step further in aggression. The name-change came in 1997 after contact from a Christian act with the same moniker. Another cover, Sepultura's 'Arise', was recorded for the *Sepulchral Feast* tribute album and a tour with Sacrilege led to a deal with Metal Blade.

Subsequent albums *Hell Is Here* and *Deathrace King* established The Crown at the edge of the Swedish scene and featured guest vocals from ex-At The Gates frontman Tomas Lindberg. Tours with Cannibal Corpse, Nile, Morbid Angel and others ensued, and Lindberg became the band's temporary singer in 2001. *Crowned In Terror* and *Possessed 13* did so well that many fans assumed the band would be around for some years to come: it was a surprise, then, when they announced a split in 2003 due to industry pressures.

RECOMMENDED ALBUM:
Crowned In Terror (Metal Blade, 2002)
www.thecrownonline.com

Cryptopsy

The Montreal technical death metal band Cryptopsy, which began life with Lord Worm (vocals), Jon Levasseur (guitar), Miguel Roy (guitar), Eric Langlois (bass) and Flo Mounier (drums), was praised for its visceral music and live appearances, which included a memorable set at the 1997 Milwaukee Metalfest.

The brutal Cryptopsy approach was first demonstrated on the four-song *Ungentle Exhumation* demo before the band released the *Blasphemy Made Flesh* album in 1994 on the German Invasion label. After a short Canadian tour the following year, the Swedish label Wrong Again Records released *None So Vile*, which had been produced by Obliveon guitarist Pierre Remillard. At this point Lord Worm, one of the most extreme vocalists in metal, was replaced by ex-Infestation frontman Mike DiSalvo. Cryptopsy subsequently signed to Century Media and continue to enthral death metal fans worldwide.

RECOMMENDED ALBUM:
None So Vile (Wrong Again, 1995)
www.cryptopsy.net

Cynic

Fusing death metal with jazz and avant-garde influences to create a unique approach, Florida quartet Cynic (vocalist/guitarist Paul Masvidal, guitarist Jason Gobel, initially bassist Tony Choy and then Sean Malone, and drummer Sean Reinert) performed progressive metal before the term was coined. Their sole album, *Focus*, contained guitar synths and vocal effects and was regarded as a landmark in the genre.

RECOMMENDED ALBUM:
Focus (Roadrunner, 1993)

Darkane – modern thrashers

Daemon

Formed in 1996 as a side-project of
Konkhra frontman Anders Lundemark and
Hellacopters/Entombed frontman Nicke
Andersson, Daemon's 'death'n'roll' approach
was underpinned on their latest album,
Eye For An Eye, by none other than
veteran thrash drummer Gene Hoglan.
A philosophical, political album, it appeared
just before the 9/11 attacks, requiring
Lundemark to explain his lyrics in case of
misunderstanding.

RECOMMENDED ALBUM:
Eye For An Eye (Diehard, 2001)

Dark Angel

One of the most technically proficient US
thrash bands of the Eighties, Dark Angel's
Slayer and Metallica influences were
apparent on their early albums, but the band
went on to produce a much more refined
sound on later releases. The fluid line-up
consisted at various points of the singers
Don Doty and Ron Rinehart, guitarists
Eric Meyer and Jim Durkin, while bass and
drums were mostly handled by Mike
Gonzalez and the band's main songwriter
Gene Hoglan respectively.

Dark Angel first appeared on *Metal
Massacre VI* before recording their intense
debut album for Axe Killer in 1985, which
led them to be labelled with the bizarre
'Caffeine Metal' tag – an apt term
recognising the taut, frantic riffing of the
band, which attracted speed metal fans in
droves. The band signed to Combat in 1986
and further albums were issued to much
acclaim. *Darkness Descends* and *Time Does
Not Heal* stand up today as thrash classics.

After a compilation album, however, the
band realised that their style was becoming
outmoded and parted ways in 1992 after the
departures of Rinehart and Hoglan. Hoglan
would go on to work with Death mainman
Chuck Schuldiner in the Nineties, as well as
drumming with Testament, Strapping Young
Lad, Old Man's Child, Punchdrunk,
Daemon and many others.

RECOMMENDED ALBUM:
Darkness Descends (Combat, 1986)

Eric Meyer on first impressions
❝When I first heard Venom, it was like,
fuck! All of a sudden your eyes just
open up. It's like, oh my God, what's
that? It was all satanic and evil and shit.
I heard Mercyful Fate for the first time
and also went, fuck! I think I've been
really lucky to have been in the right
place at the right time.❞

Darkane *(Left)*

Formed in 1998 from an old band, Agretator, Darkane is drummer Peter Wildoer, guitarists Christofer Malmström and Klas Ideberg and bass player Jörgen Löfberg. A progressive thrash sound evolved after contributing tracks to the *War Dance* compilation and a debut album, *Rusted Angel*, which featured vocals by Lawrence Mackrory. For the follow-up, 2001's *Insanity*, Andreas Sydow provided vocals. Currently the band are touring in support of the refined 2003 album *Expanding Senses*.

RECOMMENDED ALBUM:
Insanity (Nuclear Blast, 2001)
www.darkane.com

Dark Funeral

A leading Swedish black metal band, Dark Funeral evolve around the guitarist Lord Ahriman, who formed the band in 1993 with Themgoroth (bass/vocals), Draugen (drums) and Blackmoon (aka David Parland, guitar). The Dark Funeral sound is a savage, almost death metal-like onslaught which fans of the genre have hailed as a refreshing change from the usual black metal pretensions.

A self-titled mini-album in 1993 led to a deal with No Fashion, for whom a full-length album, *The Secrets Of The Black Arts*, was recorded in 1996. The band's reputation was bolstered by their live show, which featured fire-breathing, gallons of fake blood and pigs' heads thrown into the crowd. Draugen was briefly replaced by Equimanthorn, but before any new material could be recorded, the band abruptly split, leaving Lord Ahriman to continue the band alone. Undeterred, however, he recruited vocalist and bassist Emperor Magus Caligula, drummer Alzazmon and guitarist Typhos and recorded a second album, the even more devilish *Vobiscum Satanas*, in 1998.

A 2000 EP entitled *Teach The Children To Worship Satan* and the following year's album *Diabolis Interium*, plus extended tours (leading to a live record, *De Profundis Clamavi Ad Te Domine*) kept the DF profile high. However, they are without a deal at the time of writing and it is to be hoped that they come back with appropriate malevolence.

RECOMMENDED ALBUM:
Diabolis Interium (No Fashion, 2001)
www.darkfuneral.se

Dark Tranquillity

Jointly responsible for the rise of the Gothenburg sound and the New Wave Of Swedish Death Metal, the members of Dark Tranquillity – Mikael Stanne (vocals), Michael Niklasson (guitar), Niklas Sundin (guitar), Martin Henriksson (bass), Anders Jivarp (drums) and Martin Brandstom (keyboards) – create a blend of aggressive death metal with melodic qualities. The technical aspect of this newer form of death metal was primarily reflected in the vocals, the guitar solos and the production values, which tend to be more polished than in previous years.

Dark Tranquillity were formed in 1989 and moved from the lengthier, more grandiose songs of their early years to more conventional, compressed work, reflecting the spirit of the times. However, they retained the aggression required by fans of

Dark Tranquillity – leaders of the NWOSDM

old-school death metal. Their albums have displayed a consistent grasp of the methods required, from the slightly electronic feel of *Haven* (2000) to the more mellow approach of *Projector* the previous year, which was nominated for a Swedish Grammy. The current album, *Damage Done*, showcases a certain thrash metal awareness as well as the more usual crafted death approach.

RECOMMENDED ALBUM:
The Mind's I (Osmose, 1997)
www.darktranquillity.com

Darkmoon

From Charlotte, South Carolina, Darkmoon played incredibly rapid, unrelenting black metal. Formed in the mid-Nineties under the name Demonic Christ, the band released a three-song demo, *Writhing Glory*, in 1997, before self-releasing the *Vengeance For Withered Hearts* album the following year.

Music For Nations signed them up in November 1998 and an album, *Seas Of Unrest*, was released in 1999. The band claimed that it represents a protest against the falsehood of Christianity, stating that "Christ's cancerous reign on our society and nature smolders in repulsion, his vile ways shall be banished and his light dimmed for eternity." When guitarist/vocalist Jon Vesano left to join Nile in 2002, the band changed their name to Wehrwolfe and signed a deal with the Magick label.

RECOMMENDED ALBUM:
Seas Of Unrest (Music For Nations, 1999)

Darkseed

Germany's Darkseed formed in 1992, with the line-up consisting of Stefan Hertrich (vocals), Thomas Herrmann (guitar), Tom Gilcher (guitar), Rico Galvagno (bass) and the dubiously-named drummer Willy Wurm. Two demos were recorded – *Sharing The Grave* and *Darksome Thoughts* – both of which were Gothic death metal with various innovative touches. Named after a computer game and initially playing covers of Metallica and Venom songs, the band were signed to Invasion in 1994 and recorded the *Romantic Tales* mini-album the same year.

Intensive tours followed, with Pyogenesis, Amorphis, Crematory and Lacrimosa. In 1996 the band signed to Serenades Records, who released the debut full-length album, *Midnight Solemnly Dance*. The band's Gothic influences were at the fore on this record, but the death roots of Darkseed resurfaced on the next album, *Spellcraft*, released in 1997 after a move to Nuclear Blast. A memorable appearance at a private party ensued, as well as further tours with a host of bands, from the melodic power rockers Blind Guardian to those blackest of metal acts, Mayhem and Dimmu Borgir.

In August 1999 Darkseed were shocked by the death of an ex-guitarist, Andy Wecker, who succumbed to cancer after a year's hospital treatment. The *Give Me Light* album was duly released to moderate acclaim, and the band retreated into their own Dark Music studio to record another CD, the *Diving Into Darkness* album. Subsequent albums have seen them expand the doomdeath template.

RECOMMENDED ALBUM:
Give Me Light (Nuclear Blast, 1999)
www.darkseed.com

Darkthrone

The world's most unswerving black metal band, Oslo duo Darkthrone prefer it to be acknowledged that there have been two distinct phases in their career. Originally formed in 1986, the band consisted of Gylve Nagell, Ted Skjellum, Ivar Enger and Dag Nilsen. Playing under the name Black Death, they performed Satanically-themed death metal. The 1988 *Land Of Frost* demo saw the name change to Darkthrone, and a two-song promo was also recorded, which the band called *A New Dimension*.

Two further tapes, 1989's *Thulcandra* and *Cromlech*, led to a deal with the UK label Peaceville. Songs from both demos were included on the debut album *Soulside Journey*, recorded in 1990 at Stockholm's Sunlight Studios. Although the album was a competent mix of technical riffing and raw aggression, Ted and Ivar decided that death metal had become over-fashionable, applied corpsepaint and started to write songs heavily influenced by Oslo band Mayhem. Other sources of inspiration were Celtic Frost and Bathory, all of which were evident on the ensuing album, *Goatlord*, on which Satyricon singer Satyr guested. However, the album was shelved and remained unreleased until 1997, when Moonfog issued it to much acclaim.

The next proper Darkthrone album, the classic *A Blaze In The Northern Sky*, was released in 1991. In true black metal fashion, the band had adopted devilish aliases – Gylve Nagell became Fenriz, Ted Skjellum was now known as Nocturno Culto and Ivar Enger became Zephyrous. Dag Nilsen had left the band, unhappy with the band's new direction.

Fenriz has since stated that the 'first' Darkthrone 'died' after *Soulside Journey* and that it was only at this point that the Darkthrone of today was born. The aggressively black metal stance continued on the next recording, *Under A Funeral Moon*, which was released in 1993. The label "True Norwegian Black Metal" appeared in the sleevenotes for the first time, and as *A Blaze In The Northern Sky* had contained one or two death metal riffs (a hangover from earlier days) it has been said that *Under A Funeral Moon* was the first wholly black metal album to emerge from the fast-growing Norwegian scene. The sleeve notes also stated "This album is for the Norwegian Black Metal Mafia."

1994's *Transilvanian Hunger* was rumoured to have taken its title from the circumstances surrounding the suicide of Mayhem singer Dead – he was wearing an I Love Transilvania shirt at the time of his death, and Mayhem guitarist Euronymous claimed to have eaten parts of the man's brain (see Mayhem entry). Whether or not this is true, the album brought Darkthrone to the forefront of the violent Norwegian black metal scene. Some of the album's lyrics were written by Burzum's Count Grishnackh, who included a backwards message at the end of the song 'As Flittermice As Satans Spys' which ran "In the name of God, let the churches burn".

Peaceville were reluctant to promote the album after the following statement by Fenriz: "We would like to state that 'Transilvanian Hunger' stands beyond any criticism. If any man should attempt to criticize this LP, he should be thoroughly patronized for his obviously Jewish behavior." Darkthrone later defended the statement by saying that the apparent anti-Semitism of the comment had been inadvertently introduced in translation, claiming that the word "Jew" is commonly used in Norway as a synonym for fool or idiot.

The band then signed to Moonfog, run by Sigurd Wongraven (aka Satyr) of Satyricon, and released the Panzerfaust album in 1994. Count Grishnackh wrote lyrics for the song 'Quintessence' and the album was dedicated to Satyr. This time around, the album sleevenotes included the statements "True Norwegian Black Metal", "Unholy Black Metal", and "The Most Hated Band In The World", but the band also stated that they are not Nazis, as had been rumoured. After the release of *Panzerfaust*, Zephyrous left the band and in 1995 Fenriz and Nocturno Culto recorded *Total Death*, with contributions from Insahn of Emperor and Garm of Ulver. A farewell gig was announced, to the surprise of the media, and played in Oslo on April 6, 1996.

However, the band returned in 1999 with an eighth album, *Ravishing Grimness*, which caused longtime Darkthrone fans' jaws to drop with its inclusion of more melody than on previous recordings. Subsequent albums such as *Plaguewielder*, released in 2002, see the band deviate not a jot from the necro production values of the old days. The Peaceville label has reissued the classic material on more than one occasion and in 2004 Fenriz assembled an old-school compilation for the label, featuring songs by Venom, Burzum and others.

RECOMMENDED ALBUM:
A Blaze In The Northern Sky
(Peaceville, 1992)
www.darkthrone.no

Darkwoods My Betrothed

Formed in 1993 under the charming name of Virgin's Cunt, Darkwoods My Betrothed recorded the *Reborn In The Promethean Flame* and *Dark Aureoles Gathering* demos the following year. After a wise name-change, a deal was signed with the Korean Hammerheart label and a debut album, *Heirs Of The Northstar*, was released in 1995.

The music was a combination of pagan and black metal with nods to Viking themes and traditional speed metal. A second album, *Autumn Roars Thunder*, released in 1996 after a move to the more conveniently-located Solistitium Records in Germany, contained rawer black metal, however, with a marked doom and Gothic atmosphere.

RECOMMENDED ALBUM:
Autumn Roars Thunder (Solistitium, 1996)
www.heathenwood.cjb.net

Death – truly influential and much missed

Death

The most influential death metal band in the world, Death's six-album career pioneered crunchy, technically-competent riffing with the complex song structures and guttural vocals that became a template for dozens of successful bands from the late-Eighties to the mid-Nineties, when melody became as important as power and the Gothenburg sound came to prominence.

A whole list of metal alumni passed through the Death ranks, with notables including drummer Gene Hoglan (ex-Dark Angel) and guitarists Andy LaRocque (King Diamond) and James Murphy (Obituary, Testament). The band always centred on the guitarist, vocalist and songwriter Chuck Schuldiner, who first formed a metal band, Mantas, in 1983. After recording several demos, including the three-song *Mutilation* cassette, Combat signed the newly-christened Death and the debut album, *Scream Bloody Gore*, was released in 1987. It has since been recognised as one of the great metal classics, along with Metallica's early albums and scene-defining records like Slayer's *Reign In Blood*.

Ensuing years saw the release of five more Death albums, all of which progressed in terms of technical competence and thematic intelligence, although some fans found the later material was too complex. Schuldiner took time out from Death after the release of *Symbolic* (1995) to work on a side project, Control Denied. For various administrative reasons the project didn't take off until after the recording of the final Death album, *The Sound Of Perseverance*, but a second attempt proved successful (see separate entry).

Death also headlined tours across Europe, Asia and the Americas, making them more or less the most well-travelled old-school death metal band ever along with Morbid Angel. Control Denied became Schuldiner's priority and Death was dissolved in the mid-Nineties, although the singer hinted that more material might be still to come.

In 1999 Schuldiner underwent an operation to remove a brain-stem tumour, and musical activity was put on hold. Although he fought the illness bravely, he lost his battle in 2001: along with that of Cliff Burton, his tragically early death robbed the metal scene of one of its finest talents. RIP.

RECOMMENDED ALBUM:
Leprosy (Combat, 1988)
www.emptywords.org

"I was searching for the heaviest stuff I could find in LA. At the time there was Motorhead, Metallica and Dark Angel, who were my old buddies from high school. I thought Metallica were alright, but they could have just been heavier. Everybody else was like oh my God, it's so intense – and I was like yes, it's wicked, it's awesome, but I'd seen Dark Angel and Slayer. When I saw Slayer I was like, this is it! Finally!

I used to soundcheck the drums for Slayer on the Haunting The West Coast tour, and all they played at soundcheck was Dark Angel songs. I remember Jeff Hanneman saying to me, dude, Dark Angel, I saw 'em back in LA, they're faster than us, they're better than us, they're heavier than us. And I was like, dude, you're in Slayer! What are you worrying about Dark Angel for?"

Death Angel

A San Francisco Bay thrash metal band, Death Angel – Mark Osegueda (vocals), Rob Cavestany (guitar), Gus Pepa (guitar), Dennis Pepa (bass) and Andy Galeon (drums) – were all cousins. The band's style was technical and complex, with the power and speed of their albums held up as promising examples

of the genre. In their heyday, they rivalled Metallica for the power of their shows. However, their career was dogged by record label disputes, management tension and a bad coach crash which left drummer Galeon unable to play for a year.

After the release of *Act III*, singer Mark Osegueda departed. The other four changed the band's name to The Organization, recording two funk-metal albums. Andy, Rob, and Mark founded a band called Swarm while Pepa played guitar in a punk band, Big Shrimp, and trained as a graphic designer. Many believed that the Death Angel story was over, but they reformed (with Ted Aguilar in place of Gus Pepa) in 2001 in the wake of the Thrash Of The Titans benefit gig in San Francisco for Testament singer Chuck Billy. Signing to Nuclear Blast and playing scintillating shows worldwide in 2004, they released an album, *The Fine Art Of Dying*, and continue to gain praise for their fantastic live performances.

RECOMMENDED ALBUM:
The Ultra-Violence (Enigma, 1987)
www.deathangel.com

Mark Osegueda on the comeback
"All of us in the band, not just me, had to get certain things out of their systems and try different things musically,

Death Angel – quintessential thrashers

because we'd only ever played with each other up to that point, and we'd only ever played thrash. Granted, we tried to push it as far as we could within the genre of thrash, but still you grow at the same time and you start looking at different types of music, and you want to try your hand at it.

We definitely needed some time to grow up. The time off we had made us appreciate that if we ever got to come back and play music together like this, we should savour every second that we have. When we're actually on stage, we're having the best time of our lives.**"**

Decapitated (Left)

Following in the footsteps of Vader and Yattering, Decapitated demonstrate that the Polish death metal scene is not one to be dismissed lightly. Formed in Krosno, Southern Poland in 1996 when the average age of the band was a mere 14, the band's *Cemeteral Gardens* and *The Eye of Horus* demos led to a deal with Wicked World/Earache. A startling debut album, *Winds Of Creation*, appeared in 2000 and tours with Lock-Up followed. In the same year Decapitated were voted Best Newcomer in *Terrorizer* magazine. The follow-up album, *Nihility*, was as brutal as its predecessor.

RECOMMENDED ALBUM:
Nihility (Wicked World, 2003)
www.decapitated.net

Bassist Martin on the Polish scene
"The Polish death metal scene is growing, it's true. Poland has been totally Westernised. It's the influence of the US. But I don't care, you know? It's good if there's a lot of places to get food and clothes. I don't mind American music and films either. Without them we would only be watching Polish music and films.**"**

December Wolves

The Boston band December Wolves formed in 1993 and recorded a demo, *Wolftread*, in 1994, which led to a deal with Hammerheart. A debut album, *Til Ten Years*, was released in 1996 and was acclaimed for its skilful combination of doom and death metal. After a move to Wicked World in 1997, the band recorded *Completely*

Dehumanized and toured widely to promote it. Since then activities have been minimal.
RECOMMENDED ALBUM:
Completely Dehumanized
(Wicked World, 1997)

Defleshed

A German death metal band, Defleshed were formed in 1992 from members of the speed metal bands Inanimate and Convulsion. The band's line-up was initially Lars (guitar) and Gustaf (ex-Crematorium, bass). The *Abrah Kadavrah* demo was recorded in 1992, containing songs which would later be released by the Italian label Miscarriage Records as a vinyl single. *Nuclear Blast* included 'Obsculum Obscenium' from the demo on the *Grindcore* album.

The *Body Art* demo subsequently inspired Invasion Records sufficiently to sign Defleshed, and a mini-CD, *Ma Belle Scapelle*, was recorded. The first full-length album was also named *Abrah Kadavrah* and was recorded in 1996. After some recognition, a drummer, Matte, was recruited and the three-piece recorded *Under The Blade* in 1997. Since then label difficulties have kept Defleshed under the radar, and Matte is now playing full-time in Dark Funeral.
RECOMMENDED ALBUM:
Abrah Kadavrah (Invasion, 1996)
www.defleshed.de

Deicide

Florida's Deicide combine extremely brutal death metal with satanic lyrics, making them one of the leading members of the state's early-Nineties scene along with Morbid Angel and Obituary. The band revolves around singer/bassist Glen Benton, whose controversial statements in the past, coupled with the deadly seriousness of the band members' Satanic beliefs – they really mean it – have made them a target for many groups. The other members of Deicide are brothers Eric and Brian Hoffman (guitar) and Steve Asheim (drums).

Originally performing under the name Amon, Deicide signed to Roadrunner in 1990 and issued a self-titled album. The band's first shows immediately invited controversy, with the players dressed in spiked "God armour", hurling pieces of meat into the audience and covered in pig's

blood. Benton also branded an inverted cross into his forehead, leaving a permanent scar, and promised to kill himself at 33 years old, when he would have outlived Jesus Christ. (The author of this book was the first to interview him after his 33rd birthday: he had changed his mind, explaining that he was young and foolish when he made the claim.)

Benton was once wrongly accused of advocating animal torture after he shot a troublesome squirrel in his back yard during a meeting with the press. This led to threats from animal rights activists, specifically from a UK-based group who promised to assassinate Benton if he ever came to England. After the release of *Legion* (1992), Deicide did in fact play in London, but the violence failed to materialise. However, a bomb did explode at a Stockholm show for reasons which remain unclear.

Further albums have continued the devilish theme, although Deicide fell into something of a rut in the late Nineties, only relieved after a move to the Earache label in 2003. The band is now at a crossroads. At their peak they were among the best at what they did: hopefully they can regain that form.

RECOMMENDED ALBUM:
Once Upon The Cross (Roadrunner, 1995)
www.deicide.com

Glen Benton juggles some terms
"I listened to everybody in the 80s, man. Black Sabbath, Venom, Sodom, Destruction, Possessed. There was no such thing as death metal when we were listening to this shit, it was just metal. It was either black metal or it was metal. And what was black metal back then is considered to be death metal now: anything that dealt with Satanism we called black metal, like Venom. I don't like the term death metal, really. It's not like when we write the songs we say, man, that's the heaviest death metal song I ever heard! Goddamn! It's not like that.

I believe a lot of the Satanic philosophies. I know what I believe, and when I write lyrics I don't write them to offend as many people as I can or to make people become Satanists. Also, people get too worked up about my private life. Who the fuck cares who the fuck I'm fucking?**"**

Deicide – Glen Benton, complete with forehead scar

Deinonychus

Deinonychus is the work of one man, the Dutch Marco Kehren, who had previously been a member of the black metal band Malefic Oath. In October 1993 he produced a demo, *Promo 1993*, which received a positive underground response and led to a deal with Cacophonous Records. An album, *The Silence Of December*, was recorded and released after a one-year delay due to distribution problems. It's best described as melancholy black metal and gained positive reviews, but little has been heard of Kehren since.

RECOMMENDED ALBUM:
The Silence Of December
(Cacophonous, 1995)

Demilich

A Finnish quartet notable for their unfeasibly low vocals and the complexity of their doomdeath sound, Demilich – Antti Boman (guitar/vocals), Aki Hytonen (guitars), Ville Koistenen (bass) and Mikko Virnes (drums) – recorded an early demo, *Four Instructive Tales Of Decomposition*, which impressed the No Fashion label enough to offer them a deal.

Their first and only album, *Nespithe*, features the turgidly-titled 'When The Sun Drank The Weight Of Water' and other equally cumbersome song titles. *Nespithe* was re-released by a series of labels, including Necropolis, Pavement, and Repulse, but the record was just too weird for most listeners and the band split in 1994.

RECOMMENDED ALBUM:
Nespithe (Repulse, 1993)

Denial Of God

The Danish black metal band Denial Of God were formed in 1991 and released a demo in the early Nineties which led to a Dark Trinity deal. The label subsequently released an EP, *The Statues Are Watching*, in 1994, which the band described as 'black horror metal'.

The first album, *The Ghouls Of DOG*, was well-received locally but failed to attract major label attention, although a deal was signed with Hammerheart. 1999 saw the release of another album, *Klabautermanden*, although touring has been hindered by line-up problems. Painkiller have since signed them for more recordings.

RECOMMENDED ALBUM:
Klabautermanden (Hammerheart, 1999)
www.denialofgod.net

Denial Of God's Ustumallagam hails as many heroes as possible in one breath
"Venom, Nuclear Death, Infernäl Mäjesty, Ripper, Witchfinder General, Genocidio, Obsession, Hellhammer, Celtic Frost, Officium Triste, Hobbs' Angel Of Death, Picture, Possessed, Living Death, Witchfynde, Judas Priest, King Diamond, Mercyful Fate, Beherit, Candlemass, Winter, Angel Witch, Voivod, Razor, Exorcist, Agent Steel, Death SS, Paul Chain, Evil, Treblinka, Preacher, Sarcófago, Von, Citron, Alice Cooper, Exciter, Blasphemy..."

Deranged

A brutal death metal band from Sweden, Deranged was formed in 1991 by the guitarist Rikard Wermen, a fan of gore and splatter movies. This obsession fuels both the lyrics and music of Deranged. The first demo, 1992's *The Confessions Of A Necrophile*, set out the Deranged stall and several songs from the band's five albums have been featured on gore/death metal compilations by various labels. They are among the finest and heaviest exponents of the old-school death metal genre.

RECOMMENDED ALBUM:
High On Blood (Regain, 1998)
http://mitglied.lycos.de/deranged

Desecration

A Welsh death metal band that makes those who regard the UK DM scene as dormant think again, the utterly heavy Desecration caused some controversy in 1995 with their debut album, *Gore And Perversion*, released by Copro. Discussing murderous subjects with unnerving frankness, the album attracted police attention and was hard to find for some years. After releasing *Murder In Mind* and *Pathway To Deviance*, and touring with Deicide, Morbid Angel, Cannibal Corpse and Vader, the band – Ollie (vocals/rhythm guitar), Mike (drums), and Pete (bass guitar) – re-recorded the debut, released it as *Gore And PerVersion 2* without a lyric sheet and thus managed to avoid legal problems.

RECOMMENDED ALBUM:
Gore And PerVersion 2 (Copro, 2002)
www.desecration.co.uk

Ollie on the art of gore metal
"I think it's ridiculous that this should be censored. It's art, you know? Music isn't forced on people. This music isn't

played on the radio. If people want it they have to look for it. I'm offended by offending people and not getting away with it!

The lyrics are just disgusting. It is well brutal and extremely sick, which is what we set out to do. We set out to do the sickest thing possible, and in my opinion we achieved it. Desecration are a sick band. We always have been. It's just that we've been stopped from being as sick as we could be."

Destroyer 666

Yet more unfeasibly aggressive Australian extreme metal comes from Destroyer 666, formed by guitarist K.K. Warslut when he left the black metal band Bestial Warlust in 1995. A debut, *Violence Is The Prince Of This World*, set out the D666 stall convincingly and its follow-up, *Phoenix Rising*, continued along similar lines.

RECOMMENDED ALBUM:
Violence Is The Prince Of This World
(independent, 1995)
www.destroyer666.net

K.K. Warslut on the dialectics of extreme metal
"Sadly, a lot of it seems to run in endless circles horizontally and never progress vertically. Metal to me is the most powerful music in the world, and thus stands in a prime position to bring forth the sharp edge of philosophy. This was happening with the early Nineties scene as a reaction against the mundane nonsense of the death metal movement. Unfortunately metal, like the mother culture that spawned it, is prone to the same inane desire of mainstream culture for simple non-confrontational entertainment."

Destruction (Right)

The German thrash metal band Destruction are, with Kreator and Sodom, one of the Fatherland's unholy trio of Eighties speed metal outfits. Founded by Marcel 'Schmier' Schirmer (bass/vocals) and including among others guitarists Mike Sifringer and Harry Wilkens, and drummer Tommy Sandmann, they signed to Steamhammer in 1984 and released the *Sentence Of Death* EP. The hard-hitting *Infernal Overkill* LP followed and three more albums showed that the band had staying power, but Schmier had had enough after the *Live Without Sense* album of 1989 and departed. The next Destruction album, *Cracked Brain*, was recorded with a new line-up but attempted to substitute heaviness for speed and the fans stayed away. After more EPs the band split and almost a decade of silence followed, broken only by the release of the poor *The Least Successful Human Cannonball* album in 1996.

In 1999 the band reformed, signed to Nuclear Blast and came back with well-received albums and a live DVD over the next few years. Judging by the resurgence in vintage thrash that has seen the three German bands tour on one dream package, it seems as if their place is assured.

RECOMMENDED ALBUM:
Eternal Devastation (Steamhammer, 1986)
www.destruction.de

Schmier unites the metal army...
"There are limits and we reached them a long time ago. A blastbeat is already the borderline for our receptivity. It's a small border between reaching the top of extremities and plain noise, especially live! Our music needs more tolerance in the scene itself! There is way too much anger and jealousy between all the different and exciting types of metal/ brutal music. Otherwise our scene will reduce itself to a die-hard minimum, like in the Nineties. United we stand..."

Dew-Scented – modern thrash metal

Dew-Scented

Named after an Edgar Allan Poe-utilised phrase, the modern German thrash/death metal Dew-Scented formed in 1992; a demo, *Symbolization*, led to a deal with SPV and tours with Overkill, Edge Of Sanity, Lake Of Tears, Morbid Angel and Arch Enemy. Releasing a series of albums whose titles all inexplicably began with the letter I, the band established a perfect crossover of extreme styles, most notable on the debut *Innoscent* and the most recent release, 2003's *Impact*.

RECOMMENDED ALBUM:
Impact (SPV, 2003)
www.dew-scented.de

Diabolic

Tampa death metallists Diabolic first came together in 1997 and recorded a demo, *City Of The Dead*, later reissued by the Fadeless label. *Supreme Evil* was released two years later by Conquest and the band embarked on heavyweight tours with prestigious bands from the region and elsewhere including Cannibal Corpse and Hate Eternal. Despite the acclaim they received as part of a touring package in 2004, they decided to part ways.

RECOMMENDED ALBUM:
Supreme Evil (Conquest, 2004)
www.diabolicblastmasters.com

Die Apokalyptischen Reiter

Germany's 'The Apocalyptic Riders' first formed in 1995 and soon established a brand of smooth, polished death metal that appeals to fans from across the metal spectrum. Using a piano for the softer textures but retaining a full assault of riffs, the band has expanded a fanbase across a sequence of albums for the German Ars Metalli label and recently Hammerheart. An unlikely touring alliance with US murder-metal fiends Macabre recently gained them exposure to a new audience.

RECOMMENDED ALBUM:
Allegro Barbaro (Ars Metalli, 1999)
www.reitermania.de

Guitarist Eric Hersemann on the extreme metal industry

❝I think the future of extreme metal is in constant jeopardy thanks in part to the independent record labels that distribute it. There is not enough experimentation going on because a lot of young bands are too busy chasing trends to get that 'record deal'. The labels need to take more chances and try to actually develop bands, instead of letting the bands and the underground do their work for them.❞

Volk-Man on the future of extremity

❝Extreme music will always search for new ways to break the old borders. Sick minds will find new combinations, sick producers will find new ways to record and mix the stuff in a more and more extreme way. The extreme genre will be a melting point of all extreme sub-genres. Extremists of all genres will fight under one flag. Everything is possible.❞

Die Apokalyptischen Reiter – experimental death metallers

Dimmu Borgir

Norway's Dimmu Borgir (an Icelandic expression meaning black castle or dark fortress) have created the ultimate in pompous, bombastic black metal, with long, complex songs chock-full of faux-classical pretensions and swathes of keyboards. The band was formed in 1993 when the death metal bassist/vocalist Erkejetter Silenoz met the Fimbulwinter guitarist Shagrath. A single, 'Inn I Evightens Marke', was issued in 1994 by Necromantik Gallery and some months later, the album *For All Tid* was released on the No Colours label after the addition of Nagash (bass), Tjodalv (drums) and Stian Aarstad (keyboard). Albums followed amid some line-up shifts – a new keyboard player, Mustis, was recruited; Nagash left to pursue a side project, Kovenant; sometime Cradle Of Filth drummer Nick Barker is a notable alumnus – and Dimmu Borgir remain the most overblown of the keyboard-based black metal bands. Their rise to prominence across several multi-layered albums is perhaps symptomatic of wider musical changes in metal. Like the only other black metal band which outsells them, Cradle Of Filth, they can command followers from the rock, gothic-metal and even progressive-rock scenes.

RECOMMENDED ALBUM:

Enthrone Darkness Triumphant
(Nuclear Blast, 1997)
www.dimmu-borgir.com

Silenoz looks back

"I remember my first ever heavy metal show, it was in '86 when Fury played at the local community hall. I was too young to get in on my own so I dragged my father there, and I guess ever since then he's not been fond of my love for metal music.

People can say whatever they want but I believe that the Eighties was pure metal, extreme or not, and we will never see anything like it ever again. It doesn't mean that I think metal is dead these days, far from it, but the feeling, the atmosphere, all of the things that involved metal in the Eighties was unique!"

Disincarnate

The US band Disincarnate was a brief side project for guitarist James Murphy, who played with Cancer, Death, Obituary and Testament. As a member of Death he brought a dose of melody to Chuck Schuldiner's brutal riffing, and the *Spiritual Healing* album was all the better for it. Similarly, Testament's album *The Gathering* bears the unmistakable Murphy touch and was hailed as their best work in ages. Disincarnate produced one album, *Dreams Of The Carrion Kind*, issued in 1993, and remain on hold.

RECOMMENDED ALBUM:
Dreams Of The Carrion Kind
(Roadrunner, 1993)
www.disincarnate.msanthrope.com

Dismember

Swedish death metal band Dismember perform a breed of intensely aggressive death metal with the classic middle-heavy guitar sound pioneered by countrymen Entombed in the early Nineties. Fred Estby (drums), David Blomqvist (guitar), Matti Kärki (vocals), Richard Cabeza (bass) and Magnus Sahlgren (guitar) came together in the early Nineties, releasing the excellent *Like An Ever Flowing Stream* album and causing problems with UK customs officials with the song 'Skin Her Alive'. The incident was resolved, and the band named their next album *Indecent And Obscene* in sarcastic acknowledgement. Subsequent releases have seen Dismember stick resolutely to the old-school style: Kärki also plays in an Autopsy tribute act, Murder Squad.

RECOMMENDED ALBUM:
Like An Ever Flowing Stream
(Nuclear Blast, 1991)
www.dismember.se

Matti Kärki on metal trends

❝Our old label kept telling us, 'Oh, you have to change your style, death metal is dead! Nobody listens to death metal any more...' So we said, fuck this. The death metal scene has grown back. It went away for a while because black metal was so popular. Everybody was going, 'Oh, let's wear corpse-paint! Evil! Kill! Burn churches!' All that stuff. It was a trend, just like death metal was a trend for a while before that.❞

Dissection *(Above)*

Swedish black metal band Dissection – Jon Nodtveidt (vocals/guitars), Peter Palmdahl (bass) and Ole Ohman (drums) – performed competent metal across three albums before being obliged to split when Nodtveidt was jailed for seven years for murder in 1998. The victim was an Algerian homosexual who the Dissection singer and a friend met in a Gothenburg park, attacked with a stun gun and then shot in the head with a pistol. Nodtveidt was released in 2004 and the band reformed, initially with ex-Emperor drummer, Bärd 'Faust' Eithun.

RECOMMENDED ALBUM:
The Somberlain (No Fashion, 1993)
www.dissection.nu

Divine Sin

Sweden's Divine Sin play competent, polished power/thrash metal with low vocals. Fredde Lundberg (vocals), Micke Andersson (guitar), Bubby Goude (bass) and Martin Knutar (drums) signed to Black Mark in the early Nineties and produced two well-executed albums. After several years of inactivity they reformed in 2003.
RECOMMENDED ALBUM:
Thirteen Souls (Black Mark, 1997)

Dødheimsgard

A modern, often avant-garde Norwegian black metal band with a varying line-up, Dødheimsgard (currently calling themselves DHG) produce music with the standard BM aggression but with unpredictable, textured progressions that have won them fans who seek more from metal than mere power. As the cybermetal movement has come and gone, so they have also utilised electronic sources, but the band is sporadically, rather than permanently, active and they remain something of an enigma. The members are known to participate in other metal bands: Aldrahn with Zyklon, Czral with Ved Buens Ende, and so on.
RECOMMENDED ALBUM:
666 International (Moonfog, 1999)
www.notam02.no/~sveinhat/dhg

DRI

Of the many hardcore punk/metal acts that plagued the humble metal fan in the Eighties, the biggest and best was always DRI (Dirty Rotten Imbeciles). Acts such as Gang Green and Cro-Mags also dabbled in metal, but were ultimately destined to push out a kind of proto-Green Day punk-lite, which many metal fans found deeply irritating. However, DRI were at least as much a metal band as a punk outfit, hence their inclusion in these pages.

Formed in 1982 by the core members Kurt Brecht (vocals) and Spike Cassidy (guitar), the band famously took its name from the insults thrown at them by Brecht's father during rehearsals. The self-released *Dirty Rotten* EP, issued in 1983, mixed hamfisted thrash metal with the gobby attitude of punk. A full-length album, *Dealing With It*, was released in 1985 and DRI embarked on a US tour. The audiences they drew were a fair mixture of punks, skinheads and extreme metal fans, and the idea of a 'crossover' movement started to grow among the commentators of the time. Slayer drummer Dave Lombardo also helped DRI along by waxing lyrical about the band at every possible opportunity.

Two more definitive albums – 1987's *Crossover* and *Thrash Zone* from 1989 – were released before the DRI star began to wane. Both showcased DRI's considerable power, although the growing strength of both the thrash and death metal scenes meant that fans had plenty of choice for other entertainment. Touring became the DRI lifestyle, whether alone or with thrash metal bands such as Testament. In April 1996 drummer Rob Rampy and Spike Cassidy were not permitted to cross the Canadian border, having previously been fined for driving under the influence, and several Canadian dates were cancelled. The band continues to play to this day.
RECOMMENDED ALBUM:
Crossover (Rotten Records, 1987)
www. www.dirtyrottenimbeciles.com

Edge of Sanity

Edge Of Sanity are an intermittently functioning Swedish death metal band consisting of Dan Swanö (vocals), Andreas Axelsson (guitars), Sami Nerberg (guitars), Anders Lindberg (bass) and Benny Larsson (drums). Like Opeth a progressive, melodic DM act, their finest moment for many was the 1996 album *Crimson*, consisting of one 40-minute song. Swanö departed after the *Infernal* album to spend time on his other bands, Unicorn and Night In Gales, and EOS recruited a new singer, Robert Karlsson (ex-Pan-Thy-Monium). More albums have expanded the expanding EOS fanbase.
RECOMMENDED ALBUM:
Crimson (Black Mark, 1996)

Einherjer

Norwegian black metal act Einherjer were formed in 1993 in the town of Haugesund and produce music with strong Viking influences (the name means a Viking warrior's afterlife). The line-up – Grimar (guitar), Ulvar (drums), Nidhogg (vocals) and Thonar (bass) – recorded a demo, *Aurora Borealis*, and signed to the Austrian label Napalm. The classic *Dragons Of The North* album was recorded at Grieghallen Studio with the renowned producer Eirik 'Pytten' Hundvin and, despite personnel changes, the band took a step up by signing to Century Media. More albums consolidated their position, but after 11 years at the forefront of the Viking genre, they split in 2004.

RECOMMENDED ALBUM:
Dragons Of The North (Napalm, 1996)

Emperor

The Norwegian band Emperor were one of the world's most inventive, technically proficient and influential black metal bands. The line-up centred on two Telemark musicians, Ihsahn (real name Vegard Sverre Tveitan) on guitar, synth and vocals, and Samoth (Tomas Thormodsæter Haugen) who played drums until 1992 before switching to guitar. Both are respected session players, Samoth in particular having played with Mayhem, Burzum, Satyricon, Gorgoroth and Arcturus. The band also features the astonishingly deft Trym Torson (ex-Enslaved, drums) and two session musicians for live shows, Charmand Grimloch (keyboards) and Tyr (bass). The story of Emperor is bound up with that of the main players in the intense Norwegian metal scene in a way that few other acts in this book can claim to be.

In 1990 Ihsahn and Samoth met at a music seminar and recorded a demo, *The Land Of The Lost Souls*, under the name Embryonic, later renaming the band Thou Shalt Suffer. 1991 saw Samoth and Insahn start to compose music outside Thou Shalt Suffer and invited a friend, Mortiis, to play bass. Shortly afterwards the name change to Emperor took place, Samoth supposedly taking the name from the song 'Dethroned Emperor' by Swiss legends Celtic Frost. A second demo, *Wrath Of The Tyrant*, was recorded in 1992, and a drummer, Bärd 'Faust' Eithun, was recruited. Emperor then recorded a split album, *Emperor/Hordanes Land*, with Enslaved, releasing it the following year. Samoth then set up a label, Nocturnal Art Productions, and released a 1993 EP of Emperor tracks, the 1000-only *As The Shadows Rise*.

In August 1992, while drummer Eithun was walking in the Olympic Park at Lillehammer, he was approached by a stranger who invited him for a walk in the woods, a well-known meeting-place for the local gay community. Eithun agreed and followed him into the forest. The stranger duly attempted to embrace Eithun, who produced a knife and stabbed him to death. Eithun walked home unhindered and found out later that the local police were mystified as to the killer's identity. A couple of days later, Burzum's Count Grishnackh, Mayhem's Euronymous and Eithun went to a nearby church, Holmenkollen, and burned it to the ground using petrol. Neither crime was traced to Eithun and he began to think that he might escape punishment.

However, in August 1993, Euronymous was murdered by Count Grishnackh (see Mayhem and Burzum entries) and the members of Emperor were arrested. During the investigations, Eithun's crimes were revealed and he was arrested for church arson and murder. He was paroled in 2003 and worked briefly with black metal band Dissection.

Samoth, who had also been involved in church-burnings, served a 16-month sentence; he had just guested on *Burzum's Aske* (Ashes) EP, which featured as its cover artwork a photograph of a burning church. Meanwhile, Emperor had completed a tour with Cradle Of Filth, and Samoth had temporarily joined Satyricon as well as becoming a session bass player with Gorgoroth. As if this wasn't enough, he had composed several new Emperor songs, which would ultimately appear on the next album, *Anthems To The Welkin At Dusk*. He had also been working on a side-project, Zyklon-B, who had recorded a mini-album, *Blood Must Be Shed*.

Samoth duly served his time and rejoined Emperor but there was some conflict within the band and Mortiis left in 1994, moving to Sweden, and establishing a career as an industrial-electronic rock musician. His place was taken by Tchort, who played bass on *In The Nightside Eclipse* in 1995. However, he too suffered from anti-social tendencies and served six months for assault with a knife, burglary and grave desecration. A new drummer was temporarily found in Hellhammer, whose band, Mayhem, was on hold following Euronymous' death, but his place was soon filled by Trym. Sverd of Arcturus was also

Enforsaken – American Euro-metal?

briefly recruited as a keyboard player. *The Reverence* EP was recorded in late 1996 with new bassist Alver, and issued in 1997, but it was immediately eclipsed by the *Anthems To The Welkin At Dusk* album, released later that year and hailed as one of the great black metal albums.

1999 saw a flurry of Imperial activity. A split album with fellow Norwegians Thorns, *Thorns Vs. Emperor*, was issued on Moonfog to moderate acclaim, but the year's triumph was undoubtedly the *Anthems…* successor, *IX: Equilibrium*, a startling, frenzied record of incredibly complex, majestic songs. The band also recorded a song for a Darkthrone tribute album: the two bands had known each other for some time, Darkthrone's Fenriz having worked closely with Euronymous. In 2001 Emperor announced that they were ceasing activities. A best-of album signalled their farewell. Ihsahn retreated to the classical-based studio project Peccatum and Samoth to Zyklon-B, later changing its name to Zyklon and earning considerable success (see separate entry). Emperor leave a formidable legacy behind them.

RECOMMENDED ALBUM:
In The Nightside Eclipse
(Candlelight, 1994)
www.emperorhorde.com

Enforsaken

Formed in 1998 by Steve Stell and Pat O'Keefe, Enforsaken are unusual at the time of writing (although the situation could well have changed if you're reading this in, say, 2008) in that they perform a very European brand of melodic death metal despite being an American band. After completing the line-up with Joe DeGroot and Steven Sagala, they recorded a demo entitled *Embraced By Misery* and signed to Lifeless in the US and Lifeforce overseas. Tours with many name acts followed and an excellent, multifaceted album, *The Forever Endeavor*, was released in 2004.

RECOMMENDED ALBUM:
The Forever Endeavor
(Century Media, 2004)

Steve Stell on the pioneers
❝There have been quite a few good extreme metal bands over the years, but the ones that I've always held in the highest regard are Carcass, Dark Tranquillity and Death. I know two of these bands aren't around any more, but what they left behind has left a huge mark on the extreme metal scene. They paved the way for all of today's extreme metal.❞

Enslaved

Norway's Enslaved was initially Trym Torson (drums), Grutle Kjellson (bass, vocals) and Ivar Bjornson (guitar, keyboards). Bjørnson and Torson joined up with Kjellson in 1990 after the split of the latter's death metal band, Phobia. Demonaz of Immortal suggested the name Enslaved and a demo, *Nema*, was recorded. Its successor, *Yggdrasill*, impressed Mayhem singer Euronymous and he offered them a deal with his Oslo label, Deathlike Silence. In accordance with the band's Wotanist interests – based on the Norse gods/ Valhalla system – the band named their album *Vikingligr Veldi*, and it was released in March 1994. Unfortunately the murder of Euronymous by Burzum's Count Grishnackh made the release of the album very difficult: Euronymous had sent the final contracts to Bjørnson on the very day of his murder, and one or two legal issues had yet to be resolved. An argument arose through the band's involvement with Voices Of Wonder, a label connected with Euronymous, but the situation was resolved when the French label Osmose stepped in with a new contract and a sharp legal team.

The first Osmose album, *Frost*, was recorded in 1994, showcasing a powerful, icy sound. Its successor, *Eld* (1997) continued the black/pagan themes even further, although the powerful drumming of Trym was lacking – he had moved to Emperor after some friction between the band members. In 1998, the line-up changed again, with a new guitarist, Kronheim, and a drummer, Dirge Rep; this version of Enslaved recorded *Blodhemn*, an epic record containing various spoken-word passages. The band continued to develop progressive tendencies until the astonishing *Below The Lights* appeared in 2003, the logical conclusion of their evolution.

RECOMMENDED ALBUM:
Eld (Osmose, 1997)
www.enslaved.no

Enthroned

A Belgian black metal band, Enthroned was formed in 1993 by Lord Sabathan (bass, vocals) and Cernunnos (drums) after the split of their previous bands Morbid Death and Blaspherion. They then recruited Tsebaoth (guitar) of the death metal band Slanesh, and released a five-track demo in 1994, as well as a split EP with Ancient Rites on the Belgian label Afterdark and an album on Evil Omen the following year. A second guitarist, Nornagest, joined the band – he had previously handled bass and vocals with the speed metal band Heresia – and Tsebaoth was replaced by Nebiros. A one-album deal was signed with Osmose in 1997, but just as the band were about to start recording *Towards The Skullthrone Of Satan*, Cernunnos committed suicide. In an interview, Nornagest explained that this happened "for the simple reason that this Christian world was not made for him... [Cernunnos wanted] to return to the Kingdom Below with Our Lord."

Towards The Skullthrone Of Satan was a minor underground success and was followed by *Regie Satanas*, apparently a tribute to Cernunnos. His replacement was Namroth Blackthorn. The album included a cover of Sodom's 'The Conqueror'. Subsequent albums have heightened the Belgians' profile, although Sabathan has been heard to complain about the fact that his band aren't taken seriously because they aren't Swedish or Norwegian.

RECOMMENDED ALBUM:
The Apocalypse Manifesto (Blackend, 1999)
www.enthroned-horde.com

Nornagest on black metal inspiration
❝Darkthrone – for the essence and blood-freezing side of their music: they always had that feeling and mystique I was searching for. Although we are a black metal band we are not afraid to mix thrash, death and heavy metal elements within our art, which gives it a different approach than many bands in this style. A 'famous' statement from a friend of mine is 'Black metal is not a trend, it's a cult'.❞

Entombed

At one time the most influential Swedish death metal band, Entombed consist of singer Lars-Goran Petrov, guitarists Alex Hellid and Uffe 'Monster' Cederlund, bassist Jorgen Sandstrom and drummer Nicke Andersson. The debut album, 1990's *Left Hand Path*, was an absolute classic, responsible for the launch of the 'Stockholm sound' – the raw production and buzzsaw guitar sound of death metal bands such as Dismember.

The roots of Entombed go back as far as 1987, when the various members were in a band called Nihilist. Their music was DRI-style crossover metal-punk, but the musicians found themselves moving away from that scene into more purposeful territory, signing a contract with Earache after playing shows with Carcass. Although the debut album set them up as a band to be taken seriously, Petrov left the band after an argument and stayed away for a year. However, he returned and the next album, *Clandestine*, was a success.

It was *Wolverine Blues*, however, which brought the band to the international stage. The US major label Columbia had bought Earache and decided to market the album using the Wolverine character from the Marvel Comics series, despite the fact that Entombed had taken the title from a novel by James Ellroy. Subsequent albums have seen the band soften their approach, however, with mellower textures appearing at times. While Entombed remain a cult act, their glory days appear to be behind them.

RECOMMENDED ALBUM:
Left Hand Path (Earache, 1990)
www.entombed.org

Ephel Duath

Italian black metal Ephel Duath formed in 1998 and recorded a demo, *Opera*, strongly influenced by the Scandinavian scene. Signing to Code666, they recorded a debut album, *Phormula*, after a fanbase had grown through extensive downloading of their music. Earache imprint Elitist then signed them and a reissue, *Rephormula*, was released in 2002. However, the band reached its potential for the first time with *The Painter's Palette*, which featured experimental sounds and unorthodox, semi-electronic instrumentation.

RECOMMENDED ALBUM:
The Painter's Palette (Elitist, 2003)

Eternal Solstice

A Dutch death metal band initially formed in 1989, the Eternal Solstice line-up stabilised into Kees-Jan Schouten (vocals), Philip Nugteren (guitar), Victor van Drie (guitar), Ramon Soeterbroek (bass) and Mischa Hak (drums), releasing a split album with Mourning in 1992. A self-released full-length album, *The Wish Is Father To The Thought*, was issued two years later and ex-Mourning drummer Andre van der Ree replaced Hak.

Poseidon Productions offered the band a deal and re-released *The Wish...*, while the band recorded a second album, *Horrible Within*, released by Poseidon in November 1995. A third album, the horticulturally-monikered *Demonic Fertilizer*, was released in 1997, containing new tracks and the songs from the earlier split CD. Since then activity has been slight.

RECOMMENDED ALBUM:
Horrible Within (Poseidon, 1995)

Ephel Duath – highly unusual

Exciter

A Canadian thrash metal band of the mid-Eighties, featuring John Ricci (guitar) and Allan James Johnson (bass), Exciter performed competently, but never innovatively enough to challenge the existing speed metal hierarchy, although their first album was recognised as a scene-setter. Drummer and vocalist Dan Beehler also sang in a wailing manner that put some fans off. However, Exciter re-emerged in 1996 with a new vocalist, releasing *The Dark Command* in 1997. Incongruously, footballer David Beckham was seen sporting one of their T-shirts in 2000.

RECOMMENDED ALBUM:
Violence And Force (Megaforce, 1984)

Exodus *(Below)*

Paul Baloff (vocals), Gary Holt (guitar), Rick Hunolt (guitar), Tom Hunting (drums) and Rob McKillop (bass) formed San Francisco's Exodus, who – like Flotsam And Jetsam after them – took years to get over their "lost a member to Metallica" stigma. Founder member and lead guitarist Kirk Hammett was poached by the soon-to-be-enormous thrashers in April 1983 after Dave Mustaine received his marching orders, it's true, but it should be remembered that Exodus continued to be an excellent thrash metal band in their own right, issuing one absolutely essential album and several fair efforts.

Hammett had already departed by the time the debut album, *Bonded By Blood* (originally titled *A Lesson In Violence*), was released in 1985. It was an intense record, comparable with the best work of Kreator or Possessed, with Steve Souza's rasping-shriek vocals perfect for the job. Souza also fronted Testament in their early days as Legacy. Six more albums ensued. The band split in 1992 after management and record company problems became too much for them, but an attempt at a comeback was made in 1996, when the band issued a new live album of old songs, including 'Impaler', co-written by Hammett and containing a riff which he later incorporated into the Metallica song, 'Trapped Under Ice'. Interest was mild at best, and the sudden death of Baloff of a stroke in 2002 seemed to seal their fate.

However, a much more serious return in 2003 with the Andy Sneap-produced *Tempo Of The Damned* album (Nuclear Blast) featuring Souza on vocals was hailed as a success.

RECOMMENDED ALBUM:
Bonded By Blood (Combat, 1985)
www.exodusattack.com

Extreme Noise Terror

Extreme Noise Terror were briefly that metal marketing man's dream – an extreme metal band with access to Radio 1 airplay. Formed in January 1985, ENT – vocalists Dean Jones and Phil Vane, guitarist Ali Firouzbakht, bassist Lee Barrett and one of several possible drummers – were offered a deal with Manic Ears Records at their very first show. The first release was the split *Radioactive* album with Chaos UK.

It initially seemed that they would go the way of the rest of the UK noise merchants, but in 1987 the late Radio 1 DJ John Peel was taken by their aggressive approach and asked them to record a Peel Session. The result was released by Strange Fruit and did so well that a second session was recorded, although it was never released.

An album, *A Holocaust In Your Head*, was then issued on Hurt Records and tours of Europe and Japan followed, as well as a third Peel Session. Through the Peel connection, ENT came into contact with Bill Drummond of the KLF, who asked them to appear on the Christmas Day *Top Of The Pops*, playing a live version of the KLF hit, '3AM Eternal'. The show was duly recorded, but the BBC decided that the song wasn't 'suitable' for daytime TV. Angered, the KLF boycotted *TOTP*. The song was ultimately released as a limited edition single and the two bands performed live at the 1992 Brit Awards. ENT decided to fire blanks from a machine gun at the audience, causing the tabloids to get into a pious froth. An album, *The Black Room*, was recorded with the KLF (whose famous ambient album had been called *The White Room*), but when Drummond and his co-conspirator Jimmy Cauty announced the KLF's retirement, they also deleted the recordings.

Extreme Noise Terror have continued to tour and release sporadic albums, although nowadays their activities are minimal. A vocalist shuffle with Napalm Death caused some controversy in 1995, but it would appear that the BBC-baiting days of ENT are over. Their music has turned far more towards generic death metal in the new millennium.

RECOMMENDED ALBUM:
A Holocaust In Your Head (Hurt, 1988)
http://get.to/ent

Fear Factory

Fear Factory are probably the first band to find mainstream success in the modern world by blending death and industrial metal in a chart-friendly format. The Los Angeles band was formed in 1990 by Burton C. Bell (vocals), Raymond Herrera (drums) and Dino Cazares (guitar). Signing to Roadrunner, the band released their debut album, *Soul Of A New Machine*, in 1992. It featured bassist Andrew Shives, later replaced by Christian Olde Wolbers.

The follow-up, *Fear Is The Mind Killer* (a quote from Frank Herbert's *Dune* novel) saw the Factory hand over songs from *Soul…* to remixers Rhys Fulber and Bill Leeb. After much touring and some line-up shuffles, Fear Factory released a second album in 1995, *Demanufacture*. A highly influential techno/metal remix album, *Remanufacture (Cloning Technology)*, followed in 1997, but the band was moving more towards nu-metal and reached the genre completely with 2000's *Digimortal*. However, in 2003 a split with Cazares (Wolbers took up guitar and Strapping Young Lad bassist Byron Stroud was recruited) saw the revitalised band head straight back into death metal with a new album, *Archetype*.

Fear Factory also worked on several side projects. Perhaps the most notorious was the Mexican drug-ring spoof Brujeria, while Nailbomb saw Cazares team up with Soulfly's Max Cavalera (see separate entries).

RECOMMENDED ALBUM:
Demanufacture (Roadrunner, 1995)
www.fearfactory.com

Fleshcrawl

A German death metal band, Fleshcrawl signed to Black Mark in 1992 after producing a series of successful demo tapes. The debut album, *Descend Into The Absurd*, was recorded later that year and received underground praise. After the release of a second album, 1994's *Impurity*, the band embarked on extended tours with Deicide, Cathedral, Brutal Truth, Sinister and Kataklysm.

The start of a long and fruitful relationship with Peter Tägtgren occurred in December 1995, when Fleshcrawl entered the Hypocrisy guitarist's Abyss studio. The result, *Bloodsoul*, was a stunning album of vicious death metal received ecstatically by both fans of Fleshcrawl and fans of Tägtgren's raw production. Further touring ensued and the fourth album, *Bloodred Massacre*, took a mere two weeks to record in August 1997. The album was also notable for its cover of Slayer's 'Necrophiliac'. One of Fleshcrawl's assertions has always been that they will not change for the sake of fashion: subsequent albums have proved this to be true. Additionally, they have toured with death metal acts such as Six Feet Under.

RECOMMENDED ALBUM:
Bloodsoul (Black Mark, 1995)
www.fleshcrawl.de

Fleshgrind

The American death metal band Fleshgrind were assembled in 1993 by guitarist/vocalist Rich Lipscomb, drummer Dave Barbolla, guitarist Steve Murray and bassist Casey Ryba. A demo, *Holy Pedophile*, was recorded the same year and sold 2500 copies. The next demo, *Sorrow Breeds Hatred (Bleed On Me)*, recorded in 1995, led to a one-album deal with Pulverizer.

The album in question, *Destined For Defilement*, which was released in 1997, was plagued by administrative problems; due to cash flow obstacles the label were unable to press the CD, handing the masters over to the band who distributed the album themselves. At this point Casey Ryba was replaced by Ray Vazquez, who, however, didn't stay long, and Barbolla was ejected from the band after some disagreements with the other members. Both men were replaced and after rehearsals, the band started touring, playing with Broken Hope, Malevolent Creation, Deicide, Cannibal Corpse, and Mortician among others. Since then little activity has been reported from the band.

RECOMMENDED ALBUM:
Destined For Defilement (Pulverizer, 1997)

Fleurety

Norwegian black metal act Fleurety's 1993 *Black Snow* demo led to a deal with Aesthetic Death, who issued the 'A Darker Shade Of Evil' single the following year. Signing to Misanthropy, the *Min Tid Skal Komme* (My Time Shall Come) album was a work of uncompromising craft, with unexpected nods towards the melodies of Sixties folk with female vocal parts. Sessions with Mayhem and others gave the members black metal credibility by association, but by the turn of the century, Fleurety's own music had diverged almost entirely from the metal genre.

RECOMMENDED ALBUM:
Min Tid Skal Komme (Misanthropy, 1995)

Flotsam And Jetsam

Arizona thrashers Flotsam And Jetsam – Eric 'A.K.' Knutson (vocals), Ed Carlson (guitar), initially Jason Newsted and later Jason Ward (bass), Michael Gilbert (guitar) and Kelly David Smith (drums) – play all-out thrash with no death, black or doom pretences and what's more, do it extremely well. Like Exodus, the millstone of being 'the band that your friend deserted to join Metallica' has been a little heavy at times, but despite the loss of the nimble-plectrummed bassist Newsted, F&J's albums have remained worth a look for anyone remotely interested in challenging, non-clichéd metal. They continue to this day and maintain a dedicated US fanbase.

RECOMMENDED ALBUM:
Doomsday For The Deceiver
(Metal Blade, 1986)
www.flotsam-and-jetsam.com

Craig Nielsen on narrow-minded headbangers
❝I wish metal fans were more diverse in their tastes. It seems these days that you can only enjoy this or that style, and there is no wide crossover of tastes. Maybe that's why back in the day 10,000 kids would show up for a great metal tour, and today you are lucky to see 1000, unless you are on a giant festival package.❞

Forbidden

A seminal Bay Area thrash band of the late Eighties, Forbidden produced high-quality speed metal. Initially known as Forbidden Evil, they are now largely remembered for the fact that Robb Flynn (Vio-lence and Machine Head) was once a member, although he never recorded with the band.

The Gathering – no longer extreme

Forbidden also harboured future Slayer drummer Paul Bostaph, who must have needed every ounce of talent he possessed when taking over from Dave Lombardo. More permanent members included Russ Anderson (vocals), Craig Locicero (guitar), Tim Calvert (guitar), Matt Camacho (bass) and Steve Jacobs (drums). The band split in 1998 after the release of *Green*, with various members defecting either to Nevermore or Manmade God.

RECOMMENDED ALBUM:
Forbidden Evil (Combat, 1988)

Frostmoon

Norwegian black metal band Frostmoon were initially the duo Massacra and Tundra, who formed the band in 1997 and created a demo, *Nordgesriket Hylles*. Tundra left shortly afterwards and Massacra continued alone. Oskorei Productions signed him after a series of demo recordings and Vinterfrost was recruited to the band. A debut album, *Tordenkrig*, was released in 1999. Choirs and complex vocal arrangements gave the music an epic edge. Frostmoon are currently on hold, however.

RECOMMENDED ALBUM:
Tordenkrig (Sound Riot, 1999)

G

Gates Of Ishtar

Formed in '92 by Mikael Sandorf (vocals), Andreas Johansson (drums), Stefan Nilsson (guitar), Tomas Jutenfäldt (guitar) and Harald Åberg (bass), Swedish melodic death metal act Gates Of Ishtar recorded the *Seasons Of Frost* demo and signed to the Finnish label Spinefarm. Moving to the German label, Invasion, they recorded *The Dawn Of Flames* and, after undergoing some line-up changes, toured. After releasing *At Dusk And Forever*, the band fell silent.

RECOMMENDED ALBUM:
The Dawn Of Flames (Invasion, 1997)
www.solace.mh.se/~jsf/ishtar.old

The Gathering

Formed in 1989, Holland's The Gathering started life as a death metal outfit with hints towards the experimentalism of Celtic Frost. Their 1992 debut album, *Always*, was more or less a conventional doom record, and it wasn't until the follow-up, 1993's *Almost A Dance*, that a more atmospheric approach was pursued, concentrating less on guitars. However, public response was minimal and, dumping frontman Bart Smits, the band recruited a new singer to help pick up where they had left off.

Anneke van Giersbergen was the person they eventually recruited, a 21-year-old fan of the extended explorations of Dead Can Dance and Pink Floyd. A landmark record followed, the almost psychedelic *Mandylion* of 1995, produced by the experienced Waldemar Sorychta, who had previously worked with acts as diverse as Tiamat, Moonspell and Sentenced.

The following year saw The Gathering appear at the Dynamo Open Air and Pink Pop festivals to good response by fans. The atmospherics of *Mandylion* translated well to the live setting and, encouraged, the band took the approach a step further on 1997's *Nighttime Birds* album, produced in various Amsterdam studios. The line-up – Rene Rutten (guitar), Hugo Prinsen Geerligs (bass), Frank Boeijen (keyboards), Hans Rutten (drums) and, making his last

Gathering appearance, Jelmer Wiersma (guitar) — has now more or less stabilised, issuing a follow-up to *Birds* and a live album in 2000. They are now a mainstream rock act with little metal in their sound.
RECOMMENDED ALBUM:
Mandylion (Century Media, 1995)

Hans Rutten on metal irony
❝My first experience of extreme metal was the first Napalm Death album. I was shocked. And when I saw Carcass live somewhere in 1989, I lost my appetite after seeing a gig of them showing pictures on the backdrop of carcasses, slaughtered meat... Later on I heard they were vegetarians, and the coin dropped.❞

Goat Of Mendes

Goat of Mendes is a black metal band with folk influences from Germany. Formed in 1994 by vocalist Surtur, Matthias Freyth (guitar), Winnie Freyth (drums) and Jens Weiss (bass), the band recorded a demo called *Hymn to One Ablaze*, which included poetry by Surtur. A deal with the Perverted Taste label followed. Line-up shuffles

Goat Of Mendes – black metal with folk elements

followed and GOM moved towards the growing pagan metal scene. Their next album was duly entitled *To Walk Upon The Wiccan Way*. After a label split, the band recorded the *Paganborn* demo and self-released an album, *Thricefold*.

RECOMMENDED ALBUM:
To Walk Upon The Wiccan Way
(Perverted Taste, 1997)
www.goatofmendes.de

Surtur on the commercialisation of the scene

❝I fear that the extreme metal scene will no longer be the refuge from commerciality it was before. The exploitation of its resources has already begun as more and more bands who are sounding more or less like some big and commercially successful act are being released and supported by the companies. They are used as additional cash-ins in the shadow of the bigger bands and will be dropped quite quickly as soon as commercial taste changes.❞

God Dethroned

Holland's God Dethroned were formed in 1991 by Henri Sattler, producing a demo which led to the recording of 1992's *The Christhunt* album, released on an independent German label. However, all was not to Sattler's taste: he had wanted a picture of a dissected rat to be used on the sleeve, but the label refused. Nonetheless

Sattler's virulently anti-Christian message was clear and the black metal underground's interest was awoken. Henri then formed a thrash metal band, Ministry Of Terror, which released the album *Fall Of Life* in 1994 and toured with Impaled Nazarene. However, many fans asked Sattler about God Dethroned, and on returning he recruited three musicians – Jens, Beef and Roel – recorded a demo and signed to Metal Blade. A second GD album, *The Grand Grimoire*, was issued in 1997, selling well through North America and Europe.

Tours supporting Six Feet Under ensued and *The Christhunt* was re-released. In April 1998 God Dethroned played the No Mercy Festivals with Cannibal Corpse, Immortal, Marduk, Obituary and Angel Corpse throughout Europe. 1999 saw the release of a third Dethroned album, *Bloody Blasphemy*. Subsequent albums have continued the GD satanic template, with the recent *Into The Lungs Of Hell* opus their most ambitious for some time.

RECOMMENDED ALBUM:
The Grand Grimoire (Metal Blade, 1997)
www.goddethroned.com

God Forbid

Alongside Chimaira and Shadows Fall, God Forbid are among the new wave of US metal bands receiving current exposure. Assembling in 1995 and releasing two demos on the 9 Volt label, GF rapidly signed to

God Forbid – NWOAHM stalwarts

Century Media and released a debut album, *Determination*. Building a hardcore/thrash approach that enthralled American audiences, GF toured incessantly before recording *Gone Forever*, a heavy, melodic album that seemed to encapsulate US metal in the early millennium. They are currently receiving much attention in the media.

RECOMMENDED ALBUM:
Gone Forever (Century Media, 2003)
www.godforbid.com

Gorerotted – UK grindcore

Gorerotted

From London, Gorerotted – Ben 'Goreskin' McCrow (vocals), Tim 'Fluffy' Weatherley (guitar), Matt 'Robin Pants' Hoban (guitar), The Wilson (bass) and Junky Jon Rushforth (drums) – are a death metal/grindcore act in a country where such acts are few and far between. Demonstrating a warped, violent sense of humour on a 1998 self-financed EP, *Her Gash I Did Slash*, Gorerotted signed to Dead Again two years later and released an album, *Mutilated In Minutes* (reissued in '02 by Relapse in the rest of the the world). A follow-up, *Only Tools And Corpses* (do you see what they did there?) appeared on Metal Blade in 2003 and tours with Pungent Stench, Vomitory and Cannibal Corpse restated their claim as UK extreme metallers to watch for the future.

RECOMMENDED ALBUM:
Mutilated In Minutes (Dead Again, 2002)
www.deadagain.fsnet.co.uk

Tim 'Fluffy' Weatherley on the state of the extreme scene
❝Fucked.... There are too many bands right now that have record deals when they can't even play in time. People new to the scene have to wade through so much shit and boring music to find the good stuff, it's no wonder they never get

past what's on MTV. Boring bands need to fuck off, too. We need personalities back in music, we need more Ozzys, Glen Bentons, Gene Simmonses and the like back in heavy metal for it to survive. We need the Eighties metal attitude back and we need it now.❞

Gorgasm

A grind/death metal band from Chicago, Gorgasm was formed by guitarists Tom Tangalos and Tom Leski in 1994, recruiting bassist Russ Powell, and sharing vocals between them. The band recorded a demo in 1996, a six-track tape that Gorgasm released independently the same year. A drummer, Derek Hoffman, was added and the band recorded an album, *Stabwound Intercourse*, released on Pulverizer in 1998.

It was an immediate success among grind fans and the band went on to play shows such as the Milwaukee Metalfest and the Ohio Deathfest. There is also a French band of the same name.

RECOMMENDED ALBUM:
Stabwound Intercourse (Pulverizer, 1998)

Gorgoroth

Swedish black/death metal band Gorgoroth – named after the evil dungeons in Tolkien's *Lord Of The Rings* – consisted originally of Pest (vocals), Tormentor (guitar), Infernus (guitar), Ares (bass), Vrolok (drums) and Daimonion (keyboards) on its formation in 1994. Similar in many ways to

the evil black/thrash metal of early Emperor and Dark Funeral, their music is a pounding mixture of speed and aggression, makng them a popular fixture on European festival bills.

The band issued three old-school black metal albums for Malicious before moving to Nuclear Blast and producing a slightly more commercial (if such a word can be applied to vicious black metal) record, *Incipit Satan*. It features a guest appearance by Ivar of Enslaved, who brings his Viking fixations to the lyrics, and the new singer Gaahl and new bassist T Reaper add a certain freshness to the somewhat hackneyed BM recipe. *Twilight Of The Idols* followed in 2003 amid more personnel changes.

RECOMMENDED ALBUM:
Destroyer (Malicious, 1998)
www.gorgoroth.org

Gorguts

Canadian death metal band Gorguts first formed in 1989 with Luc Lemay (vocals/guitar), Sylvain Marcoux (guitar), Eric Giguere (bass) and Stephane Provencher (drums). Two albums were released by Roadrunner, *Erosion Of Sanity* (which featured guest appearances from Death guitarist James Murphy and Cannibal Corpse vocalist Chris Barnes) and *Considered Dead*. The band then toured with Anthrax in support of *Obscura*.

Like many of the more experienced extreme metal acts, Gorguts promised that they would never change their style, and subsequent albums have shown this to be true, although the band do occasionally dabble in acoustic guitar introductions and other such fripperies before plunging back into the patented death grind. Two drummers occupied Provencher's drum-stool in recent years, Patrick Robert and Steve MacDonald, the latter of whom committed suicide in 2002. The *And Then Comes Lividity* demo anthology was the most recent Gorguts release.

RECOMMENDED ALBUM:
Considered Dead (Roadrunner, 1993)
www.gorguts.com

Grave

One of the original Swedish death metal bands, Grave – Jorgen Sandstrom (guitar/vocals), Ola Lindgren (guitar),

Grave – classic death metal fury

Jensa Paulsson (drums) and Jonas (bass) – issued their debut, *Into The Grave*, in 1991, following it up with a string of shows in Europe and America. The following year's *You'll Never See…* demonstrated a more polished sound and marked the departure of Jonas, who had grown disillusioned with touring. Sandstrom moved to bass and an EP of rare and remixed Grave tracks *…And Here I Die… Satisfied*, was recorded in 1993. As with the earlier albums, Grave recorded their third album, *Soulless*, with legendary producer Tomas Skogsberg at Stockholm's Sunlight Studios in 1994. It showed a slightly different approach, combining the power of before with a newer, almost catchy edge. This new territory was explored further on 1996's *Hating Life*, with the switch to vocals of Lindgren after Sandstrom left to join Entombed. A live album was then issued, *Extremely Rotten Live*. After a six-year hiatus Grave returned with *Back From The Grave* and a limited-edition six-vinyl LP box set, *Morbid Ways To Die*, for which the author of this book provided the sleevenotes.

RECOMMENDED ALBUM:
Into The Grave (Century Media, 1991)
www.intothegrave.com

The Great Deceiver

Named after a King Crimson song, The Great Deceiver was the new project of At The Gates singer Tomas Lindberg when ATG split in 1997. The sessions took a long time and no genuine album appeared until 2001, although the 1998 *Cave-In* EP raised some interest. When *A Venom Well Designed* appeared it led to a deal with UK label Peaceville, with a second album, *Terra Incognito*, cementing the band's formidable reputation in 2004. Lindberg's presence in many bands – grind supergroup Lock-Up among them – makes him a kind of respected metal everyman for the Noughties.

RECOMMENDED ALBUM:
Terra Incognito (Peaceville, 2004)
www.thegreatdeceiver.com

Green Carnation

Norwegian death metal act Green Carnation were formed in 1990 in Kristiansand, recording the *Hallucinations Of Despair* demo the year later. In 1992 they disbanded when guitarist Tchort joined

Emperor (see separate entry and also Blood Red Throne). However, in 1998 he reconvened the old band, recorded the *Journey To The End Of The Night* album and released it via Germany's Prophecy Productions in 2000, a decade after the band was first assembled. The follow-up, *Light Of Day, Day Of Darkness*, was more ambitious – a single 60-minute song featuring 600 samples, 150 recording tracks and choirs. Their third album, *A Blessing In Disguise*, was released by Season Of Mist in 2003.

RECOMMENDED ALBUM:
Light Of Day, Day Of Darkness
(Prophecy, 2002)
www.green-carnation.tk

Grief Of Emerald

A Swedish black metal band formed in 1990 as Mandatory and then Emerald, this act evolved from a gore outfit to a more developed, philosophical band with atmospheric keyboards on a demo, *The Beginning*, later released by the Deviation label (in Scotland, of all places). Signing to the Listenable label, GOE recorded *Nightspawn*, a powerful set of songs with death metal elements.

RECOMMENDED ALBUM:
Nightspawn (Listenable, 2003)
http://griefofemerald.cjb.net

Grip, Inc.

A proficient US semi-thrash metal band, Grip Inc. centred on Slayer drummer Dave Lombardo, who promised that he would return with a new band after leaving the LA quartet in 1992. Also including vocalist Gus Chambers, guitarist and producer extraordinaire Waldemar Sorychta and bassist Stuart Caruthers, the debut Grip Inc. album, *Power Of Inner Strength*, was released in 1995. It was a polished but powerfully aggressive record in which Lombardo's remarkable skills were showcased to the full.

The follow-up of two years later, *Nemesis*, was a much more versatile record, incorporating more electronic experimentation as well as the speed of before, and 1999's *Solidify* took the band to the next stage. A fourth album was released recently but Lombardo's return to Slayer in 2001 means that GI are inevitably on hold.

RECOMMENDED ALBUM:
Solidify (Metal Blade, 1999)

Hate Eternal – multilayered death metal

Hades

American thrash outfit Hades' first recording appeared on the Metal Blade compilation *Metal Massacre VI*. The band, Alan Tecchio (vocals), Ed Fuhrman (guitar), Dan Lorenzo (guitar), Scott LePage (bass) and Dave Lescinsky (drums), recorded the acclaimed *Resisting Success* and *If At First You Don't Succeed* albums, released by the now-folded Torrid label. However, the stresses of an extended European tour caused the band to split in 1989.

Tecchio and Lorenzo started the band Non Fiction but occasionally performed Hades reunion shows when fans demanded it – leading to a live Hades album, *Live On Location* – and on the demise of Non Fiction the duo recorded a new studio album, *Exist To Resist*.

Eight years after the band's original split, a new Hades album, *SaviorSelf,* was recorded and released in 1998. All the original Hades players reunited for the album, and the band continues to be periodically active, recording a follow-up in 2000. Lorenzo is a respected performer in his own right, releasing well-crafted solo material.

RECOMMENDED ALBUM:
Exist To Resist (Black Pumpkin, 1996)
www.danlorenzo.net

Hate Eternal

Producing extremely intense death metal, the American trio Hate Eternal are at the forefront of the current wave of brutal DM and are focused on the frantic, super-dexterous guitar riffing of ex-Morbid Angel axeman Erik Rutan. The band also includes ex-Suffocation guitarist Doug Cerrito, bassist Jared Anderson and drummer Tim Leung. Two albums to date – *Conquering The Throne* (1999) and *King Of All Kings* (2003) – have admirably shown that the old style is alive and well.

RECOMMENDED ALBUM:
King Of All Kings (Earache, 2003)
www.hateeternal.com

The Haunted

Leaders of the neo-thrash movement by a long way, The Haunted take the melodic approach of At The Gates (the old band of the two main songwriters, the Björler brothers Anders and Jonas) and combine it with the clean speed of Slayer for a highly refreshing new take on the old idiom. Leaving ATG in 1996 and hooking up with ex-Séance guitarist Jensen, drummer Adrian Erlandsson and ex-Mary Beats Jane singer Peter Dolving, the Björlers hit on the new band name after alternatives such as Death & ? Inc., The Promised Land and The Lost Dimension were rejected.

Earache, ATG's last label, expressed interest in The Haunted and offered the band a slot on the *Earplugged 2* compilation. This led to the band's classic self-titled debut album of 1998, voted album of the year by several metal magazines. A short tour of the UK with Napalm Death followed, but Dolving left the band to join a now-defunct outfit called Zen Monkey. His replacement was ex-Face Down singer Marco Aro, whose gruffer, rawer approach worked well on the next album, *The Haunted Made Me Do It*, a vicious collection of seething songs. Erlandsson left to join Cradle Of Filth and was replaced by Per Moller Jensen, who debuted on a tour with Testament.

Since then the band has gone from strength to strength, although it has to be said that their approach has not progressed radically over the last two albums, *One Kill Wonder* (2003) and *Revolver* (2004) – for which Dolving returned to the band. But that hardly matters - The Haunted are exactly what was needed to revive the dormant late-Nineties extreme metal scene, and long may they reign.

RECOMMENDED ALBUM:

The Haunted Made Me Do It
(Earache, 2002)
www.the-haunted.com

Hecate Enthroned

Hecate Enthroned was first formed in 1993 under the name Daemonum. Jon (vocals/bass), Nigel (guitar), Marc (guitar) and a drummer and keyboard player formed the original line-up, but before any recording could be attempted, Jon was recruited to Cradle Of Filth. Daemonum recorded a demo without him in 1995, but he returned shortly after – Cradle had found their permanent vocalist, Dani Davey – and Daemonum became Hecate Enthroned. Another demo, 1995's *An Ode For A Haunted Wood*, led to a deal with the Oxfordshire label Blackend, who remixed it and renamed it *Upon Promeathean Shores (Unscriptured Waters)* before releasing it in 1996. The following year saw the band record an album, *The Slaughter Of Innocence*, and after touring in Europe and the UK, a follow-up, *Dark Requiems And Unsilent Massacre*, was released. Several line-up changes ensued, leaving Nigel as the only original member. Later albums traversed more experimental territory before returning to extremity on *Redimus* (2004).

The Haunted – kings of neo-thrash

Hecate Enthroned – UK black metal

RECOMMENDED ALBUM:
Dark Requiems... And Unsilent Massacre
(Blackend, 1998)
www.hecate-enthroned.co.uk

Bassist Dylan on the future of extreme metal

❝I think extreme metal will slowly creep into the mainstream, because kids like the look of a lot of extreme bands (especially black metal bands) and will get into them on that alone, the music will follow. I don't think it will be totally absorbed but certain aspects will: guitar and drum sounds/techniques.❞

Hell-Born

Polish death metal band Hell-Born were formed in 1995 by Behemoth members Baal and Les as a thrash metal side-project. A self-titled album was released by Pagan Records, but then activities lapsed, with the band only returning to life in 2000. Recruiting bassist Jeff and releasing new material under the title *Hellblast*, the band toured with Damnation. Moving to the Conquer label after a US tour, Hell-Born then recorded *The Call Of Megiddo*, much praised by the press. 2003 saw the release of *Legacy Of The Nephilim*, Hell-Born's best album to date.

RECOMMENDED ALBUM:
Legacy Of The Nephilim (Conquer, 2003)
www.hell-born.com

Jeff on the extreme metal pioneers

❝Venom were black metal gods and pioneers of extreme metal. In my opinion all the extreme music scene would not be in today's place without their heritage. Possessed's *Seven Churches* is the first death metal album for me and it is still a great inspiration for Hell-Born. Slayer's first three albums are the bible of thrash metal. Since *Show No Mercy* they keep the thrash metal throne on the earth. Death metal means Morbid Angel. *Covenant* is our endless inspiration about sound and production. All four studio albums with David Vincent are death metal masterpieces. Metal, leather and hell forever!❞

Hellhammer

The legendary Hellhammer was the first project of future Celtic Frost mainman Tom G Warrior (real name Thomas Gabriel Fischer). The band recorded a 1985 album, *Apocalyptic Raids*, for the Noise label, and contributed two songs, 'Messiah' and 'Revelations Of Doom', to an early compilation entitled *Death Metal*, but the production and playing competence were barely of demo quality. On the arrival of future Frost bassist and drummer Martin Eric Ain and Stephen Priestly, Warrior dissolved the band, regarding it as having reached its limitations. Many bands have since acknowledged *Apocalyptic Raids* as a masterpiece, however, and its influence can certainly be heard on early Celtic Frost albums. Noise repackaged and reissued it in 1990, retaining Ain's creepy artwork on the cover.

RECOMMENDED ALBUM:
Apocalyptic Raids
(Noise, 1985; reissued 1990)

Hirax

Currently Katon W. De Pena (vocals), Glenn Rogers (lead guitar), Dave Watson (guitar), Angelo Espino (bass) and Jorge Iacobellis (drums), LA thrash metal act Hirax began their career in 1984 as contemporaries of San Francisco acts such as Slayer, Metallica, and Exodus, with whom they played after moving to San Fran in disgust at LA's hair-metal scene. After a demo and a track on Metal Blade's *Metal Massacre VI*, Hirax also contributed a song called 'Destruction And Terror' for the Earache label's debut release, the *Angelican Scrape Attic* 7" flexidisc. Metal Blade then released the first Hirax album, *Raging Violence*, which attracted both hardcore punks and metal fans. A second album, *Hate, Fear And Power*, appeared in 1986.

At this point Hirax's fortunes changed and, instead of following the Bay Area thrash contingent onwards and upwards, they fell out with their label and demoed more songs themselves. In 1988 De Pena left the band, after a brief project called Phantasm with ex-Metallica bassist Ron McGovney. His place was temporarily taken by sometime Exodus frontman, Paul Baloff.

A reunion took place in 1997, leading to the *El Diablo Negro* EP (the name of the record label which De Pena had set up in the meantime). More releases built towards the excellent 2003 album, *The New Age Of Terror*.

RECOMMENDED ALBUM:
Raging Violence (Metal Blade, 1985)
www.hirax.org

Katon DePena on race in metal
❝You need idols no matter who you are. I was the only black kid in my neighbourhood... so I heard a lot of heavy rock music. When I first saw what Jimi Hendrix and Phil Lynott (Thin Lizzy) looked like I believed I could play heavy metal music too.❞

Houwitser

A now-defunct death metal act obsessed with warfare, the Dutch band Houwitser was formed in 1997 by members of Sinister and Judgement Day. Signing to Displeased, they released an album, *Death... But Not Buried* two years later. *Embrace Damnation* followed in 2000, *Rage Inside The Womb* in 2001, but it was 2003's unbelievably intense *Damage Assessment* (which sampled gunfire from the movie *The Predator*) that gained them most fans. However, the band split the following year.

RECOMMENDED ALBUM:
Damage Assessment (Displeased, 2003)

Hypocrisy

The project of the renowned Swedish death metal producer Peter Tägtgren (vocals, keyboards, guitar), Mikael Hedlund (bass) and Lars Szoke (drums), Hypocrisy were formed by Tägtgren in 1990 as a European reaction to the rapidly-rising US death metal scene. He also plays in the band Pain, and over the course of Hypocrisy's ten-year-career, it has persistently been rumoured that every Hypocrisy release would be its last and that Pain would become the guitarist's full-time project. The Hypocrisy sound is a brutal, semi-melodic brew, which in itself has attracted many bands to his studio, the famous Abyss. With the reputation of both his production and his band in the ascendant, it seems that Tägtgren will remain a prominent member of the death metal scene for some time to come.

RECOMMENDED ALBUM:
Osculum Obscenum (Nuclear Blast, 1993)
www.hypocrisy.com

Hypocrisy – Peter Tägtgren

Ice Age

An all-female thrash metal band from Sweden, Ice Age were touted in the late Eighties as 'the female Megadeth', which was trite but it pointed to their skills with a technical riff. Initially with Tina Strömberg on drums, Pia Nyström on guitar, Sabrina Kihlstrand on guitar and vocals and Vicky Larsson on bass, the band recorded demos, *General Alert* and *Instant Justice*, and toured with Defender. After line-up changes they prepared to release an album, having signed to the AVM label, but before they could do so, the band split permanently.
RECOMMENDED ALBUM:
Instant Justice (demo, 1989)

Imagika

Neo-thrash act Imagika, named after a mythical world created by horror novelist Clive Barker, formed in San Francisco in 1994, toured with Vicious Rumors, Forbidden and Machine Head and released a self-titled debut album in 1996 on Headless Corpse Records. *Worship* followed in 1998 and tours with Grave Digger and Iron Savior followed. Their best work to date is 1999's *And So It Burns*.
RECOMMENDED ALBUM:
And So It Burns (Headless Corpse, 1999)
www.imagikametal.com

Steven Rice on the ideal metal scenario
❝I think that when some band finally finds the perfect blend of dark aggressive music with a top-notch vocalist that will be it. Imagine something like Emperor or Dimmu Borgir with Rob Halford or Geoff Tate singing awesome hooks and melodies! Still yet to be done. Music is probably one of the most subjective art forms there is. Noise to one person is beauty to another and that is what makes music such an amazing facet of our lives. You can never hear it all and there's always something awesome to discover.❞

Immolation

The New York black/death metal band Immolation – Ross Dolan (bass, vocals), Robert Vigna (guitar), Thomas Wilkinson (guitar) and Alex Hernandez (drums) – were originally formed under the name Rigor Mortis in 1986, recording a series of demos and receiving fanzine and live interest. Releasing *Dawn Of Possession* for Roadrunner and *Here In After* on Metal Blade, Immolation set themselves up as a truly uncompromising band and performed regularly on summer festival slots in the USA and Europe. Subsequent albums have assured the band's place in the extreme metal scene, with 2002's *Unholy Cult* containing some of their best work to date.

RECOMMENDED ALBUM:

Here In After (Metal Blade, 1996)
www.everlastingfire.com

Immortal *(Below)*

One of several Norwegian black metal bands with some involvement in the 1993 Oslo murders (see Mayhem; Burzum), Immortal was formed by Abbath Doom Occulta and Demonaz. In 1991 they secured a deal with Osmose and the following year, the first album, *Diabolical Fullmoon Mysticism*, was released. Demonaz had known Mayhem's Euronymous for some time, and Immortal appear from time to time in the sequence of events surrounding the latter's death. The 1993 follow-up, *Pure Holocaust*, contained what the band called 'holocaust' metal – extremely fast black metal with plenty of blastbeats. The velocity was maintained on succeeding albums, although the band's unswerving commitment to badger-like corpsepaint raised a few sniggers in the metal press here and there. Demonaz also retired from the band in 1997 with

acute tendonitis in both arms. After a series of excellent albums, the band called it a day in 2003: they are much missed.

RECOMMENDED ALBUM:
At The Heart Of Winter (Osmose, 1999)

Impaled Nazarene

Finland's Impaled Nazarene were originally formed in 1990, consisting of Mika Luttinen (vocals), Kimmo Luttinen (drums), Mika Pääkkö (guitar), Ari Holappa (guitar) and Antti Pihkala (bass). A demo tape, *Shemhamforash*, was recorded on a two-track tape recorder – leading to the worst sound quality possible – but a better attempt, 1991's *Taog Eht Fo Htao Eht* (read it backwards) led to a one-single deal with an Italian independent label. The *Goat Perversion* EP was duly issued and vanished without trace. However, the French label Osmose stepped in and offered the band a deal, who signed the contract in their own blood.

In 1993 *Tol Cormpt Norz Norz Norz* was released and entered the Finnish charts at No. 40, an unheard-of occurrence. The *Ugra-Karma* album and the *Satanic Masowhore* EP followed, with the former the object of protests by Finnish Hare Krishna organisations over its artwork, a legal battle which would not be resolved until 1999, when a settlement was made out of court and the cover art changed. The third album was originally to be titled *Hail To Finland*, but the band changed it to *Suomi Finland Perkele* at the last minute and the album was issued in late 1994. The song 'Total War–Winter War' was denounced by a Parisian youth movement as offensive and the FNAC chainstore was obliged to withdraw the albums from its shops. However, the management confused the barcodes and *Ugra-Karma* was withdrawn instead of *Suomi Finland Perkele*.

In 1996 Impaled Nazarene recorded both the *Latex Cult* album and the *Motörpenis* EP. Jani Lehtosaari took over on bass in time to record a single, 'I Am The Killer Of Trolls', which was included on Osmose's *World Domination II* compilation. Later that year, a Nazarene show in Paris had no power for 50 minutes as a result of sabotage by the aforementioned youth organisation. Unfortunately for those responsible, the power was cut during the support band's act and Impaled Nazarene played their set unhindered.

The most recent album, *All That You Fear*, was released in 2004 and proved that IN still have what it takes to play the harshest form of metal.

RECOMMENDED ALBUM:
Tol Cormpt Norz Norz Norz
(Osmose, 1993)
www.impnaz.com

Impetigo

Illinois death metal band Impetigo – Stevo De Caixo (vocals/bass), Mark (guitar), Scotty (guitar) and Dan (drums) – were formed in 1987 and recorded a demo, *All We Need Is Cheez*. Signing to the Italian label Wild Rags, they recorded an album, *Ultimo Mondo Cannibale*, but local authorities objected to the artwork, which was toned down for release. They split in 1993.

RECOMMENDED ALBUM:
Ultimo Mondo Cannibale (Wild Rags, 1990)

Impiety

Founded in 1990, Singaporean black metallers Impiety recorded a demo two years later called *Ceremonial Necrochrist Redesecration* and signed to the local Shivadarshana label. The band – frontman Shyalthan, guitarist Leprophiliac Rex, guitarist Abyydos, bassist Rex and drummer Iblyss – then recorded an album, *Asateerul Awaleen*. Line-up changes preceded the 1999 album *Skullfucking Armageddon*, before a label change to Osmose. *Two Majesties: An Arrogant Alliance Of Satan's Extreme Elite* was the result.

RECOMMENDED ALBUM:
Skullfucking Armageddon
(Iron Pegasus, 1999)

Imprecation

Dave Herrera (vocals), Phil Westmoreland (guitar), Victor Zamora (guitar), Mark Beecher (bass), Ruben Elizondo (drums) formed Houston black metal band Imprecation in 1991. Demos included *Ceremony Of The Nine Angels* and *Theurgia Goetia Summa* and, while a single entitled 'Sigil Of Baphomet' was also issued, the band never progressed as far as a long-term record deal or album. After they split, members went on to form Infernal Dominion and Adumus.

RECOMMENDED ALBUM:
Theurgia Goetia Summa (demo, 1992)

In Flames

Swedish band In Flames successfully fuse the melodic influence of Iron Maiden with modern death metal. After leaving Ceremonial Oath (see separate entry) in the late Eighties, guitarist Jesper Stromblad presented this blend of influences to Wrong Again Records, who signed the nascent In Flames.

1993's debut *Lunar Strain* drew immediate attention to the band, who toured and recorded at regular intervals, making the most of the public's new taste for clean, well-produced metal. Another record, *Subterranean*, was released in 1994 before In Flames signed to Nuclear Blast two years later. Two more albums followed before the IF line-up finally stabilised, with Bjorn Gelotte (drums), Anders Friden (vocals), Peter Iwers (bass) and David Svensson (drums) accompanying Stromblad. The sixth album, *Colony*, was released in 1999, placing In Flames at the forefront of the Gothenburg sound. Since then they have shot to prominence on the international metal scene and show no sign of slowing down.

RECOMMENDED ALBUM:
Whoracle (Nuclear Blast, 1997)
www.inflames.com

Anders Fridén on metal now and then
"Me and Tomas from At The Gates come from the same neighbourhood. We were riding into the city one day many years ago, and he showed me the demo of this band, Malevolent Creation. I was like, 'Fuck, what is this?' It was so good! I worked in a store in Gothenburg, and when the Ten *Commandments* album came in it went straight onto the turntable. I was so stoked. It was amazing!

For some reason, more people think metal is cool now. In every country, the people who were always true to this genre are still true, and now there is a new generation added to them which increases the numbers. The whole climate of music is totally different these days, compared to the Eighties when we were kids. The media can no longer refuse to acknowledge extreme music, because so many people like it!"

In The Woods...

An avant-garde black metal band from Norway, In The Woods... were well-known for their experimental approach to their art, including doom, ambient and orchestral touches, bearing some comparison to other versatile acts such as Therion.

Their debut album, *Heart Of The Ages,* was released by UK label Misanthropy in 1995 and featured both pure and shrieked vocals, although later albums added female singers for a more gothic feel. The most recent line-up's stage names reflect their unusual approach, with X. Botteri, Jan Transit, Chris, A. Kobro and Synne Diana exercising their talents on songs like *Strange In Stereo*'s bizarre 'More Worried Than Married'. Truly strange, but possibly the future face of one branch of the genre.

RECOMMENDED ALBUM:
Strange In Stereo (Misanthropy, 1999)

Incantation

Guitarist John McEntee has been the most constant member of the New York death metal band Incantation since its formation in 1989. Releasing two brutal singles in 1991, 'Enchantment Of Evil' on Seraphic Decay and 'Deliverance Of Horrific Prophecies' on the fledgling Relapse label, the band began to tour relentlessly. The debut album, *Onward To Golgotha*, was released on Relapse in 1992. 1994's follow-up, *Mortal Throne Of Nazarene*, was the last recording of the existing line-up and McEntee recruited three musicians for tours with Grave and Immolation in Mexico and the US. Relapse released a limited edition version of *Mortal Throne* under the title *Upon The Throne Of Apocalypse*, while the band signed a one-off deal with Repulse and toured with those vicar's tea-party favourites, Anal Cunt. The tour led to a live album, *Tribute To The Goat*. 1998's Diabolical Conquest was notable for the 17-minute 'Unto Infinite Twilight', while the most recent release, *The Infernal Storm*, kept the band's progress steady. Drummer Kyle Severn received a rare accolade when the aforementioned AC wrote a song about him called 'Kyle From Incantation Has A Moustache'.

RECOMMENDED ALBUM:
Mortal Throne Of Nazarene
(Relapse, 1994)
www.incantation.com

Infernal Majesty

Toronto thrash band Overlord were formed in 1986 by Rick Nemes (drums), Psycopath (*sic*) (bass), Kenny Hallman (guitar), Steve Terror (guitar) and Chris Bailey (vocals). During the recording of a demo, it became apparent that another band using the name Overlord existed and the name Infernal Majesty was adopted. A one-album deal was signed with Roadrunner and in 1987 *None Shall Defy* was released.

New members Bob Quelch (bass), Kevin Harrison (drums) and Vince (vocals) were recruited and the four-song *Creation Of Chaos* demo was recorded. Without a record deal, Infernal Majesty self-financed a second album with Scott Burns as the producer, but the album was never finished and the band split in frustration.

Vince went on to become one of Canada's most tabloid-friendly criminals, serving seven months in prison after slashing a young woman's wrist and sucking her blood. The local press called it "the Vampire Trial", although ultimately Vince was only found guilty of aggravated assault. Surreally, his victim fell in love with him and they settled down together. As for Infernal Majesty, 1997 finally saw the release of a second album, *Unholier Than Thou*, recorded with Chris Bailey.

RECOMMENDED ALBUM:
None Shall Defy (Roadrunner, 1987)

Inhume

Grindcore act Inhume were formed in 1994, inspired by Carcass and Autopsy. A demo followed shortly after, leading to gigs with Haemorrhage, Agathocles, Nyctophobic and others. Line-up changes prevented much progress, although an album finally appeared in 2000 entitled *Decomposing From Inside*. The band recently signed to Osmose and another album is scheduled for release.

RECOMMENDED ALBUM:
Decomposing From Inside
(independent, 2000)
www.inhume.nl

Guitarist Harold Gielen on his three genre-splicing bands
❝Mangled is more technical and plays brutal death metal, Inhume is more

grindcore mixed with death, crust, hardcore and all styles we listen to. Charlie★Adler is a mix between grind, metalcore and mathcore."

Inner Thought

The death metal band Inner Thought was formed by guitarist Bobby Sadzak, formerly of the Canadian thrash outfit Slaughter, in the early Nineties, alongside vocalist Kelly Montico (later replaced by Dennis Balesdent, also since departed) and guitarist Roland Murray. The band played fairly competent death metal with the added Sisters of Mercy-like twist of a drum machine, which never really found favour among death fans, but which pleased one or two industrial metal followers tired of the mainstream-isms of Nine Inch Nails and the early Marilyn Manson.

RECOMMENDED ALBUM:
Worldly Separation (Dwell, 1994)

Insatanity

A Philadelphia band who through dint of perseverance were signed to the Greek label Unisound after three mid-Nineties demos, *Insatanity, Ad Maiorem Satanae Gloriam* and *Unholiness Rising*. The band perform Satanic death metal, keeping away from the keyboards and corpsepaint of black metal but equally dedicated to an anti-Christian ethos. Two of the band are committed Satanists, following the teachings of Anton LaVey's Church of Satan to the letter in their lives apart from the band.

Insatanity were formed in 1992 by singer Mark Rhochar, who recruited guitarists Jay Lipitz and Dan Roberts, bassist Lou Suppa and drummer Matt Mazzenga. Unisound released their first album, the aptly-titled black/death fusion *Divine Decomposition*, in January 1996. Embarking on tour, the Insatanity stage show became well-known for *the* use of candelabras and fog. After 1997's *Vengeance From Beyond The Grave* album, an eight-year cessation in recording meant that no new material appeared until 2005, with an album entitled *The Day God Died* ready for release at the time of writing.

RECOMMENDED ALBUM:
Divine Decomposition (Unisound, 1996)
www.insatanity.com

Insision

A satanic death metal band of enormous power and popularity, Insision — now vocalist Carl Birath, guitarist Roger Johansson, bassist Daniel Ekeroth and drummer Marcus Johansson — were formed in 1997 and since then have used players from the bands Embalmer, Ildoor, Dellamorte and Azatoth. A demo, *Meant To Suffer*, established the band's stance against the popular melodic death coming out of Sweden at the time and the band signed to the Heathendoom label. After successful tours led to a crucial deal with Earache, two crushingly heavy albums — *Beneath The Folds Of Flesh* (2002) and *Revealed And Worshipped* (2004) — have seen them make the European old-school style their own along with new bands such as Decapitated.

RECOMMENDED ALBUM:
Beneath The Folds Of Flesh
(Earache, 2002)
www.insision.com

Daniel Ekeroth on the future of the extreme metal scene
"Trends will come and go as always. The only thing that will matter in the end are the superior bands, the ones that

follow their inner beliefs and visions. Death metal will always go on. It is timeless music. Black metal will come and go, since it is so much more based upon image. Thrash metal was more time based, like a development into death metal. Like the NWOBHM, it is forever doomed to be a retro genre.**"**

Invocator

Danish thrash metallers Invocator – formed in 1986, the great year of thrash – produced demos entitled *Genetic Confusion* and *Alterations*, which led to a deal with Black Mark. A debut album, *Excursion Demise*, sold well and tours with Paradise Lost boosted their profile. A split was followed by several years of silence but in 2002, the band reformed and released *Through The Flesh To The Soul* the following year.

RECOMMENDED ALBUM:
Weave The Apocalypse (Black Mark, 1994)
www.invocator.com

Isengard

When Darkthrone drummer Fenriz recorded some folk-influenced progressive black metal under the name Isengard (one of Tolkien's *Two Towers*), he did so to allow Darkthrone to remain true to itself without unnecessary change. Two albums, *Vinterskugge* (1994) and *Hostmorke* (1995)

contained a blend of atmospheric folk drones, clean-sung abstract whimsy and standard black metal aggression. As with Darkthrone, the production is intentionally necro.

RECOMMENDED ALBUM:
Vinterskugge (Peaceville, 1994)

Judas Iscariot

The work of one individual, the American multi-instrumentalist Akhenaten, Judas Iscariot is often compared with the Norwegian Darkthrone. Like Fenriz' band, Akhenaten plays raw black metal but also indulges in more death metal and even traditional heavy metal approaches from time to time. The debut album, *The Cold Earth Slept Below*, was released on the Moribund label in 1997 along with a single, 'Arise, My Lord' leading to great praise from those who enjoy both Darkthrone and more structured, diverse approaches.

RECOMMENDED ALBUM:
The Cold Earth Slept Below
(Moribund, 1997)

Kalmah – Finnish extremity

Kalmah *(Left)*

Finnish band Kalmah comprise Pekka Kokko (vocals, guitar), Antti Kokko (guitar), Petri Sankala (drums), Pasi Hiltula (keyboards) and Altti Veteläinen (bass) and were formed in 1998 from the ashes of the band Ancestor. A demo resulted in a deal with Spikefarm and an album, *Swamplord*, was released in 2000. Personnel changes did not hinder the progress of a second record, 2002's *They Will Return*, and the following year's Swampsong. Festival slots at Wacken and others kept awareness high.

RECOMMENDED ALBUM:
Swamplord (Spikefarm, 2000)
www.kalmah.com

Kataklysm

Canadian death metal band Kataklysm were formed in 1991 and released a demo, *Death Gate Cycle Of Reincarnation*, the following year, which landed them a deal with Nuclear Blast. Reissuing the demo as *The Mystical Gate Of Reincarnation*, the band created a name for their furious music – 'the Northern Hyperblast' – and toured widely. The *Sorcery*, *Temple Of Knowledge*,

Kataklysm – Northern hyperblast

Northern Hyperblast Live, *Victims Of This Fallen World* and *The Prophecy (Stigmata Of The Immaculate)* albums were all well-received and extended the band's fanbase to the point where they head up the Canadian death scene. 2004's *Serenity In Fire* matched up to the high standards of its predecessors.
RECOMMENDED ALBUM:
Temple Of Knowledge (Nuclear Blast, 1996)
www.kataklysm.net

Singer Maurizio Iacono on getting it right
❝The secret is just balance in the music – balancing out the melodies with the groove and the blast. Too much of one of those things can be annoying! Doing death metal is cool but it doesn't really pay all the bills. As most people know, it's something you do because you like it.❞

Katatonia

One of Sweden's more inventive death metal bands, Katatonia were initially formed in 1987 by guitarist Anders Nystrom and drummer Jonas Renkse, both of whom also handled vocals. Heavily influenced by Bathory and Celtic Frost, the band played pure black metal to mass public indifference before splitting up. Regrouping in 1992, the band recorded a demo, *Jhva Elohim Meth*, which led to a deal with No Fashion later that year – the demo was later issued by the Dutch Vic label. In late 1992, the trio signed their first deal with the Swedish label No Fashion. The first Katatonia album, *Dance Of December Souls*, was released immediately to underground interest, but attention only really started to develop when the band moved to Avantgarde – home of many experimental bands – and recorded *Brave Murder Day*, a versatile album with Renske's tuneful vocals juxtaposed against the death metal rasp of guest vocalist Mikael Akerfeldt of Opeth. Adding guitarist Fredrik Norman and Micke Oretoft on bass, the band then signed to Century Media for one album and to Opeth's label Peaceville for another. They remain one of either label's most successful acts and have become well-known as one of gothic metal's most innovative practitioners: 1999's *Tonight's Decision* is a classic of the genre. Subsequent albums have seen them expand their musical palette still further.

RECOMMENDED ALBUM:
Tonight's Decision (Peaceville, 1999)
www.katatonia.com

Jonas Renkse on the the goth tag
❝I listened mainly to Paradise Lost, which I liked because it was gloomy. I was a big goth when I was younger, with the black hair and so on. But I don't really think the gothic metal tag describes us perfectly. We used to be a death metal band like Entombed and Dismember. It was in '87 or '88 when I was becoming a metalhead for real. When I was about 13, the first time I heard Slayer was when a friend of mine had a tape of *Reign In Blood*, which we thought was a joke because it was so hard. But as time went on I borrowed it more and more and then I started to feel like a pervert because I liked it so much.❞

King Diamond

After leaving Mercyful Fate in 1985 (see separate entry), the uniquely-voiced King Diamond named his next band after himself and recruited guitarists Andy LaRocque and Herbie Simonsen, bassist Chris Estes and drummer Darrin Anthony. The band performed less speedy songs than those of Fate, dealing with the occult themes of before but upping the theatrical content a

notch, even including onstage actors to play the characters in the songs.

Mercyful Fate reformed in 1993 and Diamond continued to tour and record with both bands. Personnel have come and gone; notable among them was Mikkey Dee, who played drums on the first four albums before being recruited to Motörhead.

RECOMMENDED ALBUM:
Conspiracy (Roadrunner, 1989)
http://king-diamond.coven.vmh.net

Konkhra

Formed in 1989 under the name Vicious Circle in the Danish town of Køge, the original Konkhra line-up settled down as Claus Vedel (guitar/vocals), Jon Clausen (drums) and Anders Lundemark (bass) – the latter was a mere 16 years old at the time. A demo, *The Vicious Circle*, was well-received locally but led to little further activity other than a short tour of Eastern Europe providing backing music for a theatre group.

After the name change, Konkhra recorded a much more professional-sounding demo, *Malgrowth*, released in 1991 and selling several thousand copies. Unusually, the first offer of a deal came not from a label but from a tattoo magazine, *Progress*, which offered to distribute a CD with the magazine. The result, 1993's *Stranded*, sold so well that *Progress* became a record label, eventually renaming itself Die Hard.

The proper debut album, *Sexual Affective Disorder*, was recorded at Sunlight Studios in Stockholm with Tomas Skogsberg. Tours of the US and Europe with Suffocation among others followed and after *The Facelift* EP, *Spit Or Swallow* was released in 1995, produced by Dismember's Fred Estby. More touring followed and no fewer than four videos were recorded of songs from the album before the band's appearance at the Roskilde festival in 1995, leading to a live album, *Live Eraser*. A support slot with Deicide through Europe confirmed Konkhra's status among death metal cognoscenti.

Although various line-up changes had taken place over the previous three years, unprecedented developments left bassist/vocalist Anders entirely alone after the departure of the other members and he was obliged to look abroad for replacements.

Kreator – veterans going from strength to strength

Eventually adding the talents of ex-Machine Head member Chris Kontos and recruiting James Murphy as a guest player, the band released *Weed Out The Weak* which sold an unexpected 20,000 copies in Europe in less than a month.

In 1999 guitarist Jensen left to join The Haunted but the latest album, *Reality Check*, has been hailed as a return to form.

RECOMMENDED ALBUM:
Weed Out The Weak (DieHard, 1997)
www.konkhra.com

Krabathor

Although the Czech death metal Krabathor only rose to prominence in the Nineties, its roots go back as far as 1984, when it was founded by Christopher (vocals/guitars) and Bruno (vocals/bass). In 1988 three demo tapes were recorded; *Breath Of Death*, *Total Destruction* and *Brutal Death*. However, Krabathor activities had to be put on hold for a further two years as both Chris and Bruno had to do their national service in the Czech army.

1991 saw the first real Krabathor demo, *Feelings Of Dethronisation*, which attracted the attention of Monitor Records, and a debut album, the miserably-titled *Only Our Death Is Welcome* (1992). A video clip for the song 'Pacifistic Death' gained some national TV airplay and the second album, *Cool Mortification*, was released in 1993. In early 1995 Krabathor moved to the German Morbid label, releasing a limited edition vinyl EP, *The Rise Of Brutality*, before a third album, *Lies*, which revealed a new-found Krabathor social conscience. Touring extensively through Europe with death metal biggies such as Cannibal Corpse and Impaled Nazarene, the band also played their first gig outside Europe at the 1996 Milwaukee Metalfest. The 1998 album *Orthodox* was supported by even more protracted touring, in territories as far-flung as South Africa and Russia. Subsequent albums *Unfortunately Dead* and *Dissuade Truth* have seen the band continue to tour widely.

RECOMMENDED ALBUM:
Orthodox (Morbid, 1998)
www.krabathor.tk

Kreator *(Previous page)*

A highly influential thrash metal band, the German band Kreator surpassed the considerable achievements of their countrymen Sodom and Destruction, heading up the B-league of thrash after the Big Four. Like Celtic Frost and Bathory, they transcended the category into which they were placed and their influence is still felt among the death metal and hardcore punk bands of today.

Formed in the industrial gloom of Essen in 1983, Kreator revolved around guitarist and vocalist Mille Petrozza, who, with a selection of other musicians, has issued 13 albums to date. Originally named Tormentor, Kreator's first recording was the *Flag Of Hate* EP, which raised eyebrows everywhere for its unrelenting attack and the drill-like precision of the playing. The first two albums, *Endless Pain* and *Pleasure To Kill*, were immediately hailed as masterpieces and remain milestones in thrash. Petrozza's hissing, fury-filled vocal style and the blistering anger of his riffs led briefly to the band being labelled as Hate Metal, a description which fitted Kreator's enraged style perfectly.

Further albums saw the band incorporate death metal influences into their sound, while Petrozza's reluctance to stay in a musical rut as well as the diversification of the thrash genre meant that by the early Nineties, other avenues were being explored. 1992's *Renewal* – recorded at Florida's Morrisound Studios with Tom Morris – was an experimental album including touches of industrial rock. Although later albums were less successful, Kreator persevered and were rewarded in 2001 with the excellent, Andy Sneap-produced *Violent Revolution* and 2004's brutal *Enemy Of God*.

RECOMMENDED ALBUM:
Pleasure To Kill (Noise, 1986)
www.kreator-terrorzone.de

Mille Petrozza on the roots of extremity

"My first concert ever was Kiss on their 'Unmasked Tour', I think it was in 1980. I was too young to go to the show alone, so I had to go with my older cousin. The band that was opening that night was called Iron Maiden, so I went and bought their record the next day.

There was this discotheque in Essen called Kaleidoscope. We used to go there every Monday night because they would play metal for two hours, before they started their regular programme. One night the DJ played something almost disturbingly extreme. I went up to his

Krisiun – Brazilian scene leaders

booth and asked what he just played. He said that the band was called Venom. That day changed my life. **"**

Krisiun

Brutal death metal from Brazil, Krisiun were formed in 1990. The brothers Max and Moyses Kolesne (guitar and drums) and bassist/vocalist Alex Camargo resolved to be the fastest metal act from Brazil, if not the world, and have come close to achieving this on several occasions. Two demos, *Evil Age* (1991) and *Curse Of The Evil One* (1992), preceded a debut mini-album,

Unmerciful Order, in '93. Tours followed and a second record, 1995's *Black Force Domain,* was picked up by the German label Gun. A European jaunt with Kreator and Dimmu Borgir, plus the 1998 album *Apocalyptic Revelation*, led to a deal with the Brazilian arm of the Century Media label, who issued 1999's *Conquerors Of Armageddon*. The following year the band played over 120 shows, with Morbid Angel among others. Their finest hour to date is easily 2001's *Ageless Venomous*, a savage collection of tunes that redefined the cutting-edge of death metal on its release.

RECOMMENDED ALBUM:

Ageless Venomous (Century Media, 2001)

www.krisiun.com.br

Kult Ov Azazel

South Florida black metal band Kult Ov Azazel are Xaphan (vocals/guitar), Xul (vocals/bass) and Von (drums) and were formed in 1999. A self-released debut album, *Order Of The Fly* was followed by tours and Von was replaced by Hellspawn. A split CD with Krieg and a demo, *Of Evil And Hatred* (which included a cover of Mayhem's 'Chainsaw Gutsfuck'), were released shortly afterwards. Signing to Arcturus and recruiting session drummer Vetis, KOV recorded the *Triumph Of Fire* album, a raw set of songs living up to their manifesto of 'No Beauty, No Atmosphere, No Tranquillity'. The last album, *Oculus Infernum*, was recorded with yet another drummer, Hammer, and they have toured extensively.

RECOMMENDED ALBUM:
Triumph Of Fire (Arcturus, 2002)
www.kultovazazel.com

Xaphan sees the bigger picture
❝Back in 1984 I thought what I was hearing was the most extreme that it got, that it couldn't get any heavier or extreme. I was wrong, dead wrong. Perhaps extreme metal will turn into more of a movement rooted not only in music but also in ideology or maybe it will become over saturated and stagnant

Kult Ov Azazel – none more black metal

eventually leading it back into obscurity again like some many other forms of art of the past. Quod est inferius est sicut quod est superius, et quod est superius est sicut quod est inferius...❞

Lake Of Tears

Sweden's Lake Of Tears originally resembled the death/doom metal of Cemetary (whose frontman Mathias Lodmalm co-produced their debut album). A late-Sixties psychedelic tone entered some of their later compositions, betraying the early obsessions of Daniel Brennare (guitar/vocals), Mikael Larsson (bass) and Johan Oudhuis (drums). The band's four Black Mark albums demonstrated that while the band had talent in spades, the confines of the metal scene were perhaps too constricting for an outfit with so many influences, and Lake Of Tears called it a day in 1999.

RECOMMENDED ALBUM:
A Crimson Cosmos (Black Mark, 1997)

Lamb Of God

A hard-hitting and much-praised NWOAHM quintet from Richmond, Virginia, Lamb Of God were formed in 1999, after musical collaborations under several names including Burn The Priest. Signing to the Prosthetic label in 2000, the band recorded a debut album, *New American Gospel*, and toured relentlessly to support it. Three years later *As The Palaces Burn* was hailed as a new milestone in metal by various magazines and led to support slots with Slayer and others. The band's future seems assured.

RECOMMENDED ALBUM:
As The Palaces Burn (Prosthetic, 2003)
www.lamb-of-god.com

Lard

Performing a satisfying blend of hardcore punk and thrash metal, the sporadically-active Lard is a side-project of the industrial act Ministry. Sometime Dead Kennedys frontman Jello Biafra provides vocals, not for the first time in the metal arena; he has guested with a variety of thrash acts, including providing a spoken-word narrative with Body Count ('Freedom Of Speech') and writing lyrics for Sepultura ('Biotech Is Godzilla').

Ministry main-man Al Jourgensen plays guitar, along with bassist Paul Barker and William Rieflin on drums. The band address the themes of government conspiracy, paranoia and social alienation with a twisted sense of humour somewhat refreshing after all the blood-soaked gore and death metal elsewhere in this book.

RECOMMENDED ALBUM:
The Power Of Lard
(Alternative Tentacles, 1989)

Lehavoth

Israel's first successful black metal band, Lehavoth were formed in 1995 and recorded a demo, *Brith Ha Orvim*. Due to military service an extended break followed until 2000, when vocalist Molech, guitarists Gal Cohen and Nir Gutrayman, bassist Evil Haim and drummer Nir Doliner regrouped for another demo, *Iconoclastic*. In 2002 the band decamped to Sweden for the *Hatred Shaped Man* album and signed to the Fadeless label.

RECOMMENDED ALBUM:
Hatred Shaped Man (Fadeless, 2003)
www.lehavoth.com

Limbonic Art

A Norwegian duo consisting of Daemon and Morpheus, Limbonic Art played experimental black metal with classical and avant-garde elements. Five albums were recorded since their formation in 1997 and their reputation for musicianship was deserved. However, they parted ways in early 2003.

RECOMMENDED ALBUM:
The Ultimate Death Worship
(Nocturnal Art, 2002)

Living Sacrifice

Hailing from Little Rock, Arkansas, Living Sacrifice are that bizarre beast, a Christian death metal band. Originally consisting of DJ (bass/vocals), Bruce Fitzhugh (guitar), Jason Truby (guitar) and Lance Garvin (drums), the band progressed from a primitive thrash sound on their self-titled debut of 1991 to a modern death style on later releases. Fitzhugh ultimately took over vocal duties from DJ, who was ejected from the band, which along with some movement towards a punk sound led to the attraction of a rather different audience for more recent albums. Truby's brother Chris later also took over bass, but after 1997's *Reborn* (also the title of a Slayer song, although the sentiments were somewhat different) both brothers left and the band split.

RECOMMENDED ALBUM:
Metamorphosis (Rex, 1993)

Lock-Up

A death metal supergroup formed of consecutively Hypocrisy's Peter Tätgren and ex-At The Gates singer Tomas Lindberg on vocals, plus Napalm Death's bassist and guitarist Shane Embury and Jesse Pintado and ex-Cradle Of Filth/Dimmu Borgir drummer Nick Barker, Lock-Up have released two albums. Both records, 1999's *Pleasures Pave Sewers* and 2002's *Hate Breeds Suffering,* are made up of intense grindcore and will appeal to fans of any of the members' home bands.

RECOMMENDED ALBUM:
Hate Breeds Suffering (Nuclear Blast, 2002)

Lord Belial – brutal but atmospheric

Lord Belial

Swedish black metal band Lord Belial was formed in 1992 by Thomas Backelin, Micke Backelin, Anders Backelin and Niclas Andersson. Two demos, *The Art Of Dying* and *Into The Frozen Shadows* (1993 and '94 respectively) led to a deal with No Fashion, who had been impressed by the melodic, aggressive riffing combined – bizarrely – with flute. The first album, *Kiss The Goat*, was released in 1994 after various hiccups in the manufacturing process, one of which led to initial covers being printed a decidedly un-Satanic shade of pink. In disgust, Lord Belial burned the first thousand copies.

A second album, *Enter The Moonlight Gate*, was recorded in 1997, after an Iron Maiden cover, 'The Trooper', was recorded and included on a Japanese – only Maiden tribute album. Tours with Dismember and Disfear followed and another cover, Bathory's 'Massacre' appeared on a tribute record to Quorthon's band entitled *In Conspiracy With Satan*. August 1998 saw the release of *Unholy Crusade*, which featured the newly-recruited female vocalist Lamia. The band continues to tour and record, with 2004's *The Seal Of Belial* a masterfully-executed album with strong Emperor influences.

RECOMMENDED ALBUM:
Unholy Crusade (No Fashion, 1998)
www.lordbelial.com

Micke Backelin on the best of the best
❝One of my all-time favourite bands are definitely Emperor! They make extreme metal with unquestionable quality and professionalism. Other favourite bands are Cannibal Corpse, Slayer, Enslaved, Angel Corpse and Morbid Angel. Metal will never die, maybe just transform into an even more extreme form.❞

Loudblast

A veteran thrash/death metal band from France, Loudblast were formed in 1986 and released a split LP with Agressor. Three years later a debut album, *Sensorial Treatment*, was released and a series of slightly eccentric albums followed before the band split in 1998. A reformation followed in 2003.

RECOMMENDED ALBUM:
Sensorial Treatment (independent, 1989)
www.loudblast.net

Luciferion

Swedish death metal band Luciferion – Michael Nicklasson (guitar), Peter Weiner (drums), Wojtek Lisicki (guitar and vocals) and Martin Furängen (bass) – were formed in 1993, inspired by Morbid Angel, Deicide and Celtic Frost. Signing to the Listenable label after a 1994 demo, the *Demonication (The Manifest)* album was released, including a cover of Sodom's 'Blasphemer'. Wiener was replaced by Hans Nilsson and a keyboard player, Johan Lund, joined. Although the band toured widely, they split in 1996 and reconvened thereafter solely to record tribute album tracks by Metallica, Slayer, Mercyful Fate and others. However, a reformation was on the cards in 2004.

RECOMMENDED ALBUM:
Demonication (The Manifest)
(Listenable, 1995)

Macabre *(Right)*

Chicago death metal band Macabre first reared their ugly heads in 1985 and are still going strong 20 years later. Their combination of spine-chilling nursery rhyme lyrics – dealing with the lives and exploits of infamous individuals such as Jeffrey Dahmer and the Unabomber – with incredible song-speeds has led to the label 'murder metal'. The line-up – Nefarious (bass/vocals), Corporate Death (guitar/vocals), and Dennis the Menace (drums) – first displayed their talents in

1987 on the self-released *Grim Reality* album. The following year's *Shit List* demo, containing studio and live tracks, led to a deal with Vinyl Solution, who released *Gloom* in 1989, a cheerful album featuring such gems as 'Fritz Haarmann The Butcher' and the Christmas-themed 'Holidays Of Horror'.

After a deal with Nuclear Blast in 1992, a third album, *Sinister Slaughter*, was released and an extended tour followed. The weird *Behind The Wall Of Sleep* EP and the even more bizarre *Macabre Minstrels* project followed, the latter of which involved the band performing acoustic versions of their earlier songs. Macabre went on to grace the Milwaukee Metalfest in 1997 and launched a label, Decomposed, re-releasing the remastered *Gloom*. 1999 saw the band release an EP, the well-received *Unabomber*, which acted as a taster for the *Dahmer* album of 2000. They continue to record and tour, sticking ever more closely to murder themes.

RECOMMENDED ALBUM:
Dahmer (Hammerheart, 2000)
www.murdermetal.com

Machetazo

Spanish grindcore act Machetazo, who share a similar horror-movie interest with Necrophagia, were founded by three of the members of the band Frustadiccion as a

side-project in 1994. Two successful demos convinced the players to concentrate on Machetazo full-time, and split releases with Japanese bands Corrupted and Rise Above followed, as well as a deal with Razorback. The first album, the intense *Carne De Cementerio*, was compared to Carcass, Autopsy and Impetigo. Line-up shuffles plagued the band, however, and although a second album, *Trono De Huesos*, appeared in 2001, they have been off the radar since then.

RECOMMENDED ALBUM:
Carne De Cementerio (Razorback, 1999)

Machine Head

Machine Head are a popular San Francisco band playing music influenced strongly by Eighties thrash metal, but incorporating a certain modern riffing style and, as with contemporaries Korn, addressing the themes of child abuse and other unsettling subjects. Founded in 1992 by Robb Flynn (ex-Forbidden and Vio-lence, guitar/vocals) and originally including Adam Duce (bass), Logan Mader (guitar, sometime of Soulfly) and Chris Kontos (drums), the band signed to Roadrunner and released the excellent *Burn My Eyes* in 1994.

Touring with heavyweights such as Pantera, Megadeth and Marilyn Manson, and making a memorable appearance on the 1997 Ozzfest with Black Sabbath, the band immediately gained a reputation for a powerful live show. 1995 also saw an onstage collaboration with Slayer on Venom's *The Witching Hour*, later documented on the LA thrashers' *Live Intrusion* video. The second album, 1997's *The More Things Change...*, saw Mader replaced by Ahrue Luster and Kontos by Dave McClain, but the new line-up proved if anything more popular than before and the band moved from strength to strength.

The next Machine Head album, *The Burning Red*, was produced by Korn/Limp Bizkit/Slipknot producer Ross Robinson and contained a cover of The Police song 'Message In A Bottle'. Although MH came close to falling into the nu-metal style at times (Flynn has rapped on record before), they appear to have pulled back to their extreme roots with recent albums such as *Supercharger*, a difficult but worthwhile move for a band so close to becoming a mainstream metal act.

RECOMMENDED ALBUM:
Burn My Eyes (Roadrunner, 1994)
www.machinehead1.com

Malevolent Creation – apparently unstoppable

Malevolent Creation

Formed in 1987 in Buffalo, New York, death metal legends Malevolent Creation have consisted of several different musicians, hired and fired at sporadic intervals by the guitarist Phil Fasciana, who makes no apologies for his intolerant attitude, saying "If you're too slow, you've got to go". After a successful series of demo tapes and a move to Florida, the band signed to Roadrunner and released their debut album in 1991, *The Ten Commandments*. The album was noted for its relentless attack, an approach which has continued on more recent albums. Other MC releases have pursued the NY death sound to its logical limits and they remain at the absolute creative peak of the genre.

RECOMMENDED ALBUM:
Retribution (Roadrunner, 1993)
www.malevolentcreation.cjb.net

Phil Fasciana finds beauty in evil
❝I basically worshipped bands like Slayer, Dark Angel, Exodus, Destruction, Kreator and Metallica. I was attracted to the down-to-earth nature of the bands, the speed of the music and the hateful-sounding vocals. It just made me freak out.❞

Malformed Earthborn

One of the many side projects of Napalm Death, with members of Brutal Truth and Exit-13, Malformed Earthborn played industrial metal with a perceptible techno feel on their sole album, *Defiance Of The Ugly*. Metal fans stayed well away from the electronic elements, though, and the band receded into obscurity.

RECOMMENDED ALBUM:
Defiance Of The Ugly (Release, 1996)

Malignancy

The NYC-based death metal act Malignancy was founded in 1992 under the name Carcinogen. A demo, *Eaten Out From Within*, was recorded amid constant line-up changes: musicians came and went, a notable among them being future Mortician stalwart Roger J. Beaujard, who remained active until 2002. The *Ignorance Is Bliss* demo appeared in 1997, as did an album, *Intrauterine Cannibalism*. Tours followed and a 2002 CD entitled *Frailty Of The Human Condition* appeared on the Shindy label.

RECOMMENDED ALBUM:
Frailty Of The Human Condition
(Shindy, 2002)
www.malignancy.com

Malkuth

A black metal band, Malkuth were formed in 1993 and produced a demo, *Orgies In The Temple Of Christ* (Bastard Son), two years later. Another demo, *Glory And Victory*, led to a deal with Demise. Original bass player Kleudde was replaced by Flammellian Azoth and the 666-copy EP *Under Delight Of The Black Candle* was released in 1997. More personnel rearrangements ensued as drummer Invoker Diabolic Flame made way for Maniac For War. A song from *Glory And Victory* had made it onto the Cyclonic compilation, *Under The Pagan Moon*, and a keyboard player called Cyber Necro Daemon was recruited. Flammellian Azoth had also had enough: the new bassist was Foehnmephys Occultus. Malkuth supported Rotting Christ for some Brazilian gigs, and a debut album, *The Dance Of The Satan's Bitch*, was released in 1998. Even more reshuffles followed, leaving the band with Holocausto on bass and Samir on drums.

RECOMMENDED ALBUM:
The Dance Of The Satan's Bitch
(Demise, 1998)

Marduk

Swedish black metal band Marduk – named after a Babylonian god – were formed in 1990 by Abruptum guitarist Morgan Hakansson in the town of Norkopping. This extraordinary group perform extremely powerful, uncompromising metal with lyrical themes such as the life and times of Count Dracula – the albums *Heaven Shall Burn* and *Nightwing* contained several songs dedicated to the story of the bloodthirsty nobleman – and warfare on *Panzer Division Marduk*, which featured a British WWII tank on the sleeve.

1991 saw the initial line-up – Hakansson plus Rikard Kalm (bass), Joakim Af Grave (drums) and Andreas Axelsson (vocals) – record the *Fuck Me Jesus* mini-album, which was shelved when a deal with No Fashion enabled the band to release *Dark Endless*. They later moved to Osmose.

Marduk – enduring black metallers

Fuck Me Jesus was eventually released in 1995 and was instantly banned in seven countries for its cover art. What distinguishes Marduk from the morass of other corpsepaint-daubed chancers is their musicianship – new drummer Fredrik Andersson added an immediate touch of proficiency on his arrival before 1994's *Opus Nocturne* – and their vision; three of their albums formed a trilogy based on the old Bathory trio of blood, fire and death. A new vocalist, Legion (real name Erik Hagstedt) also made an immediate impact, and a tour of Germany featuring Hypocrisy's Peter Tägtgren on guitar led to a successful live album. Hagstedt was replaced in 2003 by Mortuus.

RECOMMENDED ALBUM:
Opus Nocturne (Osmose, 1994)
www.marduk.nu

Massacra

Massacra was a French 'neo-classical death metal' band and was formed in 1986. Three demos landed them a deal with Shark Records from Germany and later, the major label Phonogram. However, the band was put on hold in 1997 when a founding member, Fred Duval, died of skin cancer at only 29. Some members of the band formed an industrial band, Zero Tolerance, and released an album on the Active label.

RECOMMENDED ALBUM:
Final Holocaust (Shark, 1990)

Massacre

A death metal band from Florida, Massacre originally consisted of Kam Lee (vocals), Bill Andrews (drums), Steve Swanson (guitar) Terry Butler (bass) and Rick Rozz (guitar). Lee, Andrews and Rozz had played with Death at various points. The band recorded a groundbreaking demo, 1985's *Aggressive Tyrant*, and a 1992 EP, *Inhuman Condition*, which featured a cover of the Venom song 'Warhead'. Venom's bass player and singer Cronos appeared on the recording. The debut album, *From Beyond*, was a competent, crunchy death metal album which stands up well today.

RECOMMENDED ALBUM:
From Beyond (Earache, 1991)

Mayhem (Right)

Along with their countrymen Burzum – to which this band are, for many reasons, inextricably linked – the Norwegian act Mayhem was for some time the leading light of the black metal movement. The band is said to have taken its name from the Venom song 'Mayhem With Mercy'.

Formed in 1984 by guitarist Oystein Aarseth, who adopted the stage name Euronymous, Mayhem came to be at the centre of the Inner Circle, a disorganised

group of vaguely Satan-worshipping youths who planned the overthrow of Christianity in Norway from the confines of Helvete, Euronymous' Oslo record shop. Helvete also later became the headquarters of Deathlike Silence Productions, a record label run by Aarseth, whose first release was *The Awakening* by the local band Merciless. The first two Burzum albums also saw the light of day through Deathlike Silence.

The original Mayhem line-up consisted of Euronymous plus Manheim (drums) and Necrobutcher (real name Jorn Stubberud, bass). A session singer, Messiah, was used on two demos, *Voices Of A Tortured Skull* and *Pure Fucking Armageddon* (note the similarity of Cradle Of Filth's later *Total Fucking Darkness* demo), but neither caused many ripples in the metal swamp and a new singer, Sven Erik Kristiansen – Maniac on stage – was recruited for the first Mayhem album, *Deathcrush*, released in 1987. Neither he nor Manheim had any desire to remain in the band after the album, however, and were replaced by Per Yngve Ohlin (known professionally as Dead) and the drummer Jan Axel von Blomberg (Hellhammer).

A live album, *Live In Leipzig*, was recorded, but due to the course of events, wasn't released for some time. The first Mayhem tragedy struck when Dead, a depressive who had sometimes claimed that he 'felt dead', committed suicide by slashing his wrists and then shooting himself with a shotgun. The bullets in the gun had been sent to him as a present by Burzum's Varg Vikernes. Euronymous and Hellhammer discovered the body and took pictures of the scene before alerting the police. Hellhammer went as far as making himself a necklace from some of Dead's skull fragments, while Euronymous claimed to have cooked and eaten pieces of the dead man's brain. The highly graphic photos were later used as artwork on Mayhem recordings.

Necrobutcher, a friend of Dead, left the band and his place was taken by the young Vikernes – at the time a protégé of Euronymous' – who played bass on the first Mayhem album, *De Mysteriis Dom Sathanas*. The session vocalist Attila Csihar was used on this album and Snorre Ruch (aka Blackthorn) of the band Thorns also played guitar. However, the record remained unreleased for some time due to contractual complications caused by the death on August 21, 1993 of Euronymous, who was murdered outside his apartment by Vikernes. Having

gained access to the guitarist's flat on the pretext of wishing to discuss a Burzum contract, Vikernes stabbed him several times in the flat and on the landing outside. His motive is said to have been jealousy at Euronymous' central role in the Inner Circle, although since his arrest and incarceration, Vikernes has claimed that he acted in self-defence. The murder has since become the stuff of tabloid legend; a grim reminder of the reality behind the gory fantasies of black metal.

In a bizarre twist, it later emerged that Euronymous visited a psychic shortly before the murder, who warned him of his impending death. Vikernes was given 21 years in prison, where he remains to this day despite an escape attempt in 2003, and the dead man's parents requested that the bass tracks he had recorded for *De Mysteriis...* be removed. They were duly re-recorded by Hellhammer and the album was released late in 1993. Hellhammer took over the day-to-day running of the band, recruiting a new guitarist, Rune Erickson (also known as Blasphemer) and calling in Maniac and Necrobutcher once again. An EP, 1997's *Wolf's Lair Abyss*, was released and the band resumed activity. 1998 saw the release of a live video, *Live In Bischofswerda*, through the UK label Misanthropy, which also handled Burzum releases.

Mayhem continue to play and record to a high standard to this day. Although Maniac's penchant for cutting himself onstage can make a Mayhem show hard going, the band are still very much to metal fans' tastes. Their albums are now polished and well-produced, however, much to the regret of many old-school fans.

RECOMMENDED ALBUM:
De Mysteriis Dom Sathanas
(Voices Of Wonder, 1994)
www.thetruemayhem.com

Meads Of Asphodel

A British black metal band with folk and pagan influences, Meads Of Asphodel were founded in 1998 by singer Metatron, guitarists Jaldaboath and Zephon and drummer Urakbaramel. Three well-reviewed demos, *Bemoaning Of Metatron* (1998), *Metatron And The Red Gleaming Serpent* and *The Watchers of Catal Huyuk* (both 1999), were followed by a deal with Supernal. A debut album, *The Excommunication Of Christ*, featured guest spots from A.C. Wild (of Bulldozer), Huw Lloyd-Langton (Hawkwind) and Kobold (Old Forest).

In 2002, the track 'Christ's Descent Into Hell' appeared on the Godreah compilation *Britannia Infernus: A History of British Occult And Black Metal*. MOA then recorded the three-song *Jihad* promo which Supernal issued on a split CD with two Dead-era Mayhem songs (see above) on limited-edition 10" vinyl. Jaldaboath departed after conflict over musical direction and was replaced by J.D. Tait. The new line-up duly recorded the *Exhuming The Grave Of Yeshua* album, released in 2004 and featuring Langton again plus Alan Davey (also of Hawkwind), Mirai Kawashima (Sigh), Vincent Crowley (Acheron) and Paul Carter (Thus Defiled). They remain a unique act on the British scene.

RECOMMENDED ALBUM:
Exhuming The Grave Of Yeshua
(Supernal, 2004)
www.themeadsofasphodel.com

Metatron on his favourite extreme metal bands
❝Venom, for ripping apart the NWOBHM blueprint and igniting extreme metal as we know it. Tongue-in-cheek they may have been, but at the time, this band were a very real, ugly, metal beast spitting an aural chaos more intense than anything that was to follow, purely because they were the first to do so. Also Emperor for revitalising a genre that was never solidified until the Norwegians made black metal the most diverse extreme metal genre of them all. Take away the initial controversy of murder and desecration, and you still discover talent and daring.❞

Megadeth

For many years the biggest-selling speed metal band in the world, Megadeth revolve around the outspoken guitarist and singer Dave Mustaine, who formed the band in 1983. It's the combination of Mustaine's knack for a catchy riff, his predilection for addressing teen-friendly social issues and his unfortunate habit of slagging other bands off that fuelled the rise to prominence of his band throughout the Eighties and Nineties. Although Mustaine has struggled with heroin and alcohol addiction, much of which was responsible for his choicest outbursts, it's probable that the resentment

Megadeth – led by the troubled Dave Mustaine (second left)

he accumulated through being raised in a broken home fuelled some of his anger. Along with his old band Metallica, Anthrax and Slayer, Megadeth were one of the Big Four of Thrash in the late Eighties.

After forming Metallica in 1981 with James Hetfield and Lars Ulrich, Mustaine co-composed some of the band's early tunes before being kicked out after tension over his alcohol abuse grew intolerable across the band's journey to New York to meet Megaforce founder Jon Zazula. This was the last straw after a series of incidents – including one in which Hetfield kicked Mustaine's dog and was punched in the mouth for his pains, after which the two guitarists had to be physically restrained from throttling each other. After leaving Metallica, Dave immediately recruited bass player Dave Ellefson along with guitarist Chris Poland and drummer Gar Samuelson. Metallica replaced him with Kirk Hammett.

After touring for two years and watching Metallica go from strength to strength, Mustaine eventually signed Megadeth to Combat in 1985 and released the debut album, the much-acclaimed *Killing Is My Business... And Business Is Good!*, a technically complex, perhaps overambitious album which was promising enough, however, to attract the major label Capitol. The excellent Capitol debut of 1986, *Peace Sells... But Who's Buying?* propelled the band into the big league and eventually went platinum. Despite this success, Mustaine developed a dependency on heroin, firing both Poland and Samuelson and replacing them with Jeff Young and Chuck Behler. Both were talented musicians although Young was often the butt of jokes because of his elaborately blow-waved coiffure and his habit of playing his guitar high up – "a fucking bow-tie with strings," as Mustaine later described it. The first album with this line-up was 1988's *So Far, So Good... So What!*, which reached No. 28 in the US charts and featured a tinny cover of The Sex Pistols' 'Anarchy In The UK' with ex-Pistol Steve Jones on guitar.

In 1990 Mustaine was arrested for drink-driving and entered a rehab centre, successfully cleaning up and becoming almost humble in comparison to the foot-in-mouth braggart of before. Once again firing the two non-Daves, he recruited Marty Friedman and Nick Menza. Shred guitarist Friedman in particular was a surprising choice, having recorded several guitar-showoff albums in Yngwie Malmsteen vein, but his expert touch went down well with fans on three successive albums. *Rust In Peace* was Megadeth's best album, with dazzling riffing (the complexity of which, Mustaine has since admitted, was an attempt to out-metal Metallica), the less complex but successful *Countdown To Extinction* and a weak, rock-club-friendly drop in standards entitled *Youthanasia*. It seemed that as the Nineties progressed, Mustaine was trying to emulate Metallica and exchange extreme metal for chartbound rock.

After a rarities collection, the band depressed many fans even further with 1999's *Risk* and then *The World Needs A Hero* (2001). Mustaine then announced that he had injured his arm and that Megadeth were no more. Rumours began flying, but it emerged later that after these two albums failed to sell in large quantities, the old Megadeth line-up simply fell apart and Mustaine returned to heroin abuse. Returning in 2004 with *The System Has Failed*, on the Sanctuary label, Dave explained that he had injured the nerves in his left arm while sleeping in an uncomfortable position and that it had taken a year of physiotherapy for them to heal. He also explained that Megadeth's change in musical direction had partially come from Friedman, who had tired of metal and attempted a more alternative-rock approach. While the year was a busy one for Mustaine, there was a perceptible sense that this would have to be his last credible comeback: with so many people to blame (he also lashed out at Metallica's Lars Ulrich over an appearance he had made against his will in that band's movie, *Some Kind Of Monster*), the pressure was on him to deliver. However, *System...* was average rather than scintillating and it seems that the end is nigh for Megadeth. That's not to say that Dave himself will not return as a solo artist or in a new band: watch this space.

RECOMMENDED ALBUM:
Rust In Peace (Capitol, 1990)
www.megadeth.com

Dave Mustaine in bullet points
Songwriting: "I think it takes a really developed songwriter to make heavy melodic music. Anybody can write heavy music, and anybody can write melodic music, but to do the two is really hard, and it's even harder to write something that's your own."

Drugs: "It was harder facing up to the things I did when I was abusing drink and drugs than it was detoxing. If I wanted to have a glass of wine or a pint right now, I'd have one. You know, my life changed – people are making a big deal about me finding God. And it is a big deal. But it doesn't change my music. I'm not gonna tell you what to do. I still love blowjobs."

Fashion: "I don't think people look fondly on guys in skin-tight blue jeans any more. You've got to remember, that was a really, really long time ago, and that was what was fashionable in that scene. Turnups, hightops, denim vests covered in badges and pins..."

Melechesh

Israeli black metal band Melechesh were the first BM act from Jerusalem to sign a record deal (although the band themselves are not actually Israelis). Formed in 1993 and releasing a demo, *As Jerusalem Burns*, in 1995, they signed to the US indie label Breath Of Night and relocated to Europe in '98. Joined by Absu drummer Proscriptor and signing to Osmose, Melechesh released *Djinn*, supprted by a video clip streamed online worldwide. A third album, *Sphynx*, was recorded in Gothenburg with King Diamond guitarist Andy Larocque and released in 2004.

RECOMMENDED ALBUM:
Sphynx (Osmose, 2004)
www.melechesh.com

Ashmedi on geography

"On the heavier side of music Slayer manage to impress me with every album. Immolation and Darkthrone deliver intense music and feelings. There are many great bands out there, but unfortunately there are more and more bands that simply get signed on the basis of their demographic/ geographic status rather than their music quality and integrity."

Mercyful Fate

Along with Venom and Bathory, the Danish band Mercyful Fate established the first black metal template in the mid-Eighties, which would later be refined by the Nineties Scandinavian BM acts and which also influenced the first wave of US thrash metal. The band were recognisable for the extraordinary vocals of the ex-professional footballer King Diamond, whose operatic range stretched from the deepest Glen Benton grunt to extremely high-pitched screams. Together with guitarists Hank Shermann and Michael Denner, bassist Timi Hansen, and drummer Kim Ruzz, Mercyful Fate wrote thrash-based material with lyrics dealing with supernatural and evil forces – hackneyed by millennial standards, to be sure, but unheard-of at the time.

After only two albums, the band split after arguments with Shermann, who wanted the band to pursue more commercial avenues. Diamond formed the equally successful King Diamond (see separate entry) for some years, but in 1993 Mercyful Fate reformed and issued a series of albums throughout the Nineties. Line-up changes included the recruitment of a new drummer, King Diamond's Snowy Shaw; the replacement of Hansen by Sharlee D'Angelo on 1994's *Time*; Shaw himself being ousted by Bjarne T. Holm for 1996's *Into The Unknown*; and Mike Wead (ex Memento Mori) replacing Denner. Parallel projects include Shermann and Denner's Zoser Mez, and King Diamond itself, with whom Diamond continues to tour. They continue to draw crowds across Europe.

RECOMMENDED ALBUM:
Don't Break The Oath (Roadrunner, 1984)
http://mercyful-fate.coven.vmh.net

King Diamond on Old Nick

"People say, 'Are you a Satanist?' And I say, 'Well, first of all I need to hear your definition of a Satanist before I can say yes or no.' I can relate to the philosophies that Anton LaVey wrote about. When I read his books for the first time, I thought, 'this is the way I live my life. These are the values I have.' But at the same time, there's a big void in there – he doesn't say to anyone, 'Listen here, this is the right god and this is the wrong god.' There's nothing about gods in there. It simply tells you to pick and choose whatever makes you happy, because no-one can prove anything anyway. So if people say I'm a Satanist if I believe in the life philosophy in that book, then sure. But if they're saying, 'Do you believe that baby blood will give you extra energy, and you can conjure demons with it?' Then no, I don't believe in that."

Meshuggah

Formed in 1987 in the Swedish town of
Umeå, Meshuggah took their name from
the Yiddish for 'mad' – an appropriate
label for the band, perhaps, who combine
melodic death metal with progressive
time-signatures and generally weird and
unorthodox influences. Their initial line-up
– vocalist/guitarist Jens Kidman, guitarist
Fredrik Thordendal and bassist Peter Nordin
– used a session drummer on their debut
EP, *Psykisk Testbild*. Signing to Nuclear Blast,
an album, *Contradictions Collapse*, was
recorded in 1991 and a full-time drummer,
Tomas Haake, was added to the band.
Kidman moved solely to vocals, handing
over guitar duties to Mårten Hagstrom, and
tours to promote the album followed.
1994 saw the release of the *None* EP as well
as a series of incidents, including Thordendal
– a carpenter by trade – losing the end of
one of his fingers in a workshop accident.

Meshuggah – intense prog-death metal

The digit portion was sewn back on,
however, and the guitarist carried on
unimpaired. Not to be outdone, Haake then
injured his hand in a machine and another
EP, *Selfcaged*, was delayed due to these
events. The *Destroy, Erase, Improve* album
came out in 1995 and during a tour after its
release, bassist Nordin's balance was impaired
through illness and he failed to complete
the shows. Thordendal played his guitar parts
on a bass as a temporary measure, but
Nordin's continued ill-health meant that he
was obliged to leave the band altogether and
he was replaced by Gustaf Hielm. Moving
to Stockholm for ease of studio access, both
the *Sane* and *The True Human Design* EPs
were released in 1997.
A further album, *Chaosphere*, was
released in 1998. Tours with Cannibal
Corpse, Hypocrisy and Machine Head
followed and Meshuggah appeared at the

Milwaukee Metalfest in 1998. The *Nothing* album of 2002 and the 21-minute, one-song *I* EP two years later saw the band's popularity increase. Recently they have developed 8-string guitars for a broader range of tones.

RECOMMENDED ALBUM:
Chaosphere (Nuclear Blast, 1998)
www.meshuggah.net

Tomas Haake on evolution
❝Things are changing all the time for the better: people are more open-minded about music than they used to be. Musical influences are so widely spread now. Any one band might have many influences, which opens people's eyes to different styles. You play for yourselves, that's all. If you can evolve as a band, that gets you the greatest satisfaction. To look back a decade and see what you've accomplished since your starting-point, that's a great drive.❞

Metallica

Currently the seventh biggest-selling band on earth, Metallica have evolved from playing super-precise, extremely innovative thrash metal in the Eighties to their position today as an MTV rock band. For the band's full history, the reader is referred to the author's book *Justice For All: The Truth About Metallica* (Omnibus Press, 2004), but where Metallica concern us here is not in their sophisticated latterday incarnation but the early years of their career, when they were the absolute apogee of the thrash genre, an unsurpassed combination of neck-breaking speed and razor-sharp precision. Venom laid down the thrash template, and Slayer took the genre to previously-uncharted territories, but it was Metallica who first brought thrash to the masses.

Most of the band were initially residents of Los Angeles. The teenage drummer Lars Ulrich – a Dane who had almost followed professional tennis as a career before his love of music took over – first met guitarist James Hetfield through an LA newspaper ad in *Recycler*, which he had placed in search of like-minded musicians influenced by NWOBHM giants such as Diamond Head and Judas Priest. Nothing solid materialised for another two years, until Ulrich was offered a track on Metal Blade's forthcoming compilation, *Metal Massacre*. Contacting Hetfield again and recruiting

bassist Ron McGovney, Metallica was formed and the addition of the fiery guitarist Dave Mustaine completed the line-up in early 1982.

The flaccid LA metal scene at the time focused largely on glam-metal acts such as Mötley Crüe, causing Metallica to make regular trips to play in the much more thrash-friendly San Francisco. While a reputation began to develop around them, Ulrich and Hetfield weren't getting on with McGovney and had their eyes on the fearsomely-talented bassist Cliff Burton of the San Fran band Trauma. After extended negotiations (Burton only agreed to join Metallica if the band relocated to San Francisco) McGovney was ousted and the move took place.

In late 1982 the New York music store owner Jon Zazula heard Metallica's *No Life 'Til Leather* demo and offered to manage them if they could come to NYC. After the band made the journey, Mustaine was kicked out after a series of rows over his alcohol abuse. Fuelled by a righteous rage which he has never completely resolved, Mustaine went on to form the extremely successful Megadeth and a rollercoaster career. His replacement was the Exodus founder and guitarist Kirk Hammett (see separate Megadeth and Exodus entries).

Zazula, unable to secure a record deal for his new band with an existing label, resolved to release an album himself and formed the Megaforce label for that purpose. *Kill 'Em All*, released in 1983, was an eye-opener for thousands of fans. Ulrich's double-speed drumming, with snare on one and three in each bar, combined with Hetfield's lightning-fast power chords, was the very essence of thrash metal, a completely new experience for the vast majority of listeners. The songs 'Motorbreath', 'No Remorse' and the ultimate expression of speed metal at the time, 'Whiplash', had their roots in the speedy, raw playing of Venom but took the ferocity of the approach to a new level. In a matter of months other Californian bands were playing thrash metal influenced by the *Kill 'Em All* template, notably Exodus, Slayer and Dark Angel. Emulating Hetfield's muscular, economical guitar style – honed by years of playing Black Sabbath and Iron Maiden songs – was no easy task, and only the most proficient players survived for any meaningful length of time.

The follow-up, 1984's *Ride The Lightning*, was a different record altogether. Gone were the scratchy production values of the debut, and the band had introduced the odd acoustic guitar and even a ballad, 'Fade To Black'. However, the speed was there in spades and the opener, 'Fight Fire With Fire', remains the fastest song the band have ever recorded. Other songs such as 'Creeping Death' and 'For Whom The Bell Tolls' have entered the heavy metal canon as superb examples of non-thrash metal writing, and it was becoming clear that the band's talents would soon exceed the confines of the speedy template which they had created.

Moving to Elektra, with a deal that famously allowed Metallica a great deal of autonomy, the band's exposure to the public increased and sales of the first two albums soared. In 1985, while playing at the legendary Castle Donington festival, Hetfield responded to the small-minded listeners who had accused Metallica of softening up with the immortal line, "If you came here to see Spandex, eye make-up and the words 'Ooh baby' in every fuckin' song, this ain't the fuckin' band!" The Elektra debut, *Master Of Puppets* (1986), was one of the greatest metal albums ever recorded. Combining a new, brutally heavy sound with breathtaking speed and precision, *Puppets* revealed a complexity not seen on the first two albums. 'Disposable Heroes' and 'Damage, Inc.' were streamlined and fast, while the title track and 'Sanitarium' were glacial, mid-tempo masterpieces, and Burton even penned a blues workout on the instrumental 'Orion'. Along with Slayer's *Reign In Blood*, this album is the pinnacle of thrash metal.

Tragedy awaited in 1986. After tours with Anthrax and Ozzy Osbourne, the band's bus skidded on ice in Sweden and turned over. Burton was ejected through an open window and crushed to death underneath the vehicle. Deeply shocked and distressed, the band considered quitting but ultimately decided to continue. Flotsam And Jetsam (see separate entry) bass player Jason Newsted was recruited a mere month later and, after a whirlwind Japanese tour, the *Garage Days Re-Revisited* EP was issued to showcase his considerable skills and to prepare for an appearance at Donington in 1988. As a tribute to Burton, Metallica issued a video entitled *Cliff 'Em All,* containing old footage of the band live and in rehearsal.

Metallica's move away from thrash metal was evidenced further by ...*And Justice for All* (1988), which gained a Grammy nomination for Best Heavy Metal Performance. Unbelievably, the award went to prog-folk veterans Jethro Tull, leading Metallica to place stickers on the *Justice* album reading 'Grammy Award Losers'. When the song 'One' eventually won a Grammy for Best Video in 1990, the band good-humouredly thanked Tull for not producing any material that year. Metallica have since gone on to well-documented heights; the self-titled *Metallica* album of 1991 has sold over 20 million copies to date, while subsequent albums, *Load, Reload, Garage Inc.* and the San Francisco Symphony Orchestra collaboration of 1999, *S&M*, have seen the band rivalled in sales terms only by globally-popular bands such as U2 and REM. The downside of all this success is that old-school thrash fans deserted them in droves, with many accusing the band of selling out to commercial blandness – an accusation that spread further in 2000 when Metallica were instrumental in the downfall of Napster, the filesharing program. In 2001, Newsted left after Hetfield repeatedly refused to allow him to work with other bands: he went on to work with Voivod and Echobrain. Hetfield then went through rehab, successfully conquering an alcohol addiction, and emerged a wiser, more tolerant man as a result. 2003's *St Anger* album, which had been talked up as a return to heavier music, split the fanbase down the middle: some loved its rawness, but others hated its primitive production and uninspiring riffs. Their 2004 movie, *Some Kind Of Monster*, was revealing. While Metallica were once one of the greatest metal bands ever, their time is running out.
RECOMMENDED ALBUM:
Master Of Puppets (Elektra, 1986)
www.metallica.com

Midvinter

Swedish black metal band Midvinter were formed in 1993 by Damien (guitars and bass), Björn (vocals) and Krille (drums) and recorded the *Midvinternatt* demo. Extensive personnel problems meant that nothing else happened until 1996, when the band was joined by Kheeroth (ex-Setherial) on vocals and Zathanel (ex-Sorhin) on drums. Signing to the Black Diamond label, the band released the *At The Sight*

Of The Apocalypse Dragon album in '97. Since then the band has only been partially active.
RECOMMENDED ALBUM:
At The Sight Of The Apocalypse Dragon
(Black Diamond, 1997)

Misanthrope

The French band Misanthrope – Phillipe De L'Argilière (guitar/vocals), Jean-Baptiste Boitel (guitar), Jean-Jacques Moréac (bass) and Alexis Phélipot (drums) – play progressive death metal, including complex time changes and other musical departures in their music. Their albums to date have been interesting enough to attract a hardcore body of fans for whom conventional death metal is too unsophisticated but who enjoy the aggression of the band's sound. A box set was recently issued to celebrate 15 years of Misanthrope.
RECOMMENDED ALBUM:
Variation On Inductive Theories
(Holy, 1993)
http://misanthrope.darkriver.net

Mithotyn

Swedish black metal band Mithotyn included Viking influences in their music, most notably on their last album before splitting, 1999's *Gathered Around The Oaken Table*. Although their use of choirs and epic textures made them popular on the folk-metal scene, the band couldn't sustain a career longer than six years and went on to other projects. Guitarist Stefan Weinerhall formed the band Falconer.
RECOMMENDED ALBUM:
King Of The Distant Forest (Invasion, 1998)

Monstrosity

Florida death metal band Monstrosity were formed in 1990. The *Horror Infinity* demo circulated on the tape-trading scene and led to a deal with Nuclear Blast; the debut album, *Imperial Doom*, has become a classic among other early works from fellow Floridians Morbid Angel, Obituary and Deicide. A second album, *Millennium*, was followed by tours of South America and Europe, while its successor *In Dark Purity* contained a cover of Slayer's 'Angel Of Death'. Founder member George 'Corpsegrinder' Fisher departed to a successful career with Cannibal Corpse and a box set of the Fisher-era material was issued entitled *Enslaving The Masses*. Subsequent vocalists Jason Avery and Sam Molina assisted Monstrosity's forward progress but since then they have remained in the death metal B-league.

RECOMMENDED ALBUM:
Imperial Doom (Nuclear Blast, 1991)
www.conquestmusic.com/monstros.htm

Morbid Angel (Below)

The most influential of the Florida death metal bands, Morbid Angel were formed in 1984 by Trey Azagthoth (guitar/keyboards) with Pete Sandoval (drums), David Vincent (vocals/bass) and Richard Burnelle (guitar). Azagthoth (real name George Emmanuel III) is the principal songwriter and has become worshipped on the scene for his virtuoso guitar playing and mocked not a little for his beliefs, apparently a bizarre combination of Sumerian myth, Kabbalah lore and Satanism.

After playing UK concerts with Napalm Death in the mid-Eighties, Morbid Angel signed to Napalm's label, Earache, based in Nottingham. The debut album, *Altars Of Madness*, surprised many by reaching the top of the UK's independent charts, and has since become recognised as a groundbreaking album of the death genre. The follow-up, 1992's *Blessed Are The Sick*, was a classic, oozing sinister riffs and anchored with furious speed and aggression.

The *Covenant* and *Domination* albums saw the band step into the metal limelight, while the first two albums have each sold over half a million copies. A live album, *Entangled In Chaos*, which saw second guitarist Erik Rutan step in to replace Richard Burnelle, featured Azagthoth on his producing debut. Steve Tucker then took over bass and vocals from Vincent, who went on to the uninspiring Genitorturers, and while he is a competent frontman, recent MA albums have settled into generic rather than innovative territory. *Formulas Fatal To The Flesh*,

Gateways To Annihilation and *Heretic* have all been blastbeat-driven, mid-tempo albums which fail to match up to the earlier work.
RECOMMENDED ALBUM:
Blessed Are The Sick (Earache, 1991)
www.morbidangel.com

Steve Tucker on the roots of extremity
❝I grew up in middle fucking America! When I was a teenager I listened to anything heavy that I could get my hands on – Dio, Iron Maiden, Judas Priest, Motörhead, then Metallica, Dark Angel, Venom, Possessed, Slayer, stuff like that. The term extreme has changed over the years – what was extreme when I first heard it is by no means extreme today – but what really woke me up was when I heard 'Whiplash' by Metallica for the first time. Nothing else seemed to compare.❞

Mordred

San Francisco's Mordred started life as a thrash metal band along the lines of local rivals Exodus, producing a standard album of the genre, 1989's *Fool's Game*. Originally

Mordred – initially thrash, later funk

consisting of Scott Holderby (vocals), J. Taffer (guitar), Danny White (guitar), Art Liboon (bass) and Gannon Hall (drums), the band soon moved onto a more funk-based approach, recruiting a keyboard player and samples manipulator, Aaron Vaughn, and replacing Taffer with James Sanguinetti. The *In This Life* album and *Visions* EP of 1991 saw the band exorcise whatever funk demons lurked within them, returning to a more metal approach on their final album, 1994's *The Next Room*, which featured the tougher vocals of Paul Kimball. They split after this release, only reforming for a show in 2002.
RECOMMENDED ALBUM:
In This Life (Noise, 1991)

Morgion

From Orange County, California, death/doom metal band Morgion were formed in 1990 by Jeremy Peto (vocals/bass), Rhett Davis (drums) and Dwayne Boardman (guitar), recording a single, 'Travesty', released by Catatonic in 1993. The band recruited Bobby Thomas (guitar) and Ed

Parker (keyboards) in 1994 for their debut album on Relapse, *Among Majestic Ruin.* Morgion went on to record tracks entitled 'Innocence And Wrath' and 'The Usurper' for a Celtic Frost tribute album in 1996 and played at the Milwaukee Metalfest the following year. Thomas and Parker were then replaced by the multi-instrumentalist Gary Griffith. 1999's *Solinari* album continued the epic doom themes and, despite line-up problems and a three-year hiatus, Morgion remain active.

RECOMMENDED ALBUM:
Solinari (Relapse, 1999)
www.morgion.com

Morgoth

German death metal band Morgoth were Marc Grewe (ex-Comecon, vocals), Harry Busse (guitar), Sebastian Swart (bass), Carsten Otterbach (guitar) and Rüdiger Hennecke (drums/keyboards). They played death metal with electronic elements in the latter stages of their career, but couldn't make this a successful formula and disappeared after 1996's *Feel Sorry For The Fanatic.*

RECOMMENDED ALBUM:
Cursed (Century Media, 1993)

Mörk Gryning

Swedish black metallers Mörk Gryning were formed as a duo in 1993. Recording a demo, *When Moonshine Is The Only Light,* Draakh Kimera (vocals, guitar, drums, keyboards, screams) and Goth Gorgon (bass, keyboards, screams) signed to No Fashion and released the album *Tusen År Har Gått…* in 1995. Incorporating non-metal elements into their aggressive but atmospheric approach, MG have since released three subsequent albums, *Return Fire* (1997), *Maelstrom Chaos* (2001) and *Pieces Of Primal Expressionism* (2003). Keyboard player Aeon was recruited for later work and the band remain an interesting cult act.

RECOMMENDED ALBUM:
Maelstrom Chaos (No Fashion, 2001)
www.mork-gryning.com

Bassist Jonas Berndt on the future
❛❛The genres will mix. I don't believe that in 10 years people will talk about black or death metal, at least not in same way as today. It will develop and also more elements from non-extreme music will be included.❜❜

Mortal Sin

An Australian thrash metal band of the late Eighties and early Nineties, Mortal Sin's debut album, *Mayhemic Destruction,* a Metallica and Anthrax-influenced combination of heaviness and speed, promised great things. However, its timing meant that by the time the follow-up was issued, fans were looking more towards the death and black metal emerging from Florida and Scandinavia. After a third album the band split up, with a reunion concert and DVD in 2004.

RECOMMENDED ALBUM:
Rebellious Youth (Under One Flag, 1991)

Mortician

Combining horror themes with fast, heavy death metal and super-guttural vocals, the US act Mortician was formed in 1989 as Casket with Will Rahmer (bass/vocals) and Matt Sicher (drums). Renaming the band after the title of one of their early songs, the duo invited John McEntee of Incantation to play on their early days: Rahmer also provided vocals for Incantation at the time. In 1991 Roger J. Beaujard joined as guitarist (although he often plays drums for them live) and a deal with Relapse was signed. Sicher was asked to leave and the band began to use a drum machine, giving them an immediately identifiable sound.

After various problems the band managed to record the 'House By The Cemetery' 7" plus bonus tracks 'Scum' (Napalm Death) and 'Procreation Of The Wicked' (Celtic Frost). Once the band had hit their stride, a series of albums emerged, all more or less identical grind (as Beaujard admitted to the author in 2002) and with graphic sleeve art. Tours with Anal Cunt and Incantation kept the Mortician profile high, as did the sleeve of *Chainsaw Dismemberment.* They continue to enthral horror fans and make everyone else feel slightly queasy.

RECOMMENDED ALBUM:
Domain Of Death (Relapse, 2001)
www.mortician.net

Roger Beaujard talks extremity
❛❛A lot of bands now are pushing the envelope of extremity and speed – where is it gonna end? For me, Slayer's *Reign In Blood* was pivotal as far as

being fast goes, but you listen to it now and it's slow! The music depends on the mood I'm in and how disgusted I am with the world. There's so much bullshit in life and we take it out on the guitars, heh heh. **"**

Myrkskog

Norwegian black metal band Myrkskog was formed in 1993 by Destructhor (guitars), Master V (bass, vocals) and Lars Petter (drums). Petter was replaced in '94 by Bjørn Thomas. A demo appeared the following year entitled *Ode Til Norge* and the band recruited drummer Eek and guitarist Secthdaemon, but it was not until 1998 that any music appeared. *Apocalyptic Psychotica: The Murder Tape* appeared on Candlelight and was followed by tours: however, the band's perennial side-project status means that players have come and gone. Two more albums, *Deathmachine* and *Superior Massacre*, have been released. Destructhor and Secthdaemon also appeared in the very successful Zyklon.

RECOMMENDED ALBUM:
Apocalyptic Psychotica: The Murder Tape (Candlelight, 1998)
www.myrkskog.org

Naglfar – melodic black metal

Naglfar

Swedish black metal act Naglfar were formed in the early Nineties and pioneered a form of melodic BM not too far removed from the equivalent version of death metal. With output infrequent rather than prolific, the band debuted with the *Vittra* album in 1995 and took three years to follow it up with *Diabolical*. This was supported by live dates with Deicide, Six Feet Under and Amon Amarth, before another three-year hiatus. The *Ex Inferis* EP (2001) gave fans something to chew on, together with festival shows, before yet another extended break and the *Sheol* (Hebrew for hell) album of 2003, which was composed of nine songs corresponding to Dante's *Inferno*.

RECOMMENDED ALBUM:
Sheol (Century Media, 2003)
www.naglfar.net

Napalm Death *(Opposite)*

The pioneers of grindcore along with Carcass, Napalm Death started off as a punk-turned-metal joke, became an annoyance when they refused to go away and are now accepted as a serious death/grind band. Founded in Birmingham in 1982 by Nick Bullen (vocals), Nick Ratledge (drums), Darren Fideski (guitar) and others, the first incarnation of the band recorded the *Hatred Surge* demo, a more punk-based recording than their later music.

Digby Pearson of the fledgling label Earache was impressed by their live show and offered them a deal; the first album, 1986's *Scum*, unconventionally featured two different line-ups on either side. Mick Harris (drums), Justin Broadrick (guitar), Nik Bullen (bass/vocals) appeared on Side One, while Bill Steer (guitar), Jim Whitely (bass), and the mighty-lunged Lee Dorrian (vocals) looked after Side Two.

After the release of *Scum*, the band toured extensively, adding Shane Embury on bass. Between *Scum* and the release of a second full-length album, Napalm Death released two John Peel sessions and contributed tracks to the *North Atlantic Noise Attack* and *Pathological* compilations,

as well as recording a split flexidisc with SOB.

The second album, the mighty *From Enslavement To Obliteration*, featured no fewer than 54 tracks, many of which lasted no more than a few seconds. Hackles rose among many music journalists, who dismissed Napalm as a joke, but attention was nonetheless drawn to the band, even to the extent that BBC-2 based an *Arena* Heavy Metal Special on them in 1989. The band went on to tour Japan, but Dorrian and Steer left to form Cathedral and Carcass respectively. Their replacements were Mark 'Barney' Greenaway (ex-Benediction, vocals) and the American Jesse Pintado (ex-Terrorizer, guitar).

More touring followed, with the two new members fitting in seamlessly; successful shows with Bolt Thrower, the newly-successful Carcass and Morbid Angel ensued – the latter would later sign to Earache – before a New York concert, their first in the US. Mitch Harris (ex-Righteous Pigs; not Mick Harris) was added as a second guitarist, and the rather more sophisticated *Harmony Corruption* was recorded at Florida's Morrisound studios. Two EPs followed, *Suffer The Children* and *Mass Appeal Madness*, with thicker, more unsophisticated production values akin to the Napalm of old.

Mick Harris was the next to leave – he went on to form Scorn – and was replaced by Danny Herrera for gigs in Germany and

America with the heavyweight Brazilian thrash outfit Sepultura. A fourth album, *Utopia Banished*, and an EP, *The World Keeps Turning*, were followed by more touring, this time the legendary 'Campaign For Musical Destruction' tour of Europe with Obituary and Dismember, and with Carcass, Cathedral and Brutal Truth in the States. The *Death By Manipulation* compilation album was also released. After a tour in South Africa, a cover version of The Dead Kennedys' 'Nazi Punks (Fuck Off)' was released as a charity single benefiting anti-Nazi groups.

Fear Emptiness Despair was the title of the next ND long-player, and the band took it on tour with Entombed, Obituary and Machine Head to a rapturous response. The *Diatribes* album saw the band continue to tour, but in November 1996, Barney was replaced by Extreme Noise Terror's Phil Vane and a split EP with Coalesce was released soon after. However, Barney was reinstated for the next album, *Inside The Torn Apart*, and the line-up has since remained stable. Napalm Death remain one of the most committed extreme metal bands in any country, with subsequent albums ever more scornful of the music industry. Embury and Pintado are also part of the grind supergroup Lock-Up (see separate entry).

RECOMMENDED ALBUM:
From Enslavement To Obliteration
(Earache, 1988)
www.enemyofthemusicbusiness.com

Nasum

Swedish grindcore merchants Nasum were founded by Necrony members Rickard Alriksson and Anders Jakobsson in 1992 and released a split single with Agathocles on the Poserslaughter label. Recruiting guitarist/bassist Mieszko Talarczyk, they recorded more tracks for a split album with Retaliation, CSSO and Vivisection, released on Talarczyjk's Grindwork label. Edge Of Sanity main-man Dan Swanö assisted them on the *Industrislaven* album, an 18-song, 16-minute (yes) album, before Altoksson was replaced by Per Karlsson and then Jallo Lehto. A 1998 album was finally released by Relapse, initial copies of which came with a 7" EP of cover versions. Burst bassist Jesper Liverod joined in 1999 for American dates. More albums, 2000's *Human 2.0*, and 2003's *Helvete* (featuring the talents of Napalm Death's Shane Embury and Grave's Jörgen Sandström) have kept the Nasum flag flying high. Personnel switches have not prevented the band from touring widely and gathering a fanbase, notable among whom is Slipknot drummer Joey Jordison.

RECOMMENDED ALBUM:
Human 2.0 (Relapse, 2000)
www.nasum.com

Necromantia

Necromantia is a secretive Greek gothically-tinged black metal band formed in 1989 by the bassists Magus Vampyr Daoloth (four-string and vocals) and Baron Blood (eight-string), plus the semi-permanent musicians Inferno (keyboards), Divad (guitar) and Yiannis (saxophone/percussion), who goes by the name The Worshipper Of Pan. Magus is a renowned producer and has also worked with Rotting Christ and Diabolos Rising, as well as his own solo project and Danse Macabre with members of Ancient Rites.

The band are notable in their use of the eight-string bass in place of a rhythm guitar, which creates a necro, gloomy sound. Apart from issuing several albums through Osmose, Necromantia also issued a collection entitled *Covering Evil (12 Years Doing The Devil's Work)*.

RECOMMENDED ALBUM:
Scarlet Evil Witching Black
(Osmose, 1998)
www.necromantia.tk

Necrophagia

US death metallers Necrophagia produce crushing metal laced with unnerving movie samples and dialogue, the result of singer Killjoy's obsession with all things horror-related. He formed the band back in 1983 but, after recording demos, they split in 1987. Working on side-projects such as the Cabal thrash metal band, Killjoy reconvened Necrophagia after meeting Pantera singer Phil Anselmo, who co-wrote a new album, *Holocaust De La Morte*. The die was cast and a sequence of violent, unsettling albums that have placed Necrophagia at the cult edge of horror metal.

Killjoy (who has not used his real name since he was 15 years old) is also at the centre of Ravenous, Wurdulak, Eibon and Hellpig and other bands with musicians from such bands as Mayhem, Immortal, Gorelord and Bloodthorn. He also runs a record company and a horror DVD company together with Casey Chaos of Amen.

RECOMMENDED ALBUM:
Cannibal Holocaust (Season Of Mist, 2001)
www.necrophagia.com

Necrophobic

The Swedish death metal Necrophobic consists of Tobias Sidengård (bass/vocals), Martin Halfdahn (guitar), Sebastian Ramstedt (guitar) and Joakim Sterner (drums). They combine their death approach with black metal to provide a satisfying mixture of raw speed and complexity. An early demo, *Unholy Prophecies*, led to the release of an album, *The Nocturnal Silence,* in 1993. An early member was David Parland – also known as Blackmoon – who went on to form Dark Funeral after the release of the first Necrophobic album and its follow-up, the *Spawned By Evil* EP. The latter included three covers – Slayer's 'Die By The Sword', Venom's 'Nightmare' and 'Enter The Eternal Fire' by Bathory.

The next album, 1997's *Darkside*, was less heavy and more melodic, leading many fans to believe that Necrophobic had gone the way of so many other Swedish death metal bands, prioritising tunefulness instead of power. However, the next record, *The Third Antichrist*, was a return to form and the band toured extensively in 2002 and 2003.

RECOMMENDED ALBUM:
The Nocturnal Silence (Hammerheart, 1993)
www.necrophobic.net

Nembrionic

Formerly known by the more cumbersome name Nembrionic Hammerdeath, Nembrionic were founded in 1988 and played grindcore. A 1991 demo led to tours with Malevolent Creation and Nocturnus and the band released the *Themes On An Occult Theory* EP on the Displeased label in 1993.

A debut album, *Tempter*, followed in 1994 and tours with At The Gates and Consolation took the band through Europe. The grindcore of before now gathered certain hints of death metal and subsequent albums, *Psycho One Hundred* and *Incomplete*, showed that Nembrionic had assimilated a whole host of styles. They continue to tour and record infrequently.

RECOMMENDED ALBUM:
Tempter (Displeased, 1992)
www.deathforce.com/nembrionic

Neuraxis

Montreal death metal grindcore act Neuraxis were formed in 1994 and released a debut album, *Imagery*, two years later. It would be another four years, however, before more material appeared, but once *A Passage Into Forlorn* appeared in 2000 the band hit the road hard to support it, touring North America with Cephalic Carnage. 2002's *Truth Beyond* album preceded more touring, this time with Birdflesh and Hellblazer; at the time of writing the first three albums have just been reissued.

RECOMMENDED ALBUM:
Truth Beyond (Neoblast, 2002)
www.neuraxis.org

Guitarist Rob Milley hails the pioneers

❝Cryptopsy are a huge inspiration because of their devotion to their instruments and their amazing talent at writing extreme, technical, brutal, melodic metal. Suffocation's style of brutal technical death metal is crushing, and is very original – countless bands have imitated them. Ever since they released *Heartwork*, Carcass are the best melodic death metal band to this day. Catchy and heavy riffs, amazing solos and flesh tearing vocals.**❞**

Nightfall

Formed in 1992, Nightfall were a Greek gothic band with black metal influences, revolving around the songwriter Efthimis. A demo, *Vanity*, led to the brand-new Holy label, based in Paris, offering the band a deal. The debut album for both band and label was *Parade Into Centuries*. Subsequent albums have seen them stray into electro-goth territory (a collaboration and remix project with the German band Sabotage under the name *Sabotage/Qu'est-ce Que C'est* – one of the tracks was called 'Moon: Death Is Gay'). Tours with Slayer, Paradise Lost, Rage and Saxon demonstrated the band's popularity on many scenes. Nightfall also contributed to the soundtrack of the *Blood Kiss* vampire film.

RECOMMENDED ALBUM:
Athenian Echoes (Holy, 1996)
www.listen.to/nightfall

Nightrage

A multi-national melodic death metal band composed of the ubiquitous Tomas Lindberg (death vocals), Tom Englund (clean vocals), guitarist and songwriter Marios Iliopoulos, Brice Leclercq (bass) and Per M. Jensen (drums, although he's normally a guitarist in The Haunted), Nightrage have released one excellent album to date, 2003's *Sweet Vengeance*. As expertly performed and produced as you would imagine from its line-up and provenance, *Sweet Vengeance* was produced by Fredrik Nordström (In Flames, Arch Enemy, Opeth, Hammerfall, Dimmu Borgir) at Studio Fredman in Gothenburg, and holds great promise for the future.

RECOMMENDED ALBUM:
Sweet Vengeance (Century Media, 2003)
www.nightrage.com

Nile

The most gripping death metal band to emerge since Morbid Angel, South Carolina's Nile are currently the ultimate expression of the genre: no other band at the time of writing combines such utter brutality with mind-numbing technicality and an epic vision that dwarfs the concept behind any other album by a comparable act.

Formed in 1993 by Karl Sanders (guitar/vocals), Chief Spires (bass/vocals), and Pete Hammoura (drums), and later joined by

Nile – new hope of US death metal

Dallas Toler-Wade (guitar), Nile developed a death metal attack shaped and moulded by Sanders' obsession with (and deep, scholarly study of) ancient Egypt and its religion, sociology and history. In musical terms, this meant that Middle Eastern scales and instrumentation were deployed above the fearsome riffing; lyrically, the band sang in suitably gruff tones (there were three lead singers) words taken from or inspired by Sanders' interpretation of ancient Egyptian inscriptions, temple carvings, hieroglyphics, tomb paintings and so on.

The debut album, *Amongst The Catacombs Of Nephren-Ka*, appeared in 1997 on Relapse. Audiences were levelled by Nile's ferocity and musicianship and a buzz began to build about the band, the like of which had not been felt for some years. An 18-month tour with the aforementioned Morbid Angel and others established the Nile foothold still further. Their second album, 2000's *Black Seeds Of Vengeance*, scored hugely on a whole new level of achievement and received a

whole string of accolades in the metal press. In years to come *BSOV* will be regarded as a genre classic, replete as it is with an almost orchestral structure of layers. The lyrics took Sanders a year, while Toler-Wade spoke of requiring the same amount of time to master just one composition, 'Multitude Of Foes'. The record included African choirs, tablas, tambouras, sitars, gongs, kettle drums and Tibetan 'doom' horns and was that rare beast – an instant classic.

After touring extensively, Spires and Hammoura departed (the latter due to injury) and were replaced by Darkmoon guitarist Jon Vesano on bass and the phenomenal drummer Tony Laureano, once an acolyte of the mighty Gene Hoglan. The reinvigorated band returned to the studio and recorded *In Their Darkened Shrines*, another breathtaking record which continues the musical dexterity of *Black Seeds...* with, if it's possible, even more symphonic grandeur. If an *Extreme Metal III* comes out in 2010, I will be surprised if Nile are not one of its biggest bands. They are unique.

RECOMMENDED ALBUM:
Black Seeds Of Vengeance (Relapse, 2000)
www.nile-catacombs.net

Karl Sanders walks like an Egyptian

"In the beginning I loved Slayer, early Metallica, Voivod, Kreator, Mercyful Fate, Omen, early Megadeth... classic quality metal full of fire and power and originality!"

Novembre

An Italian metal band with equal death and doom/gothic strands, Novembre were founded in 1990 by the brothers Carmelo Orlando (guitars, vocals) and Giuseppe Orlando (drums) under the name Catacomb. The *Unreal* demo came the following year, as did a name-change and a deal with Polyphemus. In 1994 they recorded a debut album, *Wish I Could Dream It Again*, at Dan Swano's Unisound studios. A second record, 1996's *Arte Novecento*, was followed by the recruitment of Massimiliano Pagliuso (guitars) and Alessandro Niola (bass). More albums, *Classica* ('99) and *Novembrine Waltz* ('01) were supported by tours with Moonspell, Kreator, Witchery, Opeth and Katatonia, appropriate choices for the blend of gothic and death metal in which they specialised. A re-recording of *Wish I Could Dream It Again* under the title *Dreams d'Azur* is scheduled for release in 2005.

RECOMMENDED ALBUM:
Arte Novecento (Polyphemus, 1996)
www.novembre.nu

Novembre – Italian doom/death metal

Nuclear Assault

One of the second wave of Eighties thrash bands that rose in the wake of the Big Four, the classic Nuclear Assault combined high-speed riffing with an anti-nuclear, pro-environmental message which, although well-intentioned at the time, now seems somewhat naive. On leaving Anthrax, bassist Danny Lilker recruited vocalist/guitarist John Connelly, guitarist Anthony Bramante and drummer Glenn Evans to continue the precise, unhinged music of his old bands – Lilker had also performed in the speedy SOD project with Anthrax's Charlie Benante and Scott Ian (see separate entries for Anthrax and SOD).

Nuclear Assault produced five albums and an EP, 1987's *The Plague*, and while they received a certain degree of recognition, Lilker departed before the band's last album in 1993. He has since formed Brutal Truth and worked on SOD once again. A reformation took place in the early years of the new century and tours followed.

RECOMMENDED ALBUM:
Game Over (Combat, 1986)
www.nuclearassault.us

Obituary

Another of the Florida death metal pioneers, the uncompromisingly entertaining Obituary distanced themselves from the precision riffing of Death, Morbid Angel and Deicide by producing a sludgy, rapid mass of riffs with obscenely-vomited vocals. Their approach led to the label "the heaviest band in the world" and a listen to their debut, 1989's *Slowly We Rot*, makes this a charge difficult to deny.

The band was formed in the town of Brandon in 1989 by vocalist John Tardy – who on early recordings is said to have dispensed with vocals entirely, using his voice to produce belched, ultra-guttural roars to add to the generally murky vibe. Recording a single and two *Metal Massacre* compilation tracks as Xecutioner, the band were obliged to find a new moniker after legal threats from a band of the same name, at first deciding on Desecration before landing on Obituary and signing to Roadrunner.

In 1990 West was replaced by James Murphy (ex-Death, later of Cancer, Disincarnate, Testament, etc). Murphy remained in the band for a few months only, however, and West returned in time for *The End Complete* (1992). By this point Tardy's vocals had clarified somewhat, and the band toured extensively.

Obituary then took a three-year break, returning in 1997 with *Back From The Dead* and later, a live album called – appropriately enough – *Dead*. The band continued to record intermittently and even saw European chart success when they broke into the Billboard Top 40 in Germany and Finland. A few years off were followed by the predictable reunion, but in this instance it is both deserved and welcome.

RECOMMENDED ALBUM:
Slowly We Rot (Roadrunner, 1989)
www.obituary.cc

Drummer Donald Tardy on the pioneers
❝My favorite extreme metal band is Hellhammer, because they were writing such sick, heavy stuff early in metal music history. I find it amazing that Tom G. Warrior was making up such extreme, brutal ideas so long ago, I mean 1980-81 or something like that. Wow! I still listen to that album [*Apocalyptic Raids*] regularly and it still brings goose-bumps to my skin.❞

Obliveon

A thrash metal band from Quebec, Obliveon were formed in 1987 under the name Oblivion by Alain Demers (drums), Pierre Rémillard (guitar), Bruno Bernier (vocals), Stéphane Picard (bass) and Martin Gagné (guitar). The band recorded two demos, *Whimsical Uproar* and *Fiction Of Veracity Tapes*, before Active Records signed them and released a debut album, *From This Day Forward*, in 1990. The album received good reviews but was barely promoted or distributed and band and label separated.

The 1993 follow-up, *Nemesis*, sold very well, given that the band had released it independently, and Obliveon signed to ASA for a third album, 1996's *Cybervoid*. In 1998, the now-defunct label Soundscape repackaged and reissued the *Whimsical Uproar* demo as an EP, and the band contributed a cover of Ozzy Osbourne's 'Suicide Solution' to the *Legend Of A Madman* tribute released by the Olympic label.

In 1999 Obliveon recorded a video for a cover of The B-52s' 'Planet Claire' and the next album, *Carnivore Mothermouth*, was received with praise by fans and media alike. They disbanded in 2002.

RECOMMENDED ALBUM:
From This Day Forward (Active, 1990)

Obscene Crisis

A grindcore band from Quebec, Obscene Crisis were formed in 1995 by guitarists Stephane Cote (ex-Kataklysm) and his brother Jean-Pierre, vocalist Eric Fiset, drummer Stephane Chartrand and bassist Martin Riendeau, who took over from Chrystian Boyer. An album, *Silence Of The Mind*, was produced by Pierre Remillard of Obliveon.

RECOMMENDED ALBUM:
Silence Of The Mind (Relapse, 1996)

Old Man's Child *(Below)*

Renowned Norwegian black metal band Old Man's Child has seen the cream of the country's extreme metallists come through its ranks. Formed by guitarist/vocalist Thomas Rune Andersen (aka Grusom, now known as Galder), guitarist Jon Øyvind

Opeth – complex, atmospheric power

Andersen (Jardar) and Dimmu Borgir drummer Kenneth Åkesson (Tjodalv) in 1989 under the name Requiem, the early music was death metal. However, on discovering a mutual love of raw black metal, the musicians changed their name to Old Man's Child and recorded a demo, *In The Shades Of Life*, in 1994, on which ex-Dimmu Borgir bassist Brynjard Tristan also played. A deal followed with the Hot label, who released the first OMC album, *Born Of The Flickering*, the following year. Tristan was replaced by the Minas Tirith bassist and band leader Gonde. Tjodalva also left to focus on Dimmu Borgir and was replaced by Tony Kirkemo.

Signing to Century Media, OMV recorded *The Pagan Prosperity*, for which Grusom renamed himself Galder: personnel shuffles followed and only he and Jardar remained. Renowned session drummer Gene Hoglan was recruited for *Ill-Natured Spiritual Invasion*, recorded at the famous death metal studio Sunlight (the controls all had to be altered to avoid the album sounding like yet another Sunlight-recorded death metal release). After another album, *Revelation 666: The Curse Of Damnation*, was recorded with Peter

Tägtgren in 1999, Galder joined Dimmu Borgir, leaving Old Man's Child on hold. However, he did manage to record *In Defiance Of Existence* in 2003, with Dimmu/Cradle drummer Nick Barker.

RECOMMENDED ALBUM:
The Pagan Prosperity
(Century Media, 1997)
www.oldmanschild.tk

Onslaught

Bristol thrash metal band Onslaught consisted of five fine musicians – guitarists Nige Rockett and Rob Trotman, bassist Jim Hinder, drummer Steve Grice and vocalist Sy Keeler – but their superclean sound was somewhat brittle and it's this that makes them sound so dated today. Albums for Music For Nations attracted a dedicated group of fans, but on 1989's *In Search Of Sanity* Keeler was replaced by Steve Grimmett, leading to a meatier overall sound. Unfortunately, the band just couldn't compete with the might of American speed metal and folded in the early Nineties.

RECOMMENDED ALBUM:
The Force (Music For Nations, 1986)

Opeth

The progressive Swedish death metal quintet Opeth were named after a lunar city that appeared in a Wilbur Smith novel. The line-up, founded in 1990, centres on the singer and guitarist Mikael Akerfeldt, who has performed on two Katatonia albums and also on Edge Of Sanity's *Crimson*. Together with Peter Lindgren (guitar), Martin Lopez (drums) and Martin Mendez (bass), Akerfeldt performs highly complex, unorthodox metal with hints of prog-rock, acoustic balladry, doom metal and even jazz.

The UK label Candlelight Records signed the band in 1993, releasing the debut album Orchid two years later and *Morningrise* in 1996. Both albums displayed a diverse range of influences and deft playing, attracting the attention of Century Media, who licensed both albums in the US. Opeth went on to support Morbid Angel.

The next album, a concept record in which a narrative permeates each song, was entitled *My Arms, Your Hearse*. The tracks were mixed so as to blend directly into one another, while the last word of each song was used as the title of the next. The band then signed to Peaceville Records and released *Still Life* in October 1999. More albums followed until 2003, when the superb *Damnation* and *Deliverance* albums were released in quick succession: the former an atmospheric, ambient record, the latter an aggressive death metal set. Opeth remain a truly innovative band.

RECOMMENDED ALBUM:
Morningrise (Candlelight, 1996)
www.opeth.com

Mikael Akerfeldt on the classics
"I was introduced to heavy metal through Black Sabbath when I was around five years old. I remember because I was scared of the music when I first heard it. The voice in 'Iron Man' almost made me shit my pants. I was intrigued and scared at the same time. I loved it instantly, I guess. I didn't like Venom, I thought it was done by lousy players as I was more into the Scorpions. Eventually I found out about bands who could be fast and extreme but also controlled. Some of the thrash bands were really good musicians which was important to me."

Opprobrium

Initially playing under the name Incubus until the rise of the lame nu-metal act of the same name, Brazilian brothers Francis and Moyses Howard released two albums in 1988 and 1990 but came into their own with the excellent *Discerning Forces* of 2000. However, they appear to have been inactive since then.

RECOMMENDED ALBUM:
Discerning Forces (Nuclear Blast, 2000)

Overdose

Overdose are remembered today for having the potential to accompany their countrymen Sepultura out of the Brazilian slum of Belo Horizonte in the late Eighties, although they didn't rise to the same heights. Local label Cogumelo offered them a split album deal in 1985, which became the *Seculo XX/Bestial Devastation* release with Sepultura. However, their subsequent releases were only released in Brazil, with a notable exception being 1992's *Circus Of Death*. After 1995's *Scars*, the band fell into obscurity.

RECOMMENDED ALBUM:
Circus Of Death (Pavement, 1995)

Overkill

New York thrashers Overkill were founded in 1983, with Bobby 'Blitz' Ellsworth (vocals), Bobby Gustafson (guitar), D.D. Vernie (bass) and Rat Skates (drums) forming the initial line-up. They took their name from the Motörhead song of the same name. Signing to Metallica/Anthrax/Manowar label Megaforce, a self-titled EP was released the following year, which led to a long-standing deal with Atlantic, and the Overkill debut album, *Feel The Fire*, appeared in 1985.

The next album, *Taking Over*, was released in 1987 and later that year, the live EP, the very punk *Fuck You*, saw new drummer Sid Falck join the band. Bobby Gustafson left the band after 1989's *The Years Of Decay*; his replacements were Rob Cannavino and Merrit Gant. Subsequent Overkill recordings have seen personnel come and go, but Ellsworth has remained squarely committed to the band, going as far as releasing two albums in 1999, the much-praised *Necroshine* and a covers album which contained the obvious Lemmy track plus a set of punk and trad-metal standards. The most recent album, 2002's *Kill Box 13*, saw the band slow down but retain its heaviness. More importantly, Overkill are much admired among metal fans of many stripes and deserve their place in history.

RECOMMENDED ALBUM:
Taking Over (Atlantic, 1987)
www.wreckingcrew.com

Bobby Ellsworth on the politics of extremity

"We knew we never belonged anywhere but the fuckin' underground, which simplified the equation a lot, because it took popularity out of it. We were dead in 1991, we knew that. Someone said, metal's dead and so are fuckin' Overkill! But out of ignorance or determination I kept us going.

Grunge came in and deposed so many of the bands that were here, which was a thriving scene, but we looked at that as an opportunity. Change is necessary to cleanse the scene. What happens with any scene is that there are a handful of bands in a genre or subgenre, and later there comes an over-saturation of bands. The record companies are the perpetrators because they wanna get in. In our case there were so many bands who came in and wanted to be Def Leppard that the scene had to be cleansed.

Now thrash has taken on social elements and political ideology, and has progressed internally, but back then it was about release. It was about action and reaction and explosion. It was about the angry young white guy screaming at the top of his lungs, 'I'm not gonna take this shit'."

Pantera

Formed in Texas in 1981, Pantera started life as an extremely trashy glam-metal band along the lines of Warrant or early Poison. The band – later vocalist Phil Anselmo, guitarist Darrell Abbott (aka Dimebag Darrell), his brother, drummer Vincent Abbott (aka Vinnie Paul) and bassist Rex Brown – were the brunt of much ridicule for their first two albums, *Metal Magic* and *Projects In The Jungle*. These featured the vocal talents of Terrence Lee, but the recruitment of Anselmo saw the band move towards their later, much harder sound. Critics were silenced by the tougher *Power Metal* album and Pantera gained credibility.

Ironically, they went on to straddle the extreme and mainstream scenes with a satisfying blend of thrash, Southern rock and all-out heavy metal, with Anselmo's deranged roar and Darrell's meaty riffing. On July 13, 1996, the singer overdosed on heroin, 'dying' for five minutes before medics brought him back, and the band continued onward. However, the Pantera recipe became stale by the turn of the century, and amid internal strife, the band split in 2003. The Abbott brothers went on to form Damageplan and Anselmo formed Superjoint Ritual. Tragically, Dimebag was murdered on stage in late 2004: his death was widely referred to as 'metal's 9/11'.

RECOMMENDED ALBUM:
Far Beyond Driven (Atco, 1994)
www.pantera.com

Pan-Thy-Monium

Swedish death metal with a difference, Pan-Thy-Monium were the project of everyman Dan Swanö (see Edge Of Sanity) and incorporated brass and other unorthodox instruments into the standard DM riffage. Two albums, *Khaoohs* and *Dawn Of Dreams*, showcased this slightly unnerving blend.

RECOMMENDED ALBUM:
Dawn Of Dreams (Osmose, 1992)

Paradise Lost

A doomdeath band formed in Halifax, England, in 1988, Paradise Lost – named after the Milton poem – consist of Nick Holmes (vocals), Gregor Mackintosh (guitar), Aaron Aedy (guitar), and Steve Edmondson (bass), while the original drummer, Matt Archer, was eventually replaced by Lee Morris. Signing to Peaceville, the *Lost Paradise* album was released in 1990, a mixture of sludgy doom metal with Holmes' DM vocals and the odd Gothic reference. The latter aspect was fully honed on the appropriately-titled (and now-classic) *Gothic* EP of 1991 and the band signed to Music For Nations.

More albums and two EPs – 1992's *As I Die* and *Seals The Sense* of the following year – saw the band continue the literary and Sisters Of Mercy references of before, gradually edging away from death metal and towards a more electronic-based approach. Indeed, later albums such as *Believe In Nothing* and *Symbol Of Life* could be said to be more keyboard and atmosphere-based in parts than guitar-based.

RECOMMENDED ALBUM:
Lost Paradise (Peaceville, 1990)
www.paradiselost.co.uk

Paradox

A German thrash metal band, Paradox released the Metallica-influenced *Product Of Imagination* and *Heresy* at the height of the thrash movement but disbanded shortly afterwards. A revised line-up was assembled in 2000, and released the *Collision Course* album.

RECOMMENDED ALBUM:
Product Of Imagination (Roadracer, 1987)

Peccatum

A Norwegian band combining black metal with electronic and classical influences, Peccatum are ex-Emperor frontman Ihsahn and his partner Ihriel. Another member, PZ, returned to his main band, Source Of Tide. Founded in 1998 as a side-project to the much-worshipped Emperor, Peccatum have released three records to date – *Strangling From Within* (1999), *Oh My Regrets, Amor Fati* (both 2000) and *Lost In Reverie* (2003). Released on Ihsahn's Mnemosyne label, they are mysterious, captivating records that repay the listener's perseverance amply, but will probably remain of cult interest only.

RECOMMENDED ALBUM:
Strangling From Within (Mnemosyne, 1999)
www.peccatum.com

Pessimist

US death metal band Pessimist were founded in Baltimore in 1993 after founder member Kelly McLauchlin (ex-Death Force, Resistance and Cauldron) recorded demos with Rob Kline (vocals) and brothers Chris Pernia (drums) and Tony Pernia (bass). Support slots with Deicide, Incantation and Suffocation preceded the

1995 EP *Absence Of Light* and the *Let The Demons Rest* demo of 1996.

Signing to the Lost Disciple label and releasing a self-produced 1997 debut album, *Cult Of The Initiated,* Pessimist were praised for their old-school attack and went on to play with Morbid Angel, Cannibal Corpse, Immolation, Vader, Nile, Cryptopsy, Incantation, Krisiun, Monstrosity, Gorguts, Malevolent Creation, Dying Fetus, Angel Corpse, Testament and Napalm Death. In 1999 the *Blood For The Gods* album continued to make headway for the band and, despite the departure of some key members shortly afterwards, they continue to record – the latest album, *Slaughtering The Faithful*, was recorded with Erik Rutan (Morbid Angel/Hate Eternal).

RECOMMENDED ALBUM:
Cult Of The Initiated (Lost Disciple, 1997)
www.pessimist.com

Pestilence

The Dutch death metal band Pestilence produced some innovative music before calling it a day in 1995. The band, Martin van Drunen (vocals, bass), Patrick Mameli (guitar), Randy Meinhard (guitar) and Marco Foddis (drums), were talented players whose leanings towards progressive rock led to their ultimate dissatisfaction with the extreme metal scene. Their debut album, 1988's *Malleus Maleficarum*, showcased the band's skills at a time when they were happy to knock out aggressive, biting death metal without recoursing to other genres, and has since gained classic status. 1994's *Spheres* was, however, the end of a half-decade of decline away from the attack of before, and the band members seemed only too happy to form newer, non-metal projects.

RECOMMENDED ALBUM:
Malleus Maleficarum (Roadrunner, 1988)

Pig Destroyer

Virginia grindcore act Pig Destroyer were formed in 1997 by vocalist J.R. Hayes, ex-Anal Cunt guitarist Scott Hull and drummer John Evans and released a self-titled demo. This led to a split 7" with Orchid and a slot at New Jersey's Paperweight Festival. Evans was replaced by Brian Harvey and the band toured with Discordance Axis, Phobia, Daybreak, The Dillinger Escape Plan, and Cattlepress. An album, *Explosions In Ward 6*, gained them more publicity. Signing to Relapse, PD issued another split single and an album, *38 Counts Of Battery*, an intense collection based on the blast-and-growl approach. Subsequent releases *Prowler In The Yard* and *Terrifyer* kept the heaviness counts high.

RECOMMENDED ALBUM:
38 Counts Of Battery (Relapse, 2002)

Possessed

The San Francisco band Possessed were the world's first death metal act, although Death took the genre much further and the late Bathory frontman Quorthon claimed to have coined the term first. Just to confuse matters, their satanic lyrics led to them being labelled a black metal band when the term referred only to themes rather than musical style. Consisting of Jeff Becerra (vocals/bass), Larry Lalonde (guitar), Mike Torrao (guitar), and Mike Sus (drums), Possessed were formed in 1983.

Their contribution to Metal Blade's *Metal Massacre VI* album led to a deal with Combat and the first album, *Seven Churches*, was released in 1985. Along with Death's *Scream Bloody Gore*, it stands today as a landmark release in US metal and won fans' approval for its Slayer-esque thrash qualities. Later albums moved much more in a death metal direction, with Becerra's vocals pioneering the genre's guttural style. After a second album, however, friction between the musicians led to a split. 1987's *Eyes Of Horror* EP proved to be the swansong of Possessed and Lalonde went on to join psycho-funkers Primus. After the split, plans were made for a reformation, but were shelved when Becerra was left paralysed after a shooting incident just after the recording of a new demo. Torrao did attempt a comeback in 1993 with a new lineup and two demos, but the same year's best-of package was the final Possessed recording.

RECOMMENDED ALBUM:
Seven Churches (Combat, 1985)

Jeff Becerra on those damn labels
"First there was black metal, then we did death metal, later speed metal, then thrash metal. Everyone was jockeying for position for their own metal term. I wrote the song in an English class when I was supposed to be doing a test. Needless to say I flunked the test but invented the term 'death metal'."

Powermad

American thrash act Powermad were solely memorable for their appearance in the David Lynch movie *Wild At Heart*: the sight of Nicholas Cage and Laura Dern dancing along with the band's superfast song 'Slaughterhouse' is one that will remain with the viewer long after the film itself has faded from memory. Signed to the Combat label as part of the Bootcamp Series, the band released an album called *Absolute Power* and promptly broke up.

RECOMMENDED ALBUM:
Absolute Power (Combat, 1989)

Profanatica

Cult US black metal act Profanatica were formed in 1989 by Aragon Amori, Paul Ledney, Brett Makowski and John McEntee, sometime of Blood Thirsty Death and Revenant, under the name Incantation (see separate entry). However, artistic differences caused Paul, Aragon and Brett to leave and form Profanatica, recording two 1990 demos, *Putrescence Of...* and *Broken Throne Of Christ*. John Gelso (ex-Toten) was recruited and a deal was signed with After World Records, who released the *Weeping in Heaven* 7" EP.

After a move to Osmose and a split 12" with the Colombian band Masacre, extensive tours followed. Famously, the band never managed to record an album: although a set called *The Raping Of The Virgin Mary* was due to be recorded, the master tapes were destroyed in the studio (no-one knows how this happened) and the band split. A 2001 reunion was scheduled but came to nothing.

RECOMMENDED ALBUM:
Broken Throne Of Christ (demo, 1990)

Pungent Stench

Viennese death metal band, Pungent Stench were formed in 1988 by Martin Schirenc (vocals/guitar), Jacek Perkowski (bass) and the excellently-named Alex Wank (drums). After the *Mucus Secretion* demo led to a split EP with Disharmonic Orchestra, Nuclear Blast signed them and three albums followed. Labelling themselves 'Sado-Maso-Metal', the band have issued a sequence of albums with the latest, *Ampeuty*, a typically grim offering.

RECOMMENDED ALBUM:

For God Your Soul... For Me Your Flesh
(Nuclear Blast, 1990)
www.pungentstench.net

Pyogenesis

Pyogenesis's debut recording, 1992's self-titled EP, released by Osmose, was a powerful doomdeath work, as was the *Waves Of Erotasia* EP of two years later and the debut album, 1995's *Sweet X-Rated Nothings*. However, the South German band, whose most permanent members have been Wolle Maier (drums), Tim Eiermann (vocals/guitar) and Flo V. Schwarz (vocals/guitar), moved

Pungent Stench – Sado-Maso-Metal, it says here

rapidly into experimental territory, developing their use of electronics and becoming a much more alternative rock act. Quirky points like the two vocalists' duets and a cover of Toto's 'Africa' have denied them mainstream success but the band continues to be popular on the festival circuit throughout Europe. *She Makes Me Wish I Had A Gun* (2002) is the latest album at the time of writing.

RECOMMENDED ALBUM:

Unpop (Nuclear Blast, 1997)
www.pyogenesis.com

Rage

A German speed metal band, Rage avoided the rough edges of thrash and the polished blandness of much power metal and laced their tunes with hooky choruses. Driven by the nimble bass-playing and soaring vocals of Peter 'Peavey' Wagner, Rage started out in the early Eighties as Avenger, who released two more or less standard rock albums. After a name-change and an EP, *Depraved To Black*, the band moved from their original label Wishbone to Noise, home to Celtic Frost and Running Wild among others.

The debut album, *Reign Of Fear*, was followed up by tours with Destruction and Kreator and for some time it seemed that the title of leaders of the intelligent thrash scene would fall to Rage. However, despite a successful second album, 1987's *Execution Guaranteed*, the other members of the band – guitarist Guiness and drummer Jörg Michael – left and Peavey recruited ex-Warlock guitarist Rudy Graf. When Graf also departed, Wagner added Manni Schmidt (guitar) and Chris Efthimiadis (drums). The band's best-known album, *Perfect Man*, was released in 1988. Several subsequent albums have seen members come and go, but Rage remain popular on the festivals circuit, introducing classical and other diverse influences into their sound.

RECOMMENDED ALBUM:
Perfect Man (Noise, 1988)
www.rage-on.de

Ragnarok

A black metal band from Norway, Ragnarok was formed in 1994 by Jontho Pantera (guitar/keyboards) and Jerv (bass/vocals) who, along with a drummer and vocalist, Possessed Evil, had previously been in a band called Thoth. After recruiting Rym (vocals) and Thyme (guitar), Ragnarok recorded a 1995 demo, *Pagan Land*, and signed to Head Not Found. Songs from the demo were re-recorded for a debut album, *Nattferd*, which aroused some interest among black metallers, attracting the attention of Dimmu Borgir's Shagrath, who played synth on the follow-up, 1997's *Arising Realm*. After the recording of a third album, *Diabolical Age*, Thyme left and a second guitarist Sander joined the band.

RECOMMENDED ALBUM:
Nattferd (Head Not Found, 1995)
www.ragnarokhorde.com

Rakoth

From Obrinsk, Russia, black metal band Rakoth were formed as Bedevil in 1996 by Leshy (drums), Ilya (guitars), Rustam (vocals) and Miguel (bass). Line-up dissent left Rustam the sole remaining member plus new recruits Black, Den and Dy. A 1997 demo, *Tales Of The Worlds Unreal*, led to a full album, *Superstatic Equilibrium*, and a deal with the Italian label Code666. The *Planeshift* and *Jabberworks* albums have seen the band make progress internationally.

RECOMMENDED ALBUM:
Planeshift (Code666, 1999)
http://utenti.lycos.it/rakoth/home.htm

Rebaelliun

A Brazilian death metal band that plays as hard and fast as countrymen Krisiun but with a rawness that makes them a little harder to stomach, Rebaelliun were formed in 1998 by guitarists F. Penna Correa and Ronaldo Lima. Bass and vocals are handled by Sandro M and drums by Marcello Marzari. After a 1998 demo and a tour of Europe with Deicide and others, the band signed to Hammerheart and released an EP, *At War*. An album, *Burn The Promised Land*, appeared in 2000 and Rebaelliun continue to play devilishly powerful music.

RECOMMENDED ALBUM:
Burn The Promised Land
(Hammerheart, 2000)
http://listen.to/rebaelliun

Reign Of Erebus

Black metal band Reign Of Erebus – Cthonian (vocals), Crucem (guitar/bass), Ewchymlaen (synth/bass/guitar) and Xael (drums) – have two albums behind them. *Humanracist: A Higher Form Of Human* appeared in 2001 and its follow-up, *Inversion Principle*, came three years later. Having left the Blackend label, the band are currently looking for a deal.

RECOMMENDED ALBUM:
Inversion Principle (Blackend, 2004)
www.reignoferebus.com

Repulsion

A short-lived but legendary grindcore band from Flint, Michigan, Repulsion (initially Tempter, then Ultraviolence and then Genocide) originally consisted of Scott

Carlson (vocals), Matt Olivo (guitars), Sean MacDonald (bass), Matt Diffin (guitars) and James Auten (drums). After line-up changes, the band recorded a demo in 1984 that caused a buzz on the tape-trading network. A plan to join forces with Death flopped in 1985 and another demo, *Violent Death*, was released the same year. A more professional recording, *The Stench Of Burning Death*, showcased the band's insane speed and heaviness, and a self-funded album (costing $300) called *Slaughter Of The Innocent* also appeared. This was then remixed and reissued as *Horrified* by Jeff Walker and Bill Steer of Carcass – Repulsion fans who ran a label called Necrosis. The Repulsion story ended there, although *Horrified* was reissued as a double CD by Relapse in 2003.

RECOMMENDED ALBUM:
Horrified (Necrosis, 1989)

Ribspreader

Swedish death metal band Ribspreader (named after an autopsy instrument) were formed in 2003 by Rogga Johansson and Andreas Karlsson. The legendary Dan Swanö played drums as a returned favour to Johansson, who had performed death vocals on Swanö's band Edge Of Sanity's *Crimson II* album. He also contributed lead guitar to an album, *Bolted To The Cross*. A deal with Karmageddon Media followed and the band now tours.

RECOMMENDED ALBUM:
Bolted To The Cross
(Karmageddon Media, 2004)
http://listen.to/ribspreader

Rogga Johannson on classic extremity
"The classic stuff mainly represented by Death, Massacre, Grave, Entombed and Hypocrisy will always hold a special place for us. Mainly because back then nothing was dated or overused so those guys had no problem at all hammering classics wich still today kick the shit out of most bands, Ribspreader included."

Ritual Carnage

US/Japanese thrash metal band Ritual Carnage were formed in 1993 in Japan and signed a deal with Osmose shortly after. Debut album *The Highest Law* contained death metal elements, but later albums are more straightforward thrash.

RECOMMENDED ALBUM:
The Highest Law (Osmose, 1998)

Rotting Christ

The Athens, Greece black metal band Rotting Christ are Sakis Tolis (guitar/vocals), his brother Themis (drums), Costas (guitar), Andreas (bass) and George (keyboards). As it has a certain gothic sensibility, the label 'dark metal' has been applied to their music, which was first

Rotting Christ – gothic Greeks

exposed to the public in 1987 on the *Passage To Arturo* E.P. The Tolis brothers produced several albums as a duo – albeit with the help of Samael drummer and producer Xy – before recruiting the other musicians in 1998. Costas departed after the release of the latest album, *Sanctus Diavolos*.

RECOMMENDED ALBUM:
Sleep Of The Angels (Century Media, 1999)
www.rotting-christ.com

Sabbat

An Eighties thrash band from Britain that could almost stand up to the US Big Four in terms of quality and aggression, Sabbat were formed by Martin Walkyier (vocals), Andy Sneap (guitar) Fraser Craske (bass) and Simon Negus (drums) in the mid-Eighties, recording a powerful debut for Noise, 1988's *History Of A Time To Come*. The album was noted on the UK scene for Sneap's precise riffing and fans looked forward to a follow-up.

However, Sneap and Walkyier fell out over musical direction; the vocalist wanted to do more pagan-based songs, but Sneap was fed up with these. Walkyier left and formed the folk-metal band Skyclad, while Sneap recruited the singer Ritchie Desmond and a second guitarist, Simon Jones; Craske also left at this point.

The second album, *Dreamweavers*, consolidated on the debut's success but fans missed Walkyier's vocals and after a third recording with a new guitarist and bassist, Neil Watson and Wayne Banks, the band split. Sneap has gone on to be a renowned producer, with Stampin' Ground, Kreator and Exodus among others on his CV.

RECOMMENDED ALBUM:
History Of A Time To Come (Noise, 1988)

Andy Sneap on the Bay Area scene
❝When I was younger I always had this picture in my mind of the Bay Area as this huge scene which was going off, and then later when I was working out there I realised that it's more a collective group of people who all knew each other and were trying to out-shred each

other. So it wasn't as big as the magazines hyped it up to be. Really it was a few individuals who were keeping the whole thing going.❞

Sacramentum

Sweden's Sacramentum, a melodic death/black metal band, consist of Nisse Karlén (bass/vocals), Anders Brolycke (guitar) and Nicklas Rudolfsson (drums). The band was formed in 1990 under the name Tumulus and released a 1992 demo, *Sedes Impiorum*. A later recording, a five-track tape entitled *Finis Malorum*, led to a deal with Adipocere, who later released it untouched.

Sacramentum's debut album, *Far Away From The Sun*, was released after some delays in 1996 and a European tour with Ancient Rites, Bewitched and Enthroned followed. Signing to Century Media in 1997, two further albums were produced by King Diamond guitarist Andy Larocque. The band remains periodically active.

RECOMMENDED ALBUM:
The Coming Of Chaos
(Century Media, 1997)
http://fly.to/sacramentum

Sacrilege

Another Swedish melodic death metal band, Sacrilege attracted the attention of Black Sun Records in 1995 after recording two demos, *To Where Light Can't Reach* and the subsequent *And Autumn Failed*. A deal was struck after the band made it to the semi-final of the Gothenburg battle-of-the-bands competition, Rockslaget. The first album, *Lost In The Beauty You Slay*, was released in late 1996, immediately attracting fans with its melody and aggression. Vocalist Daniel Svensson adds a harmonious edge with his high, almost operatic singing style. However, the second album, *The Fifth Season*, was a far heavier and faster effort, and the band continued to play a role in the New Wave Of Swedish Death Metal. They split up at the end of decade.

RECOMMENDED ALBUM:
Lost In The Beauty You Slay
(Black Sun, 1996)

Sadistik Exekution

Sadistik Exekution, formed in Australia in 1986, play a crossover blend of black and death metal. By 1991 a stable line-up had

done some recording, with the *We Are Death Fukk You* album leading to tours in Europe with Impaled Nazarene and Absu. Shows were notable for their extreme violence, including attacks on the audience. Activity since then has been minimal.

RECOMMENDED ALBUM:

We Are Death Fukk You

(independent, 1991)

http://fade.to/sadx

Sarcophagus

A German black metal band consisting of Jay Harris (vocals, guitar, keyboards), Daniel Guenther (guitar), Andrew Kolar (bass) and Duane Timlin (drums), Sarcophagus was formed in 1991 and recorded two demos, *Cursed Are The Dead* and *Apathy*. The latter sold 1500 copies and two EPs were released by the band, *Sarcophagus* (1993) and *Deadnoise* (1994), before the band signed to Interment Records and issued the *Der Ubermensch* mini-album. After a second album, Pulverizer compiled the band's demos onto one album and Sarcophagus signed to the independent Nightfall label for one album, *Requiem To The Death Of Passion*.

RECOMMENDED ALBUM:

Requiem To The Death Of Passion

(Nightfall, 1998)

Satariel *(Above)*

Formed in 1993 by Pär Johansson, Mikael Degerman and Magnus Alakangas, Satariel started out performing drum machine-propelled black metal. A demo, *Thy Heavens*, appeared a year later and the band signed to the Impure label from France. After line-up changes another demo, *Hellfuck* (the title of which was later borrowed by Dan Swanö for his *Infestdead* album) appeared and tours with At The Gates and others followed. In 1997 they entered the Sunlight studio with Tomas Skogsberg to record a debut album, *Lady Lust Lilith*. The Pulverised label released it in '98 and later the band moved to Hammerheart. A new album, featuring a guest spot from Candlemass singer Messiah Marcolin, is set for release.

RECOMMENDED ALBUM:

Lady Lust Lilith (Pulverised, 1998)

www.satariel.com

Pär Johansson on the essence of extreme metal satisfaction

❝We write music we would like to hear ourselves, which we do not find anywhere else out there. Good music is always good music and bad music is always bad music, regardless of what it's labelled as, remember that.❞

Satyricon

A leading Norwegian black metal band, Satyricon was formed in 1992 by Satyr (vocals, guitar) and Frost (drums). Satyr runs a successful record label, Moonfog, home to Darkthrone since their split with Peaceville (see Darkthrone entry) and, although Satyricon albums are now distributed worldwide by Nuclear Blast, Moonfog continues to issue them at home in Norway. Satyr also records for his label under the pseudonyms Storm and Wongraven (the latter is his surname).

Satyricon's first demo, *The Forest Is My Throne*, set the anti-Christian tone for future releases, and was later released as one side of a split album with Viking metallers Enslaved in 1996. Their rapid, aggressive but melodic music utilises keyboards to good effect, a defining approach on their debut album, 1994's *Dark Medieval Times*. Another album, *The Shadow Throne*, featured Samoth of Emperor on guitar. A guest appearance by Darkthrone guitarist Nocturno Culto gave the second album, *Nemesis Divina*, a raw edge, while the next recording, *Megiddo*, contained remixes as well as a cover of Motörhead's 'Orgasmatron'.

Many fans will admit that it is with the third album, *Rebel Extravaganza*, that the band have finally come of age, after yet another successful EP, *Intermezzo II*. RE featured session playing by Snorre Ruch of Thorns, Darkthrone's Fenriz and non-metal artists Ra and Trine Svensen. *Volcano* (2002) was more sophisticated still.

RECOMMENDED ALBUM:
Rebel Extravaganza (Moonfog, 1999)
www.satyricon.no

Sentenced

Finnish band Sentenced are currently one of the best of the newly melodic, dark ex-death metallers. The band – Ville Laihiala (vocals), Sami Lopakka (guitar), Miika Tenkula (guitar), Sami Kukkohovi (bass) and Vesa Ranta (drums) – were formed in the early Nineties in the town of Oulu, showcasing a standard death metal approach on initial releases *Shadows Of The Past*, *North From Here* and *Amok*. An EP, the grandiose *Love And Death*, continued their move towards a more conventional, if still dark-tinged sound. Tours with The Gathering, My Dying Bride and Therion, as well as a slot at the 1997 Dynamo Festival

and gigs in South America and Japan established Sentenced still more in the Scandinavian scene. Later albums such as *The Cold White Light* (2002) saw them expand their vision still further.

RECOMMENDED ALBUM:
Amok (Century Media, 1995)
www.sentenced.org

Septic Flesh

A Greek death metal band who play rapid, brutal music tempered with clean male and female vocals, the other side of Septic Flesh is a mellow, almost ambient approach, creating atmospheric soundscapes on their albums. Formed in 1990 and signing to the Holy label, Septic Flesh pioneered what they called 'dreamy death metal' on a series of albums which feature extensive soundscapes. The line-up is currently Spiros A (death vocals and bass), Sotiris V (clean vocals and guitars), Chris A (guitars) and Akis K (drums).

RECOMMENDED ALBUM:
Esoptron (Holy, 1995)
http://go.to/SepticFlesh

Sepultura

The Brazilian thrash/death metal band Sepultura, formed in Belo Horizonte in 1984, consisted for the next 13 years of Max Cavalera (guitar, vocals), his brother Igor (drums), Paulo Jr. (bass), and Jairo T (guitar – replaced in 1987 by Andreas Kisser). Starting out as a raw, unsophisticated speed metal outfit, the band matured into a powerful, politically outspoken beast.

A split EP, *Bestial Devastation*, was released in 1985 with fellow Brazilians Overdose, but its production values were so poor that even hardened thrash fans couldn't sympathise with it and the band only started to gain a reputation after the release of an album, *Morbid Visions*. Both records were issued by the local Cogumelo label; a move to a larger company was inevitable and Sepultura moved to Roadrunner. Three classic albums followed – *Schizophrenia*, *Beneath The Remains* and *Arise*, which broke the band internationally. 1993's *Chaos AD* saw the band slow down from thrash tempos, apart from the scathing 'Biotech Is Godzilla', a Jello Biafra–penned attack on the politicians behind the 1993 Rio Earth Summit, when vagrants had been driven from the streets to present a more wholesome image to the visiting dignitaries. The album sold in huge quantities, entering the US Top 40 and also receiving praise for its innovative use of Brazilian tribal percussion. The next album, *Roots*, was a step towards the mainstream, with its slow, chunky riffs a direct influence on the nascent Korn and the nu-metal genre. Old-school fans protested.

In 1997 Cavalera left the band after internal dissent. He went on to form the successful Soulfly (see separate entry). The other members recruited a new vocalist, Derrick Greene of the US hardcore act Outface and later Overfiend. The resulting album, *Against,* was useful rather than awe-inspiring, as were its follow-ups *Nation* and *Roorback*. After a move to the SPV label Sepultura continued to play at club level. Many fans hope that the various members will one day see sense and set up a reunion with Cavalera, although this is unlikely to happen.

RECOMMENDED ALBUM:
Beneath The Remains (Roadrunner, 1989)
www.sepultura.com.br

Sepultura's 'new' line-up

Max Cavalera calls for tolerance
"If a band like AC/DC can go on forever without changing, any band can! Most metal bands are totally melodic or totally aggressive, so it's nice to be somewhere in between. I try to enjoy everything, I listen to everything. People should be able to listen to old shit and new shit and they're both great. There is a big separation – people should be able to listen to Slipknot and Manowar. It's really stupid. The barriers have got to be broken down. I've worked with Tom Araya and with Corey Taylor, to show that this is the old school and this is the new school."

Severe Torture

Founded in 1997, Dutch grind/death band Severe Torture recorded the *Baptized* demo and the 'Pray For Nothing' single on the Damnation label. A one-album deal with Fadeless followed, leading to the release of *Feasting On Blood* and tours with Cannibal Corpse, Deicide, Vader, Hate Eternal and Vomitory. Extensive tours and two more albums have followed, with the band's

equally extreme artwork and music (the vocals are the most brutal of any band in this book, except for early Cryptopsy) fuelling a degree of controversy.
RECOMMENDED ALBUM:
Feasting On Blood (Fadeless, 1998)
www.severetorture.com

Shadows Fall

One of the New Wave Of American Heavy Metal bands, Shadows Fall have perfected a melody/aggression balance that attracts fans worldwide. Releasing a debut album, *Somber Eyes To The Sky,* in 1997 through their guitarist Matt Bachand's label, Lifeless Records, the band caught the attention of Century Media, who picked the album up and signed them. The next record, *Of One Blood*, was followed by tours with bands such as Candiria, Misfits, King Diamond, Glassjaw and In Flames. 2002's *The Art Of Balance* was their most popular recording to date and was the first album in Century Media's history to sell over 100,000 copies in the US. A fourth album, *The War Within*, is set to expand their dominance still further.
RECOMMENDED ALBUM:
The Art Of Balance (Century Media, 2002)
www.shadowsfall.com

Shadows Land

A technical death metal band from Poland, Shadows Land were formed in 1995, although no music appeared until the *Epitaph* demo two years later. *Promo 99* followed and was released by the Demonic label and European tours followed. A full-length album, *Ante Christum (Natum),* showcased the band's super-aggressive, complex approach, while live shows featured their drummer wrapping himself in barbed wire.
RECOMMENDED ALBUM:
Ante Christum (Natum) (Osmose, 2004)
www.shadowsland.metal.pl

Vocalist Aro 666 muses
❝We're searching for something which will satisfy us as musicians. We're fascinated by creating new sounds. We look for the 'devil' in music, and new solutions, not boredom... The creative variety which we have built over several years in Shadows Land means that we look at music in a different and unusual way. And what is 'vision'? We simply want to make good and interesting music and to achieve satisfaction with this. That is all. The drive behind the music fills us with emotion and power –

Shadows Fall – new wave leaders

with the devil – and we get dizzy when we're playing the songs, the emotion is so strong. You fall into a trance with the pain and the obsession. Music is good or shit. That is all."

Sigh

Sigh are a Japanese metal band now signed to Century Media, but whose first album was released through Euronymous' Deathlike Silence Productions and the associated Voices Of Wonder label (see Mayhem entry). Formed in 1989 by Mirai Kawashima (bass, vocals, keyboards), Satoshi (guitar) and Kazuki (drums), Sigh recorded two demos, *Desolation* and *Tragedies*, as well as releasing a 7" single, 'Requiem For The Fools', through Wild Rags Records. Mirai

Sigh – unclassifiable, but excellent

sent the latter to Euronymous in Oslo, who offered them a deal and encouraged them to dress in black capes onstage and to wear corpsepaint.

As Japan is mostly a Buddhist country, the idea of a Satanist approach was invalid, but the band have claimed an interest in Mikkyo, a set of occult beliefs which advocate the attaining of spiritual strength through chanting mantras. Sigh play black metal with avant-garde psychedelic touches, heavily influenced by Celtic Frost and Hawkwind and balanced almost exactly by the weighty orchestration which they use, layering sampled classical instruments on the guitars and including horror-movie samples. Western reviewers have been simultaneously impressed by the refreshing approach which the band bring to the black metal formula and intimidated by the layered complexity of the music. 2001's *Imaginary Sonicscape* was an epic work which appealed to fans from almost all areas of unorthodox music. Kawashima also performs in Necrophagia and has sessioned with Meads Of Asphodel.

RECOMMENDED ALBUM:
Hail Horror Hail (Cacophonous, 1997)
http://listen.to/sigh

Sinister

A Dutch black/death metal band featuring Mike (vocals), André (guitar), Ron (guitar/bass) and Aad (drums), Sinister were formed in 1988 and released a demo, *Perpetual Damnation*, the following year. It sold 1500 copies and led to a tour in the Benelux countries with Disharmonic Orchestra and Entombed.

A self-titled EP was released in 1990 on Seraphic Decay and the band contributed two songs to a compilation album. The following year saw a split single with Monastery, and concerts with Atrocity and Morgoth. All this underground work attracted Nuclear Blast, who signed them in 1991 and released the Sinister debut, *Cross The Styx*. A female vocalist, Rachel, was recruited to extreme effect, but the band parted ways in 2004.

RECOMMENDED ALBUM:
Cross The Styx (Nuclear Blast, 1992)

Six Feet Under

Originally an Obituary side-project, Six Feet Under pursue a similarly grinding, gore-laden direction, with Chris Barnes (vocals), Terry Butler (bass), Greg Gall (drums) and Steve Swanson (guitar)

forming the current line-up. Barnes joined the band full-time after leaving fellow gore-merchants Cannibal Corpse in 1995, and the original guitarist, Obituary's Allen West, was replaced by ex-Massacre guitarist Steve Swanson in early 1998.

The band have issued an EP (*Alive And Dead*, 1996) and several albums to date, all as sludgy and lyrically repulsive as a CV for any of these three bands would indicate, although recent covers of Iron Maiden's 'Wrathchild', Thin Lizzy's 'Jailbreak' and Kiss' 'War Machine' reveal some of the band's earliest influences. The latest album, 2003's *Bringer Of Blood*, was reviewed positively by many magazines, even if the death metal scene is currently more focused on European melodic death than the pioneering American version.

RECOMMENDED ALBUM:
Maximum Violence (Metal Blade, 1999)
www.sfu420.com

Skinless

Formed in 1992 Noah Carpenter (guitars) and Sherwood Webber (vocals) are the core of death metal act Skinless; recording debut album, *Progression Towards Evil*, six years later after a variety of demos and compilation appearances. Tours with Mortician and Incantation in 1999 and 2000 gained them a fanbase and the band signed to Relapse. *Foreshadowing Our Demise* was supported by a high-profile tour with Slayer, Pantera and The Dillinger Escape Plan in 2002. The following year's *From Sacrifice To Survival* album was produced by Neil Kernon (Cannibal Corpse, Judas Priest, Nevermore, Exhumed) and took Skinless to the next level.

RECOMMENDED ALBUM:
From Sacrifice To Survival (Relapse, 2003)
www.4skinless.com

Slayer

Venom introduced the idea of thrash metal to the public, and Metallica's debut album was the genre's first masterpiece, but it was Los Angeles' Slayer who took it to the world stage. With a series of groundbreaking albums, they made thrash what it is today, becoming a profound influence on the death metal scene along the way. Although Metallica, Anthrax, Megadeth, Kreator and Testament helped raise the music's profile in the Eighties, and the leading bands of the black and death genres have surpassed Slayer in terms of pure velocity, they have retained their hard-won title of kings of thrash to this day.

Slayer were formed in 1982 in Huntington Park, California by the guitarists Kerry King and Jeff Hanneman. Recruiting bassist/vocalist Tom Araya and the drummer Dave Lombardo – who had been trained as a jazz player – the quartet initially named themselves Dragonslayer after a role-playing game. The corniness of the name was soon pointed out, however, and the band wisely decided to shorten it. Another Slayer, a rock band from Texas, started life at around the same time and one or two snide comments were exchanged about being the "first Slayer", but no long-term problems ensued and the band built up a local reputation for their powerful shows, which initially featured covers of Judas Priest, Iron Maiden and other British acts' songs.

Like many Californian thrash metal bands, Slayer's first venture onto vinyl came about after Metal Blade chief and producer Brian Slagel asked the band to record a song for his *Metal Massacre* compilation series in 1983. The song 'Aggressive Perfector' was duly recorded and Slagel signed them up. Slayer's first album, *Show No Mercy*, was issued shortly afterwards. In comparison to the band's super-crisp, super-tight later albums, *SNM* now sounds murky and hamfisted, but the unrelenting aggression of the songs turned metal fans' heads everywhere.

The *Haunting The Chapel* and *Live Undead* EPs (both 1984) continued along warp speed, foggily-produced lines: the standout track of the former was 'Chemical Warfare', hailed immediately as the fastest song ever recorded – although Slayer and several other acts would go on to break that record several times on subsequent albums – which, despite Araya's amateurish vocals and primitive lyrics, remains a thrash classic to this day. However, 1985's *Hell Awaits* saw the band take a step forward, producing murderously-threatening, precisely-performed songs that completely eclipsed their previous work. High points included the title track's ludicrous but satisfyingly spooky extended intro, formed of demonic chanting and wailing guitar screeches, the lyrically repellent but musically astonishing 'Necrophiliac', and the vampire epic, 'At Dawn They Sleep'.

At this point Slayer's fortunes changed radically, having attracted the attention of Def Jam head Rick Rubin, who despite his Run DMC and Beastie Boys pedigree was also a confirmed thrash-head. Signing them up, he then produced the definitive thrash metal album, 1986's *Reign In Blood*, which has been hailed ever since as the genre's finest record. Many fans would agree that along with Metallica's *Master Of Puppets*, it's where the entire thrash metal pantheon starts and finishes. Despite the fact that the 10 songs were squeezed into just 28 minutes, each of them is a classic. Slayer's best-known track, 'Angel Of Death', is the opener, while 'Jesus Saves', 'Criminally Insane' and the colossal 'Raining Blood' have yet to be bettered in terms of sheer power and precision. 'Necrophobic', meanwhile, accelerates past a fearsome 250bpm.

The album generated some controversy due to the subject matter of 'Angel Of Death'. The song dealt in explicit detail with the horrendous exploits of the Nazi death camp scientist Dr. Josef Mengele – although he was in no way glorified or revered in the lyrics – and Def Jam's distributor CBS refused to handle the album. The publicity gained by this did sales no harm at all and the album was ultimately distributed by Geffen.

Lombardo temporarily left the band after a disagreement over tour protocol and was replaced by Tony Scaglione of Whiplash, but returned for 1988's slower, more clean-sounding *South Of Heaven*. Araya actually sang for the first time on 'Spill The Blood' and had refined his standard bark to allow the riffs to come through more clearly.

A cover of Judas Priest's 'Dissident Aggressor' was a stand-out, as was the title track and the only real nod to the velocities of *Reign In Blood*, the 'Chemical Warfare' Part Two, 'Ghosts Of War'. Fans of Slayer's early speed were slightly put off, but many others welcomed this more considered style.

A cover of The Exploited's 'Disorder' was subsequently recorded as a duet with Ice-T for the *Judgment Night* soundtrack in 1990 – the song was acceptable, but the film was dreadful. The next album, *Seasons In The Abyss*, followed the same year and became the most positively-reviewed Slayer album after *Reign In Blood*. *Seasons...* combined the venom of the first three albums with the band's new, maturer approach, losing none of the fabled Slayer attack on the way. The opener, 'War Ensemble', went on to be an MTV 'Headbanger's Ball' staple.

1992 saw Lombardo leave the band for good, forming Grip, Inc. and his place was taken by ex-Forbidden drummer Paul Bostaph (see separate entries on Grip, Inc. and Forbidden). The legendary 'Clash Of The Titans' tour followed, which saw Slayer perform on a revolving bill with two other headliners, Anthrax (Testament In The UK) and Megadeth, supported by Suicidal Tendencies. Megadeth frontman Dave Mustaine, abusing alcohol and heroin at the time and famously difficult to work with, insisted that his band never follow Slayer, much to the other bands' amusement. Slayer chose not to dignify this with an argument and went along with Mustaine's insistence.

After the release of a double live album, *Decade Of Aggression*, a period of inactivity was followed by 1994's *Divine Intervention*. Although it was another powerful, speedy album (the song 'Dittohead' was even faster than 'Necrophobic'), many fans thought that it showed signs that Slayer were treading water. Others were repelled by a sleeve image of a fan who had carved the band's name into his arm to demonstrate loyalty.

The uncomfortably-titled *Live Intrusion* video was released before Slayer mystified many fans by releasing an album of punk covers and unreleased tracks, 1996's *Undisputed Attitude*. The record didn't sell well, unsurprisingly, and Slayer appeared to have entered a rut, from which some think they have never emerged. Bostaph was then briefly replaced by Testament's John Dette, but was reinstated for 1998's *Diabolus In Musica*. An album including modern detuned touches and some worryingly nu-metal moments on the song 'Stain Of Mind', *Diabolus* caused a few fans to desert Slayer.

However, the band regained their old aggression on 2001's competent *God Hates Us All* (released, unnervingly, on 9/11) and a career-spanning box set, *Soundtrack To The Apocalypse* (2003) sold well. *The War At The*

Slayer – perhaps the most influencial band in this book

Warfield live DVD was also a useful document. Araya guested on a Soulfly album and King on a song by Sum 41, which – while not exactly signs that they are sticking to their old-school roots – are clear indications that for a new generation of metallers, they are still as respected today as they always were. A 2003 tour on which they played the *Reign In Blood* album in its entirety was an earth-shattering experience for many fans.

RECOMMENDED ALBUM:
Reign In Blood (Def Jam, 1986)
www.slayer.net

Tom Araya on society
❝We need to start keeping an eye on each other. Look at the shit that's going on now. People just aren't happy: they'd rather see people die... you need to be aware of what's going on around you. Anything can happen. 9/11 just opened up our eyes. We need to be aware of who our neighbours are, and just get to know each other, because we've been strangers too long.

People find solace in good songs, wherever that song may take them. Society is a tough place to be. We no longer have a free society. Social commentary is a common theme we all share. There's always something to say, because there's always a critic.**❞**

Kerry King on survival
❝Every album we do has one or two semi-experimental songs, but never too much. We're just not into it. I was pissed off through the whole of *God Hates Us All*, man. Now we're working on the new record I'm thinking 'Wow, I really fucked myself up with all that hate on the last one, it's gonna be hard to outdo!' But I'm sure we'll pull it off... just put me on the freeway for an hour and I'll find somebody to yell at.

What I've realised in my older age is that a fan helps everything. You just have to get the air moving. I always thought fans were for pussies, but they've become a necessity in order to actually finish a show. I remember playing shows in Europe two years ago and it was so hot, I was on the brink of heat exhaustion. I was behind my rig, just dry-heaving. I wasn't drunk, I don't do drugs – it was just the heat.**❞**

Slipknot

Bursting onto the metal scene in 1999, the nine-man masked, overalled nu-metal outfit Slipknot emerged from the bleak environs of Des Moines, Iowa with a self-titled album. Fuelled by their death metal backgrounds, their music is extreme enough for them to warrant entry in this book, despite their own admission that they have as much in common with Korn as they do with Morbid Angel.

DJ Sid Wilson, drummer Joey Jordison, bassist Paul Gray, percussionists Chris Fehn and Shawn Crahan, guitarists James Root and Mick Thompson, sampler Craig Jones and vocalist Corey Taylor go by numbers rather than names – 0 to 8 inclusive – and initially donned masks to avoid the usual process of listeners judging them by their faces rather than their music.

Slipknot were formed in 1995 and self-released an album, *Mate. Feed. Kill. Repeat,* the following year. Jordison and Gray came from the death metal band Anal Blast, while Thompson had played in the grindcore outfit Body Pit, and the death influences in the Slipknot sound were immediately obvious. They signed to Roadrunner in 1997 via the I Am label of producer Ross Robinson and released *Slipknot,* an unrelenting record with a hidden track including the sound of the band reacting in nauseous amusement to a coprophagiac porn film.

The early Slipknot shows were frenzied affairs. Taylor's onstage tricks included offering fans the chance to inhale through an oxygen mask plugged into his rectum, as well as Crahan's habit of opening a jar containing the carcass of a decaying crow, sniffing deeply and vomiting into the crowd. Memorable UK appearances included a stage-dive by DJ Wilson off a 35-foot balcony at London's Astoria.

All this aggro led to immense expectation for the second Roadrunner album *Iowa,* which debuted at No. 1 on the UK album chart in 2001. A dark, depressed record, it spawned a major hit single in 'Left Behind' and became the biggest-selling extreme metal album in history. 2004's third album, *Volume 3: The Subliminal Verses,* was a major change in style: the band had spent the years since *Iowa* exorcising some demons in the side-projects Stone Sour, Murderdolls and To My Surprise and the result was a more multifaceted approach, with orchestral ballads and even acoustic folk songs. The fanbase was split and Slipknot's future, while still assured, is not as predictable now as it once was. For more Slipknot information, the reader is directed to the author's *Slipknot Unmasked* (Omnibus Press, 2001; revised 2003).

RECOMMENDED ALBUM:
Slipknot (Roadrunner, 1999)

Joey Jordison on the extreme metal pioneers

❝My favourite Morbid Angel album is *Blessed Are The Sick* – I think it's untouchable. *Altars Of Madness* is old school, man, that's going back. I think they really came into their own around the time of *Domination*, when they started tuning down low. 'Where The Slime Lives' is one of the best songs they've ever written. They are the prime top-of-the-line death metal band. I'm a big fan of Dark Funeral. That's a band we want to take out. I'm more into black metal, honestly, than death metal. I'm an avid follower. I love the old Marduk. I really like Raging Speedhorn, I think they're great. I think Immortal's *Damned In Black* is one of the finest black metal releases ever. They're one of the prime black metal bands.**❞**

SOD

After the demise of the hardcore/thrash project MOD led to three of the members forming Anthrax (see separate entry), guitarist Scott Ian, drummer Charlie Benante and bassist Danny Lilker (who had played in Nuclear Assault and Brutal Truth) regrouped from time to time to form Stormtroopers Of Death, or SOD. Along with frontman Billy Milano, SOD issued an album, 1985's *Speak English Or Die*. While

SOD – sporadically hard-hitting

the musicianship was superb (Ian's rhythm guitar in particular points directly to the precision of Anthrax) the band went for a sludgy production and a front cover by Benante, featuring the demonic Sergeant D, a character who appears in many of the songs. Unbelievably, the album, recorded in three days, went on to sell over 900,000 copies.

Controversy arose over the album's misogyny (Sergeant D promised to "kidnap your sister… and mail back her tits") and the band's supposed racial prejudice on 'Fuck The Middle East'. However, Ian has since claimed that they were being ironic; parodying, not espousing, right-wing values. After seven years, 1992 saw the release of the recorded-in-America *Live At Budokan* album, featuring an hilarious cover of Nirvana's 'Territorial Pissings'.

After SOD played support slots in 1997 with Anthrax in support of the latter's *Volume 8* album, Nuclear Blast signed them up and after another seven-year period since the previous album, the band issued a new record, *Bigger Than The Devil*, in 1999. The cover featured the inimitable D taking the place of Eddie on a copy of Iron Maiden's *Number Of The Beast* sleeve. The album includes a Slayer spoof, 'Evil Is In' and two old tracks from the *Speak English* days, 'Aren't You Hungry' and 'Kill The Assholes'. SOD now appears to be on permanent hold.

RECOMMENDED ALBUM:
Speak English Or Die
(1985; reissued by Megaforce, 1995)
www.sodpit.com

Scott Ian on 'Fuck The Middle East'
❝Yes, I've been challenged on it, but you know what? Most of the time I won't even defend myself. If you want to think I'm a racist, then think I'm a racist. I don't give a fuck what you think of me. I've got a very sarcastic sense of humour. We're not afraid to say anything or approach any subject. I'll say, take babies and burn them at the stake. You can say anything, it's just words. People may not like what you're saying, but that's the point.

When that song was written there was probably some specific incident somewhere in the world, the hijacking of a plane or something. The song actually was a pro-peace song, because Israel and Egypt at that time were going through their peace talks, and you had all these other countries who kept stepping in and fucking things up. If anything, this was a song that backed Israel and Egypt and said, 'why can't you all just get along?'❞

Sodom

One of the biggest of the second wave of thrash bands that followed in the wake of the Big Four, Sodom are a German band who continue to push out raw, unsophisticated metal to a devoted audience. Formed in 1980 by Tom Angelripper (bass/vocals), Chris Witchhunter (drums), and Aggressor (guitar) the band signed to Steamhammer and began a long and almost distinguished career, commencing with 1985's *In The Sign Of Evil* EP. Witchhunter and Aggressor were later replaced by a long string of musicians, with only Angelripper staying the distance.

Despite their lengthy pedigree, there isn't an awful lot to be said about Sodom, except that their chainsaw-wielding cover star Knarrenheinz has entered the metal mascot Hall Of Fame alongside Iron Maiden's Eddie and SOD's Sergeant D.

RECOMMENDED ALBUM:
Agent Orange (Steamhammer, 1989)
http://sodomized.info

Soilwork

A Swedish band specialising in melodic death metal, Soilwork rose to prominence after their debut album, *A Predator's Portrait* (2001). Its follow-up, *Natural Born Chaos*, was produced by none other than Devin

Soilwork – more melodic death from Sweden

Townsend of Strapping Young Lad (see separate entry). Tours through America and Japan with Hypocrisy, Killswitch Engage, In Flames and Pain saw SW gain a new fanbase, in time for their next record, *Figure Number Five*, recorded with Frederik Nordström at Studio Fredman, the current must-use studio in this genre of music.

RECOMMENDED ALBUM:
Natural Born Chaos (Nuclear Blast, 2002)
www.soilwork.org

Solefald

Vocalist/guitarist/bassist Cornelius Jakhelln and vocalist/keyboardist/drummer Lazare Nedland (also of Borknagar) form Solefald, a Norwegian melodic black metal band with experimental elements. 1997's debut album, *The Linear Scaffold*, was based thematically on the art of Odd Nerdrum, the poetry of Lord Byron, the music of Beethoven, Norwegian pantheism, and existentialist philosophy. Later albums such as *Pills Against The Ageless Ills* and *In Harmonia Universali* almost reach progressive rock territory, with the black metal template blurred beyond recognition.

RECOMMENDED ALBUM:
In Harmonia Universali (Avantgarde, 2003)
www.solefald.org

Soulfly

Just creeping into this book thanks to the thrash metal elements of some of their more recent songs, Soulfly are more commonly associated with the now-dying nu-metal genre. Having left his old band Sepultura in 1996 in acrimonious circumstances, leather-throated singer and guitarist Max Cavalera recruited former Seps roadie Marcello D. Rapp (bass), Roy "Rata" Mayorga (drums) and Mike Doling (guitar) for his next band, Soulfly. The formation came at a tricky time for him – his adopted stepson Dana Wells had just been murdered – and Max has admitted that musically, Soulfly functioned as therapy. Their self-titled album, released in 1998, contained a message to Wells' still-unidentified killers and bore some of the most anguished, enraged lyrics of Cavalera's career.

Always politically outspoken, Cavalera has also engaged in extra-curricular activities such as speaking at CMJ's New Music Marathon with Moby and Marilyn Manson and Holland's Crossing Boarder Festival, both in 1997. He also appeared on The Deftones' *Around The Fur* album, and perhaps surprisingly – given his anti-corporate stance – sang a Brazilian TV jingle for the soft drink Sprite.

Max is a popular figure on the extreme metal and wider musical scene, attracting a host of guest appearances for the first Soulfly album, including Burton C. Bell, Dino Cazares and Christian Olde Wolbers (at the time all in Fear Factory), Fred Durst and DJ Lethal from Limp Bizkit, Chino from Deftones, Benji from Dub War and Eric Bobo from Cypress Hill. Slipknot and Korn producer Ross Robinson – who had worked with Sepultura on their *Roots* album – made the album a moderately heavy experience. A limited edition with a bonus disc of live and remixed tracks was also made available.

However, fans of Max's faster playing with Sepultura were only partly satisfied by Soulfly's mid-tempo riffing. The second album, *Primitive* (2000), featured Slipknot singer Corey Taylor on the song 'Jumpdafuckup', and Slayer frontman Tom Araya on 'Terrorist', which featured a fast break at the end. Better still, 2002's *3* album featured some all-out thrash metal, such as 'Tree Of Pain'. The band split after the *Prophecy* album in 2004, leaving Cavalera to recruit a new set of musicians.

RECOMMENDED ALBUM:
3 (Roadrunner, 2002)
www.soulfly.com

Soulreaper

Formed by ex-Dissection members Tobias R. Kellgren (drums) and Johan Norman (guitar) with the aim of playing brutal death metal, despite being in the Gothenburg area, Soulreaper (initially simply Reaper) added Mikael Lang (bass), Christoffer Hermansson (guitar) and Christoffer Hjerten (vocals) in 1997. A debut album, *Written In Blood*, was

Solefald – experimental black metal

Soulreaper – not overly melodic

released in 1999. Hermansson was then replaced by Stefan Karlsson and the band signed to Nuclear Blast, the home of Dissection. The *Liferazer* album appeared in 2003.

RECOMMENDED ALBUM:
Liferazer (Nuclear Blast, 2003)
www.soulreaper.tk

Mikael Lang on the problems ahead
❝The extreme metal scene is gaining more and more fans every day. But it will never be as big as the ordinary heavy metal/hard rock scene. The scene would also be bigger if the downloading of music from the internet would stop. But you guys out there who read this, keep on banging your head until the reaper of souls gets you (I know he will).❞

Stampin' Ground

The British hardcore punk/thrash metal band Stampin' Ground have risen from their punk-club roots to the point where they can claim a fanbase in countries worldwide, thanks to constant touring and a way with a catchy, extreme riff. Formed

in Cheltenham in 1995, SG became the first English band of their genre to tour the US without having an album released there. The *Demons Run Amok* and *An Expression Of Repressed Violence* albums, released independently, led to a deal with Century Media, who released their finest moment, 2001's *Carved From Empty Words*. A US tour followed as American audiences warmed to the band's expert metal and chaotic live shows. Another album, *A New Darkness Upon Us*, was produced by Andy Sneap and released in late 2003, taking the band to previously untried territory - musically and geographically.

RECOMMENDED ALBUM:
Carved From Empty Words
(Century Media, 2001)
www.stampin-ground.com

Strapping Young Lad

The excellent main project of the much-in-demand musician and producer Devin Townsend, Strapping Young Lad is a multifaceted band including guitarist Jed Simon, bassist Byron Stroud, drummer Gene Hoglan (ex-Death/Dark Angel) and keyboard player Matteo Caratozzolo. Townsend has worked on projects as diverse as Steve Vai's Frontline Assembly, Metallica bassist Jason Newsted's IR8 band and Sabbath bassist Geezer Butler's outfit G/Z/R. He has also contributed to the Rush tribute album *Working Man*, and – at the other end of the metal spectrum – performed vocals on James Murphy's solo album.

Townsend formed the band in 1994 and issued the *Heavy As A Really Heavy Thing* album the following year. A 1997 European tour as part of the Full Of Hate shows with Entombed and Obituary was followed by a two-month US tour support slot for Testament. A second album – the classic *City* – was also released in 1997 and a live EP was released after concerts in Melbourne. The title, *No Sleep Till Bedtime*, once again demonstrated Townsend's insane sense of humour. Strapping Young Lad were often namechecked by Emperor, among others, and their self-titled album of 2002 was another masterpiece.

RECOMMENDED ALBUM:

City (Century Media, 1997)

www.strappingyounglad.com

Strapping Young Lad – prog madness

Devin Townsend gets sensitive

❝Heavy metal gets a bad rap because it's represented in a really fucking stupid way. At the end of the day the people who play this kind of music tend to be pretty sensitive. I think there's a lot of repressed sensitivity in metal which manifests itself as aggression.❞

Suffocation

A classic New York death metal band comprised of Frank Mullen (vocals), Terrance Hobbs (guitar), Doug Cerrito (guitar), Chris Richards (bass), and Doug Bohn (drums – later Dave Culross, ex-Malevolent Creation), Suffocation play high-quality, aggressive DM with plenty of technical riffing and the usual complex song structures. Formed in 1990, the band released a three-song EP, *Reincremation*, before signing to Nuclear Blast for one album. This was followed by a move to Roadrunner, with whom the band remained for three highly-acclaimed albums. However, they split after 1998's *Despise The Sun*.

A reformation came in 2002 with Mike Smith (drums), Terrance Hobbs (guitar), Guy Marchais (guitar), Frank Mullen (vocals), and Derek Boyer (bass). Appearances at the New England Metal and Hardcore Festival, Maryland Deathfest and Milwaukee Metalfest preceded an intense new album, *Souls To Deny*.

RECOMMENDED ALBUM:
Human Waste (Nuclear Blast, 1991)
www.suffocation.us

Frank Mullen on the future of extremity
❝Although my favourite bands are the old school – Carcass, Pestilence and Atrocity – I think right now the future is huge for extreme metal. With the resurgence of Headbanger's Ball and Fuse's Uranium the future is vast for this music, and it's about time!❞

Suidakra

German black metal band Suidakra were formed in 1994 by Arkadius Antonik und Stefan Möller under the name Gloryfication. After line-up shuffles and two demos, Daniela Voigt, Marcel Schoenen und Christoph Zacharowski were also

recruited and the name was changed. An album, *Lupine Essence*, was released in 1997 and the band continues to record. Five more recent albums for Century Media have seen the band expand their fanbase in their homeland.

RECOMMENDED ALBUM:
Emprise To Avalon (Century Media, 2002)
www.suidakra.com

Bassist Marcus on extremity
❝All of us in Suidakra listen to a wide range of different music. It goes from Deicide and Death to 16 Horsepower and Backyard Babies, from good old Elvis to modern bands like Tool, Korn or Slipknot. We don't care about images or trends or maximum extremes as long as the music is superior in an individual way. It always depends on the mood and actual situation what's the best to listen to.❞

Susperia

Formed by Tjodalv (Dimmu Borgir, Old Man's Child) and Cyrus (Satyricon, Old Man's Child) in 1998, black metal band Susperia added vocalist Athera, bassist Memnock and guitarist Elvorn. The *Illusions*

Suidakra – German black metal

Of Evil demo followed, leading to 10 record label offers: the band went with Nuclear Blast and released their debut album, *Predominance*, in 2000. Tours with Dimmu Borgir, In Flames, Nevermore and Lacuna Coil followed and they headlined the Extremo Open Air Festival in Portugal. Another album, *Vindication*, appeared in 2002 to mass acclaim.

RECOMMENDED ALBUM:
Predominance (Nuclear Blast, 2000)
www.susperia.net

Terrorizer

A classic 'one album band', Terrorizer were Oscar Garcia (vocals), Jesse Pintado (guitar), David Vincent (bass) and Pete Sandoval

Susperia – BM supergroup

(drums). The last two musicians were, of course, the rhythm section of death metal legends Morbid Angel for many years, while Pintado went on to become a mainstay of Napalm Death. One album, *World Downfall*, made the band's name, but they split soon after. Garcia vanished from the music scene and the others moved onwards. Slipknot later covered Terrorizer's 'Fear Of Napalm'.

RECOMMENDED ALBUM:
World Downfall (Earache, 1989)

Testament

A proficient, technically-gifted thrash metal band, Testament started out as Metallica copyists before refining the Bay Area template and ultimately heading up the thrash B-league with Kreator and Sodom. The Nineties saw them turn more towards a death metal style, with long-serving frontman Chuck Billy's powerful, guttural

Thanatos – Dutch pioneers

vocal style at the centre of the sound. This development was also the result of Testament's temporary recruitment of guitarist James Murphy, whose melodic death style was beneficial for several other bands featured in these pages.

The Californian band were originally called Legacy and featured vocalist Steve Souza, who left to form fellow thrashers Exodus. After adding the iron-tonsilled Billy, the line-up remained relatively stable, with the more permanent members including the principal songwiter Alex Skolnick (guitar), Eric Peterson (guitar), Louie Clemente (drums) and Greg Christian (bass). Testament have also at some point hosted all three of Slayer's drummers, with Paul Bostaph and John Dette working on several albums and one excellent long-player, *The Gathering,* featuring the considerable talents of Dave Lombardo. Former Death drummer Gene Hoglan also appeared on one album.

After issuing three successful albums in the Eighties, Testament gradually became unhappy with Atlantic's promotion of their work and negotiated a release from their contract after 1994's *Low.* Skolnick had departed after the previous album, and together with the aforementioned Murphy, Billy et al set up a record label, Burnt Offerings, through which one live and one studio album were subsequently issued. The band then moved to the small Mayhem and Spitfire labels, normally the sign of a band on a steep downward spiral, but Testament showed no sign of slowing down, even despite Billy's battle in recent years with cancer. A re-recording of early material entitled *First Strike Still Deadly* appeared in 2002 to much praise.

RECOMMENDED ALBUM:
Practice What You Preach (Atlantic, 1989)
www.testamentlegions.com

Eric Peterson remembers how it went
❝The order was: Metallica, Slayer, Exodus, Possessed, Death Angel, Legacy. Possessed were the Bay Area black metal band. They were a little too much like Slayer, I think. The fact that they were later known as a death metal band is probably just a political thing – just journalists with their labels. We used the term speed metal before thrash metal. A lot of us did a lot of speed. We'd go out on Friday night and come home from, say, Paul Baloff's house on Sunday morning! We were up all night, tripping on dark things. Everything was real dark, satanic and trippy. But it was definitely a clan. There was definitely something in the air.

It's weird how they say 'the Big Four Of Thrash', because they left out Exodus and Testament. We weren't chumps, we sold millions of records too. We definitely made our mark. It's bullshit, because it made us the underdogs, which is bull.❞

Thanatos

Holland's first death metal band, Thanatos – Stephan Gebedi (guitar/vocals), Paul Baayens (guitar), Marco De Bruin (bass) and Yuri Rinkel (drums) – recorded underground demos and played shows with Napalm Death, Kreator, Sepultura, Bolt Thrower, Autopsy, Death Angel and Messiah. Signing to the Shark label and releasing a debut album, *Emerging From The Netherworlds* (1990) and a follow-up, *Realm Of Ecstasy* ('92), tours with Cannibal Corpse and Exhorder were cancelled amid label problems. The band was shelved for seven years, reforming at the end of the decade and signing to Hammerheart. *Angelic Encounters* appeared in 2000 and successful tours followed.

RECOMMENDED ALBUM:
Emerging From The Netherworlds
(Shark, 1990)
www.thanatos.info

Stephan Gebédi of Thanatos on playing heavy
❝It comes straight from the heart. It's pure but it's also a challenge to play this music tight at neckbreak-speed. I think this is the way extreme metal should sound. Although I'm not stating we have a totally original sound, I won't hesitate to say that we found our own little niche, our own particular sound within the death/thrash movement.❞

Theatres Des Vampires

A dramatic black metal band from France, Theatres Des Vampires take their image straight from Ann Rice's *Lestat* novels and produce gothic music with heavily theatrical overtones. A 1996 album entitled *Vampyrìsme, Nècrophilie, Nècrosadisme, Nècrophagie* led to a deal with the UK's Blackend label and *Bloody Lunatic Asylum* followed in 2001. 2002's *Suicide Vampire* album was to feature a cover of Kylie

Theatres Des Vampires – theatrical metal

Minogue's hit 'I Can't Get You Out of My Head', amended to 'I Can't Get You Out Of My Grave', but Minogue's lawyers failed to provide permission and the album was recalled. *Nightbreed Of Macabria* (2004) continued along similar lines.

RECOMMENDED ALBUM:
Bloody Lunatic Asylum (Blackend, 2001)

Fabian of Theatres Des Vampires on evil... and the evil empire

❝I think that 'evil' doesn't mean fast guitar riffs and grind drum tempos. At all. I think that evil is what we feel inside... and often the gothic atmospheres are more near my concept of evil and extreme. Today to be 'extreme' in the US market you must be a kind of nu-metal idiot.**❞**

Therion *(Left)*

Like many other metal bands, Therion – formed in 1987 by Christofer Johnsson (vocals, guitar), Peter Hansson (guitar), Oskar Forss (drums) and Erik Gustafson (bass) – have progressed from a simple death metal style to a more technical, progressive approach, although recent albums have seen the band nod towards earlier influences with covers of Manowar's 'Thor' and Accept's 'Seawinds'.

1991's *...Of Darkness* debut album consisted of melodic metal, and the *Beyond Sanctorum* album of the following year continued along these lines. However, the ponderously-titled *Symphony Masses: Ho Drakon Ho Megas* of 1993 showcased a more experimental concept, due to Johnsson's recruitment of a new line-up, Magnus Barthelson (guitar), Andreas Wallan Wahl (bass) and Piotr Wawrzeniuk (drums). This new style was taken to the next level on *Theli*, released in 1996, which featured keyboards and other instruments, although the band retained a certain metallic edge. A covers album, *A'arab Zarah Lucid Dreaming*, included strings and woodwind arrangements played by the Barmbek Symphonic Orchestra and featured covers of Iron Maiden's 'Children Of The Damned' and Judas Priest's 'Here Come The Tears'.

The eclectic approach persisted on what many regard as the best Therion album, 1998's *Vovin*, which was recorded by yet another line-up: the indomitable Johnsson plus guitarist Tommy Ericsson, singers Martina Hornbacher and Sarah Jezibel Diva,

drummer Wolf Simons and bassist Jan Kazda. The female vocals established the band in quite another arena to death metal, but the album was snapped up by fans nonetheless, as was a later release, *Deggial*. Therion are lucky to have an understanding set of followers: subsequent albums have seen them maintain their experimental edge.

RECOMMENDED ALBUM:
Theli (Nuclear Blast, 1996)
www.megatherion.com

Thokk

An American black metal band who released one album, *Of Rape And Vampyrism*, and then vanished, Thokk were the side project of Kaiaphas from the band Ancient. After the album was released, Kaiaphas returned to his main band.

RECOMMENDED ALBUM:
Of Rape And Vampyrism
(Hammerheart, 2000)

Thorium

Danish death metal band Thorium – Morten Ryberg (guitar), Allan Tvedebrink (guitar), Michael H. Andersen (vocals) and Jesper Frost Jensen (drums) – formed in 1997 as a side project to Andersen's band Withering Surface. Two albums showcase their dexterity and aggression.

RECOMMENDED ALBUM:
Unleashing The Demons (Die Hard, 2002)

Thornspawn

Texan black metal band Thornspawn debuted in 2000 with the crushing *Blood Of The Holy, Taint Thy Steel*, which was later reissued by the Osmose label. Stepping up a level with the Morrisound Studios-recorded *Sanctified By Satan's Blood*, the band went on tour through Mexico with Summon and Excommunion. They remain at the darker end of the US black metal scene.

RECOMMENDED ALBUM:
Sanctified By Satan's Blood
(Osmose, 2002)

Thou Art Lord

Formed in the early Nineties by Magus (Necromantia) and Sakis (Rotting Christ), the Greek black metal band Thou Art

Thyrfing – Viking black metal

Lord added Mortify vocalist Gothmog and released a series of limited-run recordings, the first of which was the *Diabolou Archaes Legeones* EP. Signing to the Unisound label and recording an album, *Eosforos*, the band toured extensively. The *Apollyon* album was a step up in production quality but the musicians then returned to their main bands.

In the early Noughties Thou Art Lord returned with a new vocalist, Seth of Septic Flesh, and drummer Akis K of various acts. *DV8* was the next album and TAL appear to have a promising future ahead of them.

RECOMMENDED ALBUM:
Apollyon (Unisound, 1995)
www.thouartlord.tk

Thou Shalt Suffer

After rejecting Xerasia, Dark Device and Embryonic as possible band-names, Norwegian musicians Ihsahn and Samoth chose Thou Shalt Suffer for their first band, formed in 1991. Producing death metal with an avant-garde edge, the duo then formed Emperor (see separate entry) but contined working with TSS from time to time. 1997 saw the release of *Into The Woods Of Belial* on Samoth's Nocturnal Art label. In the year 2000 Ihsahn signed a deal for Thou Shalt Suffer with Candlelight (also home to Emperor) and released a studio album, *Somnium*.

RECOMMENDED ALBUM:
Into The Woods Of Belial
(Nocturnal Art, 1997)

Throne Of Ahaz

Swedish death metal band Throne Of Ahaz were formed in 1991 by vocalist Veretorn and bassist Taurtheim. The 1992 demo *At The Mountains Of The Northern Storms* led to a debut album on No Fashion entitled *Nifelheim* two years later. Adding guitarist Vargher of Bewitched and Ancient Wisdom, the band recorded more sessions (including a cover of Black Sabbath's 'Black Sabbath') and *On Twilight Enthroned* appeared in 1996. The band parted ways that same year.

RECOMMENDED ALBUM:
On Twilight Enthroned (No Fashion, 1996)

Thy Primordial

Swedish black metallers Thy Primordial (originally Carcharoth, then Lucifer, then Primordial) released two demos, *En Mörka Makters Alla* and *Svart Gryning*, which led to a deal with Pulverised for *Where Only The Seasons Mark The Path Of Time*. The line-up – singer Michael Andersson, bass player Jonas Albrektssson, guitarists Karl Beckmann and Stefan Wienerhall and drummer Jocke Petersson – issued *The Crowning Carnage* in 2002 and continue to tour.

RECOMMENDED ALBUM:
Where Only The Seasons Mark The Path Of Time (Pulverised, 1996)
www.thyprimordial.com

Thyrfing

Viking, black and folk metal sounds all combine in the music of Thyrfing, a respected Swedish outfit formed in 1995. After two demos led to a deal with

Hammerheart, they recorded a self-titled album with Tomas Skogsberg at Sunlight Studios and released it in 1998. Thyrfing followed up the second record, *Valdr Galga*, with tours alongside Six Feet Under, Vader, Enslaved, Cryptopsy and Nile. In the meantime Hammerheart reissued the two demos as a limited album entitled *Hednaland*. Subsequent albums such as 2003's *Vansinnesvisor* included more unorthodox instrumentation and cemented the band's position still further.

RECOMMENDED ALBUM:
Vansinnesvisor (Hammerheart, 2003)
www.thyrfing.com

Patrik Lindgren on the prospects for the extreme scene
❝I think it has a bright future, if I may use that expression in this case. It seems to grow bigger and bigger with many new bands. OK, most bands lack what it takes to catch my interest, but it's all a matter of selection and taste. Album sales are going down for most bands, but from what I've heard it's not as bad as with other musical genres.❞

Tiamat – highly experimental

Tiamat *(Previous page)*

Originally based in Sweden before moving to Dortmund in Germany, Tiamat are a revered experimental death metal band consisting of Johan Edlund (guitar, vocals, keyboards), Anders Iwers (bass) and Lars Sköld (drums). The band were originally called Treblinka, but, becoming aware of the dubious pedigree of the name, changed it to Tiamat – the name of the Sumerian goddess of chaos, married to Absu (see separate entry). Two demos, *Crawling In Vomits* and *Sign Of The Pentagram*, led to a single release, 'Severe Abominations' through Mould In Hell Records, which in turn alerted the Metalcore label, to which the band signed for one album.

Their initial recordings were death metal with black touches, a formula that made a success of their debut album, 1990's *Sumerian Cry*. Subsequent albums, *The Astral Sleep* (1991) and *Clouds* (1993) saw Tiamat incorporate atmospheric keyboards and an overall ambient element into the sound, but it was 1994's *Wildhoney* which – like Therion's *Vovin* – saw much more public attention drawn to the band. Since then, Tiamat albums have stuck close to the ambient-death template: *Skeleton Skeletron* featured a slightly more Gothic feel and included a bizarre cover of The Rolling Stones' 'Sympathy For The Devil'. Personnel have come and gone over the years, notably including the producer and keyboard player Waldemar Sorychta. *Judas Christ* (2003) extended some religious and philosophical elements into the Tiamat approach.

RECOMMENDED ALBUM:
Wildhoney (Century Media, 1994)
www.churchoftiamat.com

Triumphator

Signing a deal with Necropolis after a 1996 demo, Swedish black metal band Triumphator perform malevolent music with a definite Marduk influence (due in part to the presence of Marduk drummer Fredrik Andersson on sessions). After a hiatus, the *Wings Of Antichrist* album was released in 2000. Since then, the band has only been sporadically active.

RECOMMENDED ALBUM:
www.triumphator.tk

Tsjuder

Founded in 1993 by guitarist Berserk and bassist/vocalist Nag, Norwegian black metal band Tsjuder added guitarist Drauglin and recorded a 1995 demo, *Ved Ferdens Ende*. Berserk departed and temporary drummer Norvus assisted on the *Possessed* demo. After more personnel changes, the *Throne Of The Goat* EP was released on Solistitum Records and a full-length album, *Kill For Satan*, appeared on the Drakkar label. In 2002 *Demonic Possession* was released and a deal with Season Of Mist followed.

Nag on being truly metal
"Celtic Frost, Bathory, Destruction, Sarcofago – these bands made music with the true feeling and no compromises. There is no good thing about our music. We play raw black metal which we've always done, and we'll always continue doing that. If you listen to bands with synths, female vocals and all that crap, Tsjuder is not for you!"

Tsjuder – uncompromisingly raw

Twin Obscenity

Formed in 1991 by singer/guitarist/
keyboardist Atle Wiig, bassist Jo-Arild
Toennessen and drummer Knut Naesje,
Norway's Twin Obscenity established a
black/death metal style over three demos:
Ruins, Behind The Castle Walls and *Revelation
Of Glaaki.*

Head Not Found signed them and a
debut album, 1997's *Where Light Touches
None,* received positive reviews. Signing to
Century Media, the band recorded *For
Blood, Honor And Soil.*

RECOMMENDED ALBUM:

Where Light Touches None

(Head Not Found, 1997)

Ulver

Norwegian band Ulver – named after the
native word for wolves – perform aggressive
black metal with the odd death metal riff.
They also include more atmospheric
passages with acoustic instruments. The
band were formed in the early Nineties
by vocalist Garm (Kristoffer Rygg, aka
Trickster G) and have developed a very
modern metal image, lounging around in
suits and providing intelligent, restrained
comments in interviews. Other members
include guitarists Haavard and Aismal,
bassist Skoll and drummer Aiwarikiar.
With a strong anti-Christian message and
an Enslaved-style desire to return to pre-
Christian social structures evident in their
music, Ulver have based each of their
records on a concept. *Bergtatt* (1995)

portrayed a Norse myth concerning ancient underworld creatures, *Kveldssanger* (1996) was nothing less than a collection of acoustic folk music and *Nattens Madrigal* (1997) handled the 'wolf' theme. However, their most ambitious moment has been 1999's *Themes from William Blake's The Marriage Of Heaven And Hell*, and on the follow-up, *Perdition*, they moved into more experimental, electronic territory.

RECOMMENDED ALBUM:
Kveldssanger (Head Not Found, 1996)
http://ulver.cjb.net

Unleashed (Left)

A Swedish Viking band formed of Johnny (bass, vocals), Tomas (guitar), Fredrik (guitar) and Anders (drums), Unleashed pursued a black metal-influenced approach but avoided the usual keyboards and other atmospherics in their sound, preferring to record straight-up metal that tied in with their Nordic message.

A solid base of fans was built through Europe, to which the band paid homage in 1994 by rushing out a live album to combat an over-expensive bootlegged version. They split after 1997's *Warrior* but later reformed for 2002's *Hell's Unleashed*.

Century Media released a six-LP box set of Unleashed albums in 2003, featuring sleevenotes by the author of this book.

RECOMMENDED ALBUM:
Where No Life Dwells
(Century Media, 1991)
www.unleashed.nu

Unlord

A Scandinavian black metal act formed in 1989, Unlord recorded three now-unavailable demo tapes and signed to the Displeased label. A collection of melodic, aggressive songs, under the title *Schwarzwald*, appeared in 1997 and a follow-up, *Gladiator*, came three years later. Their finest moment came with 2001's *Lord Of Beneath*, with cover art by Marduk and Motörhead artist Joe Petagno.

RECOMMENDED ALBUM:
Schwarzwald (Displeased, 1997)

Vader

A death metal band possibly named after the *Star Wars* Dark Lord, Vader are a death metal band from the industrial town of Olsztyn, Poland. Formed in the pre-perestroika days of 1986, it says something for the lateral approach of the UK's Earache label that Vader became the first Eastern Bloc metal band to be signed to a Western record company.

The first two Vader albums, *The Ultimate Incantation* and *The Darkest Age: Live '93*, were followed up by an EP, *Sothis*, before the band moved to Impact in 1996 and began extended touring and releases throughout Europe and the US. Support slots with Deicide, Cannibal Corpse, Broken Hope and Malevolent Creation helped spread the Vader message, but it was 2000's utterly scorching *Litany* album that elevated them to their current position. A fast, heavy album produced with precision, the album was compared with Slayer's *Reign In Blood* and placed them at the forefront of European death metal. Subsequent albums such as *Revelations* continued Vader's rise.

RECOMMENDED ALBUM:
Litany (Metal Mind, 2000)
www.vader.pl

Varathron

Formed in 1989, Greek black metal act Varathron recorded the *Procreation Of The Unaltered Evil* demo and signed to the Black Vomit label for an EP entitled *One Step Beyond Dreams*. A split album with Necromantia called Black Arts Lead To Everlasting Sins followed, with the albums *His Majesty At The Swamp* (1993), *Walpurgisnacht* (1995), *Genesis Of Apocryphal Desire* (1997) and *The Lament Of Gods* (1999) keeping the dark flame burning.

RECOMMENDED ALBUM:
His Majesty At The Swamp
(independent, 1993)

Vassago

Named after a demonic prince of hell, Vassago comprises Lord Belial's Pepa Af Vassago (guitar) and Sin (drums and vocals). Bloodlord plays session bass. Playing thrash/death metal with alternated screams and death vocals, the band were at their best on the *Knights From Hell* album of 2002. The members returned to their main bands after its release.

RECOMMENDED ALBUM:
Knights From Hell (Mercenary Musik, 2002)

Ved Buens Ende

Avant-garde, experimental black metal from members of Arcturus and Dodheimsgard, Ved Buens Ende released two albums for the UK's Misanthropy label, *Written In Waters* (1995) and *Those Who Caress The Pale* (1997). Such an approach was never likely to win a great number of fans, of course, and the band fell silent after their second album.

RECOMMENDED ALBUM:
Written In Waters (Misanthropy, 1995)

Venom

The band which started the extreme metal scene in the early Eighties, Venom even preceded Metallica, whose 1983 debut album *Kill 'Em All* owed much of its themes and speed to early Venom recordings. The Newcastle three-piece, consisting of vocalist/bassist Cronos (Conrad Lant), guitarist Mantas (Jeff Dunn) and drummer Abaddon (Tony Bray), watched in bewilderment as the world grabbed their musical ball – so to speak – and ran with it, leaving them with a rather lower profile than those who refined the original primitive style and turned it into megabucks. Few bands can claim to have started a whole musical trend off; even fewer can claim to have started two – but Venom's speedy metallic tunes formed the basis of the thrash approach, while their second album, 1982's *Black Metal*, is directly responsible for the satanic gibberings of Mercyful Fate and Bathory, and thus for a whole range of bands following a clear line as far as today's Cradle Of Filth and Satyricon.

Venom first formed as the quintet Oberon in the late Seventies before trimming down, changing their name and speeding up considerably. Influenced by Motörhead, Judas Priest and Black Sabbath, the first three Venom albums, *Welcome To Hell*, *Black Metal* and *At War With Satan* established a new approach to metal. The American Big Four – Metallica, Anthrax, Megadeth and Slayer – had transformed Venom's beery style by the mid-Eighties, however, and the trio became increasingly irrelevant to all but their loyal fans in Britain and Europe. The legendary Venom shows remained strong crowd-pullers, though, even featuring Metallica in support on the very early 'Seven Dates Of Hell' tour.

Venom were a volatile set of individuals, and arguments during the recording of 1985's less-successful *Possessed* album provoked Mantas into leaving the band after the subsequent *Eine Kleine Nachtmusik* tour in the US. Venom replaced him with two guitarists, Mike Hickey and Jimmy Clare, recording 1987's *Calm Before The Storm* with this line-up. The new Venom was no more peaceful than before, however, and this time it was Cronos who departed in a huff to form a new band under his own name. Mantas stepped back in with a new guitar player, Alan Barnes, while Tony 'Demolition Man' Dolan (ex-Atomkraft) took over bass and vocals. This line-up recorded no fewer than four albums, the best of which is generally regarded to be the first, *Prime Evil*.

Abaddon persuaded Cronos to return for a headlining appearance at 1995's Waldrock Festival in Holland and the following year's Dynamo Festival. The latter was made memorable by an incident during the song 'Countess Bathory'; the pyrotechnics set off during the song dislodged the Venom backdrop, an enormous sheet of cloth which settled slowly onto Abaddon. Roadies struggled for some time to free the hapless drummer and the event went down in history as a moment of pure *Spinal Tap* surrealism.

In 1997 the trio released another album, *Cast In Stone*, popular among nostalgic fans but not exactly a musical landmark. By now Cronos was working as a fitness instructor, Mantas as a martial arts centre manager (he has a third degree Tae Kwon Do black belt) and Abaddon as a studio owner and head of the Hardware label. Since then Venom activities have been few and far between, although Cronos did appear on Cradle Of Filth's *Dusk And Her*

Embrace album and in a Diabolos Rising video. A reunion of Mantas and Cronos with new drummer Anton for 2000's *Resurrection* album came and went, although Mantas now has a self-titled project up and running. They remain a band responsible for much musical change, for which they have – perhaps unjustly – never been rewarded. Their place in the Metal Hall Of Fame is assured, however.

RECOMMENDED ALBUM:
Black Metal (Neat, 1982)
www.venomslegions.com
www.mantas666.co.uk

Jeff Dunn on how it all started

❝I think the metal-buying public was just ready for something different. We had the punk attitude and we were described in the early days as long-haired punks. People used to say, 'You're making such a fuckin' racket...' We went out there and thrashed it up and the audiences loved it. The other bands were doing their best to be good musicians and everything.

It just happened, although it's probably fair to say that the first thrash metal song we did was 'The Witching Hour'. Like Paul Stanley said, when someone asked him how they came up with the Kiss make-up and all that, he said, 'If someone falls into the Mississippi and comes up with 16 gold nuggets, you're not going to call them a fuckin' genius.' What we did was just what we did, it wasn't contrived. For the publicity, we said we were going to be the biggest and the fastest and all that shite like every band says – but I think we achieved it to a certain degree. I think we opened the floodgates for a lot of other acts to come through and do this kind of stuff, too.❞

Viking Crown

Viking Crown was the side project of Anton Crowley (a combination of the names of Satanists Anton LaVey and Aleister Crowley – actually Phil Anselmo of Pantera) and Killjoy, of the death metal band Necrophagia. Their sole album to date includes material taken from Eibon, Anselmo's earlier collaboration with Fenriz of Darkthrone and Satyr of Satyricon (see separate entries). Viking Crown produced extremely powerful black metal - an outlet

for Anselmo, whose regular band at the time would have been committing commercial suicide had they released it themselves.

RECOMMENDED ALBUM:
Unorthodox Steps Of Ritual
(Baphomet/Hammerheart, 1999)

Vile

A Californian death metal band formed by Colin Davis, Aaron Strong, Tyson Jupin and Juan Urteaga, Vile were formed in 1996 from the ashes of Thanatopsis, Entropy, Lords of Chaos and Sporadic Psychosis. Demo tapes and a tour with Deeds Of Flesh followed, with a 1999 album *Stench Of The Deceased* leading to deals with the Listenable and then Unique Leader labels.

RECOMMENDED ALBUM:
Stench Of The Deceased (Relapse, 2001)

Colin Davis on why he bothers

❝I play death metal music because it's inside of me. I don't care how it looks to others, but it's never been about me trying to rebel. It's just a natural thing. I don't look at it like it's a lifestyle that you must live and die for. Music is not about proving something to anybody. It's about your own expressions and there is no reason to judge people based on what they listen to, who they support or don't support and how long they keep it in their lives. I am a born slave to music and I will probably die with it as a big part of my life.❞

Vintersorg

Formed in 1994 as Vargatron (which means Wolfthrone), guitarist and singer Vintersorg's intention was to create heavy music with clean vocals and acoustic guitars. The early line-up disintegrated two years later and Vintersorg continued alone under his own name. An EP, *Hedniskhjärtad*, was released in 1998, along with an album, *Till Fjälls*. Folk music influences abounded on both releases and continued on the *Ödemarkens Son* album the following year. Along with a newly-recruited guitarist, Mattias Marklund, Vintersorg continues to release albums at a prolific rate, with the latest recording, *Cosmic Genesis*, entering progressive-metal territory.

RECOMMENDED ALBUM:
Cosmic Genesis (Napalm, 2000)
www.vintersorg.com

Vital Remains

Death metal band Vital Remains formed in 1989 in Providence, Rhode Island, and signed to the Deaf label after recording two demos. *Let Us Pray* followed and introduced the band's particular brand of blasphemous DM to the scene, which responded with enthusiasm and the band released a follow-up, *Into Cold Darkness*. Switching to Osmose, Vital Remains then released *Forever Underground* and *Dawn Of The Apocalypse*. A line-up change came in 2001 when main-man Tony Lazaro, together with drummer/bassist Dave Suzuki, asked Deicide frontman Glen Benton to record an album with them: the result was the much-praised *Dechristianize*, recorded at Morrisound Studios, gaining the band a new fanbase.

RECOMMENDED ALBUM:
Dechristianize (Century Media, 2003)
www.vitalremains.com

Voivod

Along with their early Swiss labelmates Celtic Frost, the Canadian band Voivod were responsible for much of the technical, experimental side of Eighties thrash metal, influencing many bands with their deftly-performed, dense music. Originally consisting of Denis D'Amour (guitar), Michel Langevin (drums), Denis Belanger (vocals) and Jean Yves Theriault (bass), their first album, *War And Pain*, was released in 1984.

1986's weirdly-named *Rrröööaaarrr* and the following year's *Killing Technology* saw Voivod refine their complex style to moderate acclaim, receiving a leap in popularity on the release of the acclaimed *Dimension Hatröss* in 1988. Theriault departed in 1991, as did

Vital Remains with Deicide frontman Glen Benton (centre)

Belanger two years later, and a new member, Eric Forrest, replaced them. The band continued to make albums, hindered only slightly by a 1998 bus crash in which Forrest broke some bones in his lower back. He made a full recovery and the band continued, with their profile boosted in 2002 by the surprise recruitment of ex-Metallica bassist Jason Newsted, who signed them to his Chophouse label and funded the recording of a self-titled album.

RECOMMENDED ALBUM:
Killing Technology (Noise, 1987)
www.voivod.com

Vomitory

Formed in 1989 by vocalist Ronnie Olsson, guitarists Urban Gustafsson and Ulf Dalegren, bassist Tomas Bergqvist and drummer Tobias Gustafsson, Sweden's Vomitory play hard-hitting death metal and head up their niche of the scene with one or two other bands yet to gain widespread exposure.

After the band recorded a demo in 1992, the Swiss Witchhunt label released a Vomitory EP, *Moribund*, which rapidly sold 2000 copies. A second demo, *Through Sepulchral Shadows*, also sold well in 1994 and the band followed it up with a tour through Poland. After appearing on the 1995 Repulse compilation *Repulsive Assault*, the band were signed by the Dutch Fadeless label and recorded their first album, *Raped In Their Own Blood*, the following year. After new bassist Erik Rundqvist and vocalist Jussi Linna were added to Vomitory,

the band toured with Deranged and recorded a second album, *Redemption*. More tours in Europe and the UK followed and the band continue to ply their aggressive trade on the European circuit. 1999 also saw a Vomitory EP celebrating 10 years in death metal. Subsequent albums have seen the band raise their death metal aggression even higher.

RECOMMENDED ALBUM:
Redemption (Fadeless, 1999)
www.vomitory.net

Von

San Francisco trio Von were a mysterious entity that formed in 1988 and consisted of Von (guitars, vocals), Kill (bass) and Snake (drums). Their sole album, *Devil Pigs*, has entered cult status for its abysmal production, necro sounds and the fact that the band, Bathory-like, received hardly any publicity.

RECOMMENDED ALBUM:
Devil Pigs (split CD reissue with Dark Funeral, Karmageddon Media, 2004)

Vondur

Super-evil Swedish band Abruptum formed a side-project, Vondur, and signed to Necropolis for the release of *Stridsyfirslysing*, a suitably extreme album, in 1995. Vondur has released nothing else to date and no information is forthcoming, as is fitting for Abruptum, one of the black metal scene's more enigmatic acts.

RECOMMENDED ALBUM:
Stridsyfirslysing (Necropolis, 1995)

Whiplash – pure thrash mayhem

Whiplash *(Previous page)*

New Jersey thrash metal band Whiplash performed competent, high-velocity metal characterised by the powerful style of drummer Tony Scaglione. Along with Tony Bono (bass) and Tony Portaro (guitar, vocals) – yes, three Tonys – the band came and went, always appearing to be on the point of splitting but always making comeback albums successful enough to justify another period of activity.

Two demos recorded in the early Eighties led to a deal with Roadrunner, who issued the band's first three albums; Whiplash faced an early threat when Scaglione accepted a temporary offer from Slayer to fill in for Dave Lombardo after the latter walked away from the band in 1987. However, Lombardo returned to the fold in due course and Scaglione was back in the B-league. The band is currently on hold.

RECOMMENDED ALBUM:
Ticket To Mayhem (Roadrunner, 1987)

Tony Scaglione on the start of it all

❝The first concert I ever attended was Black Sabbath and Blue Öyster Cult at Madison Square Garden in New York. That concert really blew me away and I quickly got more and more into the whole metal scene. Soon after I discovered Motorhead, which was totally different than the standard metal of the day. Eventually this all led up to Metallica, Exodus and Slayer and the whole thrash scene. I guess my first really influential experience of extreme metal had to be the first time I heard the *No Life 'Til Leather* demo by Metallica, which was like nothing I had heard before. It was so fast and heavy (maybe not by today's standards) that everyone I knew who had heard it was just blown away.❞

Witchery *(Left)*

From Gothenburg, Sweden, Witchery are the project of ex-Mercyful Fate and Illwill bassist Sharlee D'Angelo, as well as the vocalist Toxine, guitarists Richard Corpse and Patrik Jensen and drummer Mique. The debut album, 1998's *Restless And Dead*, was a mixture of Eighties thrash, standard metal and a touch of Gothenburg melody. This satisfying mixture continued on the follow-up EP, *Witchburner*, and the album *Dead, Hot And Ready*.

After 2002's *Symphony For The Devil*, guitarist Patrik Jensen's other band The Haunted took off and Witchery seems to have been put on hold.

RECOMMENDED ALBUM:
Restless And Dead (Necropolis, 1998)

Xenomorph

A Dutch death metal band, Xenomorph was founded in 1994 by bassist Dennis and drummer Ciro. Two demos, *Carnificated Dreams* (1994) and *Passion Dance* (1995) were recorded and sold well on the tape-trading circuit. After some personnel shifts in 1996, the Teutonic Existence label released the two demos as an album. Limited to a thousand copies, the *Acardiacus* album raised interest in Xenomorph, who then recorded *Promo 98. Baneful Stealth Desire* followed in 2001.

RECOMMENDED ALBUM:
Acardiacus (Teutonic Existence, 1997)
www.x-morph.com

Xentrix

Metallica-copyists Xentrix were originally formed in 1987 under the name Sweet Vengeance in Preston, Lancashire. Recording a demo, *Hunger For...,* and performing covers by the Bay Area thrashers was sufficient to attract Roadrunner, who signed them up and released an album, 1989's *Shattered Existence*. In 1990 a 12" single was issued, a cover of Ray Parker Jr.'s *Ghostbusters* movie theme, which led to legal threats from Columbia Pictures, who were annoyed that Xentrix had used the film logo without permission. Later in the year, another album, *For Whose Advantage?* was released, which revealed that Xentrix were more than mere Hetfield clones.

After two more albums, 1991's *Dilute To Taste* and 1992's *Kin*, the band split briefly, uncertain of their place in the era of Nirvana and Tool. The split was short-lived, however, as the band regrouped with a new vocalist, Simon Gordon. The next album, *Scourge*, was released after a four-year hiatus in recording activities and was geared more towards power metal than the speed of yore. However, it failed to gain much attention and the band split again, this time for good, although rumours of a reunion persisted throughout 1999.

RECOMMENDED ALBUM:
For Whose Advantage (Roadrunner, 1990)

Yattering

Polish death metal band Yattering were formed in 1996 by Hudy (guitar), Svierszcz (bass and vocals) and Zobek (drums). *The Human's Pain* album was released by an indie label and a new guitarist, Thrufel, was recruited. A 2000 album, *Murder's Concept*, was followed by European tours, and the *III* album was recorded but remained unreleased. However, a 2002 deal with the British label Candlelight was a step up and the *Genocide* album saw Yattering compared favourably with Vader.

RECOMMENDED ALBUM:
Genocide (Candlelight, 2002)
www.yattering.pl

Zemial

After forming in the early Nineties and recording demos, Greek black metal band Zemial – Archon Vorskaath and his brother Eskarth the Dark One – relocated to Australia in 1994 and recorded *Sleeping Under Tartarus* for the Gothic label. After label problems, a 1997 demo, *Necrolatry*, led to a deal with Iron Pegasus, who issued

For The Glory Of Ur, and a vinyl version of *Necrolatry*. After the release of *Face Of The Conqueror* in 2002, Zemial returned to Europe and recruited Melechesh main-man Ashmedi.

RECOMMENDED ALBUM:
For The Glory Of Ur (Iron Pegasus, 2000)
www.zemial.com

Zyklon *(Right)*

Initially a side-project called Zyklon-B, featuring the Emperor mainmen Insahn on keyboards and Samoth on guitars, Frost of Satyricon and Draug Aldrahn of Dødheimsgard, this Norwegian band was renamed Zyklon after the demise of Emperor and evolved into a powerful death/black metal outfit which combined the best of both approaches.

Centring on Samoth (guitar) plus Trym (drums), Destructhor (of Myrkskog, guitar) and Daemon (of Limbonic Art, vocals), the first incarnation of the band released the *World Ov Worms* album in 2001, featuring a guest spot from Kristoffer Rygg (Ulver, Arcturus). A cold, merciless set of songs, it attracted much attention and led to a world tour with Morbid Angel. The follow-up, recorded at Akkerhaugen Studios and mixed at Studio Fredman in Sweden, was *Aeon*, a similarly aggressive, honed album which featured lyrics by Bård 'Faust' Eithun (see Emperor) and Secthdaemon on bass and vocals after the departure of Daemon.

RECOMMENDED ALBUM:
Aeon (Candlelight, 2003)
www.zyklontribe.com

Samoth on the early days
❝At some point somebody gave me a copy of Mayhem's *Deathcrush* EP on tape, and that was by far the most intense, sick shit I'd ever heard. I soon discovered more brutal bands like Morbid Angel, Death, Obituary, Cryptic Slaughter and Sepultura. I also became very interested in black metal... I was already familiar with bands such as Bathory, Venom, Celtic Frost and Possessed, of course, but at that point things started to happen in Norway and there was a new movement on the rise.❞

FURTHER READING

Many of the bigger bands featured in this book have had biographies written about them, but for a more detailed look at the extreme metal scene, try the following:

The Great Metal Discography
(Martin C. Strong, Canongate)
A detailed look at the histories and releases of over 800 bands, Strong concentrates mainly on mainstream metal, but some extreme acts are featured too.

Lords Of Chaos: The Bloody Rise Of The Satanic Metal Underground
(Michael Moynihan and Dirk Soderlind, Feral House)
The well-known examination of the Scandinavian black metal scene, starring Burzum and Mayhem. The authors also examine the social and psychological roots of the genre.

Goldmine Heavy Metal Record Price Guide
(Martin Popoff, Krause)
A massive collection of album reviews. Check out Martin's other books for his immensely knowledgeable take on many genres of music.

Metalheads: Heavy Metal Music and Adolescent Alienation
(Jeffrey Jensen Arnett, Westview Press)
Ever wanted to know why you are what you are? This book will tell you.

Headbangers: The Worldwide Mega-Book Of Heavy Metal Bands
(Mark Hale, Popular Culture)
A large reference work. Good for traditional heavy metal.

Also by Joel McIver for Omnibus Press:

Slipknot Unmasked (2001)

Nu-Metal: The Next Generation Of Rock And Punk (2001)

Slipknot Unmasked Again (2003)

Justice For All: The Truth About Metallica (2004)

ONLINE RESOURCES

Since *Extreme Metal* was published in 2000, the internet has at least octupled in size, so sit back and let Google do the work for you. However, the following websites are a good place to go for your daily metal fix.

Infernal Dominion
www.angelfire.com/mi/demonzine/links.html
An excellent online magazine, ID provides over 5000 links to band websites.

Metal Update
www.metalupdate.com
This site offers an invaluable free weekly e-mailed news update with details of releases, tours etc.

DeathMetal.com
www.deathmetal.com
Excellent links to official death metal band sites.

Metal Blade
www.metalblade.com

Displeased
www.displeasedrecords.com

Peaceville
www.peaceville.com

Necropolis
www.necropolisrec.com

Roadrunner
www.roadrun.com

Osmose
www.osmoseproductions.com

Blabbermouth
www.blabbermouth.net